D0762659

THE BIG BLACK BOOK

THE ESSENTIAL VIEWS OF
CONRAD AND BARBARA AMIEL BLACK

BY MAUDE BARLOW AND JAMES WINTER

Stoddart

Published in 1997 by Stoddart Publishing Co. Limited
34 Lesmill Road, Toronto, Canada M3B 2T6

Distributed in Canada by General Distribution Services Limited
34 Lesmill Road, Toronto, Canada M3B 2T6
Tel. (416) 445-3333 Fax (416) 445-5967
Email Customer.Service@ccmailgw.genpub.com

Distributed in the U.S. by General Distribution Services Inc.
85 River Rock Drive, Suite 202, Buffalo, New York 14207
Toll-free tel. 1-800-805-1083 Toll-free fax 1-800-481-6207
Email gdsinc@genpub.com

01 00 99 98 97 1 2 3 4 5

Cataloguing in Publication Data

Barlow, Maude
The big Black book : the essential views of Conrad and Barbara Amiel Black

ISBN 0-7737-5904-2

1. Press and politics. 2. Black, Conrad — Political and social views. 3. Amiel, Barbara — Political and social views. I. Winter, James P. (James Patrick), 1952– II. Title.

PN4913.B56B37 1997   070.5'092'2   97-931932-3

Cover design: Bill Douglas @ The Bang
Text design: Tannice Goddard
Computer layout: Mary Bowness

Printed and bound in Canada

We gratefully acknowledge the Canada Council for the Arts and the Ontario Arts Council for their support of our publishing program.

To my dear friends, the staff of the Council of Canadians
—MB

To Gail Robertson, my favourite journalist
—JW

And to all of the journalists whose livelihoods
have been taken from them

CONTENTS

ACKNOWLEDGEMENTS

We would like to thank our two researchers on this project, Karen McRorie and Dawn McLean, without whom this book could not have been written. Their enthusiasm, diligence, and many other talents are deeply appreciated. We also wish to acknowledge the work of David Robinson, whose research on media concentration and whose proposals for legislation were enormously helpful in the writing of this book. Our thanks to all the members and supporters of the Campaign for Press and Broadcasting Freedom, and to those dedicated journalists who continue to struggle against management and corporate influence. Bob Hackett at Simon Fraser University has been an inspiration as well. Thanks also to Keith Davey and Tom Kent, who had the foresight to examine the problem of corporate concentration in the news media in its relative infancy.

Special thanks to Jack Stoddart, who had the chutzpah, commitment, and vision to support this project through to its conclusion. And our thanks to the terrific team at Stoddart Publishing — editor Don Bastian, Angel Guerra, Marnie

Kramarich, Jeannine Rosenberg, Terry Palmer, and the rest —
for making this book such a joy to write.
— MAUDE BARLOW AND JIM WINTER

I would like to thank the wonderful, supportive staff team at the
Council of Canadians: Peter Bleyer, Joanne Polsky, Jill Anderson-
Piche, Angela McGonigal, David Curning, Brant Thompson,
Victoria Gibb-Carsley, Marilyn Chute, David Hendrick, Steven
Staples, Manon Charron, and Suzette Wollinger. Very special
thanks to Patricia Armstrong, my assistant and guardian angel,
who keeps me sane.

Thanks also to the board and executive of the Council of
Canadians, who had the courage to undertake the tough fight
against Hollinger, and to our lawyer and friend, Clay Ruby, who
made us proud in court. I am grateful to Gail Lem, my co-chair
on the Campaign for Press and Broadcasting Freedom, for her
unswerving support. Finally, thanks to my wonderful family for
their love: my husband Andrew; my mother and father, Bill and
Flora; and Charles, Lynn, Bill, Pam, Pat, Christine, and Carole
Anne.
— MB

I would like to thank my departmental staff Ann Gallant and
Sandy VanZetten for their assistance, as well as Sheila LaBelle,
Lina Beaudry, and my colleagues and students. I am especially
grateful to my colleague and friend Barrie Zwicker for his
support and assistance, and his tireless dedication to improving
Canadian journalism. Thanks to my wonderful family: my
parents Margaret and Ken; my siblings Janet, Judy, Joel, John,
Peggy, and Justin; my delightful children Kaeleigh and Kieran;
and of course, my partner, Gail.
— JW

PROLOGUE

In November 1969, a youthful but bellicose Conrad Black appeared before the Special Senate Committee on Mass Media, chaired by Liberal senator Keith Davey. The submission by the twenty-five-year-old Black, who at the time owned one small daily newspaper in rural Quebec, has gained some notoriety owing to his personal attack on journalists as, among other things, "ignorant, lazy, opinionated, and intellectually dishonest." For good measure he added that they are "aged hacks" who are "decrepit" and "alcoholic," words which have endeared him to the journalism profession ever since.[1]

Far less attention has been paid, however, to the substance of Black's submission and presentation to the Davey Committee. Black complained to the committee that as a small-circulation independent newspaper proprietor he couldn't reasonably be expected to own his own press, and was reliant on a competitor, Paul Desmarais's Power Corporation, to print his paper, the Sherbrooke *Record*, thirty miles away in Granby, Quebec. Black decried the existence of the Power Corp. media "colossus" in Quebec as well as the development of monopolistic chains in general. "Further consolidation" toward monopolistic situations "is reprehensible," and "monopolies are undesirable," Black wrote. "Diversity of opinion and aggressive newsgathering tend to disappear with the disappearance of competition, and public opinion could thereby become more of a hostage to private interests than a master to public policy."[2] (When his submission was released publicly, Power Corp. cancelled its printing agreement in response to the criticism. The appendix to Black's submission read as follows: "So serious was the deterioration of our relationship with our printers subsequent to the writing of this brief, that we were obliged to transfer our business to the only other printer in our geographic area, whose place of business is in the state of Vermont. We hold the unreasonableness of our former printers to be the total cause of the regrettable development."[3])

By the time Black wrote his memoirs in 1993, his perception of the "total cause" had changed. "Since the former owners' [of the Sherbrooke Record] press had been repossessed, David [Radler, one of Black's partners] determined that the most economical printer, given prevailing exchange rates, was in Newport, Vermont. We thus became the only daily newspaper in world history to be printed in a foreign country."[4]

On May 27, 1997, a greying and puffy press baron named Conrad Black looked out sleepily at the audience assembled in the Design Exchange auditorium on Bay Street in Toronto, his eyes forming little more than slits in his round face. It was just moments after 11 a.m., and Black, who dislikes rising early, may have been a little grumpy. Outside, a street demonstration sponsored by the Campaign for Press and Broadcasting Freedom greeted arriving Hollinger Inc. board members, soliciting spare change to raise $1,000 in court costs for a lost appeal of the decision by the Federal Competition Bureau allowing Black's 1996 takeover of Southam Inc. newspapers.

Inside, the occasion was the Hollinger annual shareholders' meeting, which Black, as chairman of the board, called to order. He resented having to slip in through a back entrance to avoid a confrontation with the protestors. Black had someone introduce the members of the board of directors, which included his wife, Barbara Amiel Black. They stood on command and were recognized. Then Black launched into a twenty-minute harangue, interrupted sporadically by applause and laughter from the mostly appreciative audience of shareholders, board members, employees, and various members of the Toronto establishment. After making it clear that comments and questions would only be accepted from shareholders, Black railed at "the politically primitive" country of Australia, which he said he was forced to exit when their foreign ownership controls wouldn't allow him to increase his stake in the Fairfax newspaper chain. He lashed out at the former Southam management, which he had recently fired. Speaking to the assembled media, he sent a warning to Southam minority shareholders that they should accept his buyout offer of $23.50 and not hold out for a better one, as "arithmetically-challenged fools and their money are soon parted." Of his attempt to take the company private by buying up 100 percent of the shares, he warned, "we are the last train leaving the station."

Black also ranted about the CBC, in particular the French-language network, which he described as "a house-organ of the separatist movement of Quebec." He said that endless concessions to separatists only seem to have brought separatism closer. "There is no point throwing more raw meat to constitutional cannibals," he said. And he lambasted former reporter Gail Lem, now with the Communications, Energy and Paperworkers Union, when she asked him why he didn't seek political power through public office rather than through control of the nation's press. "Her perceptions are even more deranged than I imagined," Black said, before launching into an attack on the unions which he said have "hobbled" the newspaper industry.

But Black reserved most of his venom for "the lords of our national media," the Toronto press such as *The Globe and Mail* and *The Toronto Star*. His complaint? That an opinion poll about Quebec separatism commissioned by his company, Southam, and presumably run in his own sixty of 105 Canadian dailies, was ignored by the Toronto papers. (*Toronto Star* publisher John Honderich said later, "When Southam buys a poll, they run it. When *The Star* buys a poll, we run it. We don't run each other's polls — and Mr. Black knows that very well."[5]) As a result, Black told shareholders that Hollinger was contemplating starting its own Toronto-based national newspaper, and that a decision would be made soon. Black would not be ignored. He also used the occasion to express his contempt for the Council of Canadians and its protest of his recent takeovers. He said the council would only have a case if he were buying up *The Globe and Mail* and *The Toronto Star*, or making major incursions into the television industry. "Owning Moose Jaw and the *Corner Brook Western Star* and the *Medicine Hat News*, in febrile Maude Barlow's little mind that may make me [some] kind of a Goebbels of Canada but it doesn't," he was quoted as saying.[6]

In the nearly thirty years that have elapsed between these two public performances, Conrad Black has radically altered the landscape of the Canadian news media. He has gone from owning one daily newspaper to owning sixty, including all of the newspapers in the provinces of Saskatchewan, Newfoundland, and Prince Edward Island. Observers at the Senate Committee hearing in 1969 might have been amused — or perhaps taken aback — by the strong words he used at the time. In 1997, some observers were alarmed by the display of raw power, anger, and arrogance, and the blind obeisance of the assembled crowd. Even *The Toronto Star*, duly chastened, felt compelled to report on Black's Southam poll the next day in its story on Conrad Black's meeting.

Black and Amiel have written hundreds, if not thousands, of columns, and both have written memoirs. They are the two most influential figures in Canadian journalism today, yet few Canadians understand their views on the central issues confronting our society.

Readers should prepare themselves for a shock.

1

CITIZEN BLACK

"Where had I seen Black's manner? Of course: Orson Welles in Citizen Kane. *I was talking to Citizen Black."*
— ROBERT FULFORD

"I don't think Conrad wants to be prime minister, but he really does *want to be the power behind the throne and feels his money will buy him that . . . He is one of the few people I know for whom attaining power is an all-consuming goal."*
— LAURIER LaPIERRE

There is something chilling and strangely medieval about one family administering its views to an entire population, yet that is exactly what is happening in Canada today. Together, Conrad Black and his wife, Barbara Amiel Black, have an astonishing influence over the Canadian news media. Barbara Amiel is arguably the most widely read columnist in the country, with a piece in *Maclean's* magazine reaching half a million families every month, and columns in (potentially) 72 out of 105 Canadian newspapers, through 60 papers in the Southam-Sterling-Hollinger chain, the 11-paper Sun chain, and *The Financial Post*. In fact, her potential newspaper audience is about three million families in Canada alone.

While Amiel's columns may seem to be the most obvious outlet for their views, the Blacks' true and primary influence comes through Conrad Black's corporate holdings, most importantly the newspaper/media giant, Hollinger Inc., where Barbara is vice-president editorial, and Conrad is chairman of the board and CEO, and Southam Inc., in which Black now has controlling interest. But the dozens of newspapers under his direct control extend his influence even further into the Canadian media by providing much of the material disseminated by the Canadian Press (CP) and its Broadcast News and Press News services. CP operates as a cooperative, with a relatively small newsgathering staff, and most of its employees involved in redistributing news collected by its member newspapers. Black's overwhelming membership in CP means that he reaches past his own newspapers to 9 Thomson papers, 10 in the Sun chain, those of Power Corporation and Quebecor Inc., and about a dozen independents. In all, CP is used by 86 of 105 dailies.

All but Four Papers

In the final analysis, then, through his own holdings and CP subscribers, *Conrad Black reaches every newspaper in Canada but four*: the *Times-Globe* and *Telegraph-Journal* of Saint John, New Brunswick, owned by the Irving family, the Sherbrooke *Record* (ironically one of Black's earliest acquisitions), now owned by Quebecor, as well as the *Sentinel-Review* of Woodstock, Ontario, owned by Newfoundland Capital Corporation.

Newspapers are not the only medium in the Blacks' kingdom. CP's Broadcast News wire goes into 140 radio stations, 28 television stations, and 36 cable outlets in Ontario alone. The total across the country is: 425 radio stations, 76 television stations, and 142 cable outlets. CP's Press News service is picked up by CBC radio and television, and 110 outlets in business, government, schools, and other "non-news" outlets.[1] So, through CP, Conrad Black reaches 753 private and public educational broadcasting outlets across the country, plus all of the CBC radio and television stations.[2] The CBC owns 89 stations, 1,160 CBC rebroadcasters, 31 private affiliated stations, and 292 affiliated or community rebroadcasters.[3]

Through Southam, Black also partially owns Coles Bookstores, which merged with SmithBooks in March 1995 to form Chapters Inc., a megachain of 430 bookstores with about 35 percent of the national book market. Such concentration is not without its effects. Jacquie McNish of *The Globe and Mail's* Report on Business notes that "Chapters now employs one team of only nine buyers for about 400 stores. That leaves publishers with no national alternative if Chapters shows little or no interest in a book."[4]

And the tentacles reach beyond Canadian borders. Through his personal holding company, the Ravelston Corporation, and his partnership in Sterling Newspapers and Hollinger with David Radler and Peter White, Black controls an international newspaper empire consisting of hundreds of dailies, weeklies, and free shoppers. Although this empire started with what were once modest Canadian holdings, Black's purchase of the London *Daily Telegraph*, *The Jerusalem Post*, and the Chicago *Sun-Times* in the late 1980s and early 1990s established his presence internationally. Over the decade between 1985 and 1995, his former U.S. subsidiary, American Publishing Inc. (since folded into Hollinger International Inc., another Hollinger Inc. subsidiary), under the stewardship of David Radler, was accumulating small papers throughout the U.S. at an astonishing rate. The Canadian expansion really began in 1992, when Black bought a 21 percent share of Southam Inc., the country's largest publisher. When Montreal financier Paul Desmarais also bought into Southam in 1993, Black and Desmarais together had control of the company and effectively formed a partnership. In 1995 and 1996, Black was buying up Canadian as well as American newspapers from Ken Thomson, and decided to consolidate his control over Southam by buying out Paul Desmarais in May 1996. Subsequently he increased his holdings to more than 50 percent. Thus, in the short span of about three and a half years between late 1992 and the spring of 1996, Black leapt from his position as a very minor player in Canadian newspapers to become the dominant force in Canadian news media.

Not that Black was a new figure in Canadian business. His takeover of holding company Argus Corporation in the late 1970s, his dismantling of Dominion Stores Ltd. and Massey-Ferguson Ltd. early in the 1980s, his attempted takeover (through the Calgary-based mining company Norcen Energy Resources) of Hanna Mining Co. of Cleveland — all of these machinations and more gained Black tremendous notoriety. Indeed, in 1982, Peter C. Newman of *Maclean's* magazine published *The Establishment Man*, a book about none other than Conrad Black.[5]

"People will think what I tell them to think"
Back in November 1966, Peter White, who at the time was executive assistant to Quebec's Union Nationale premier Daniel Johnson, offered his chum Conrad Black a half interest, for under $500, in two small weekly newspapers in the Eastern Townships, forty-five miles east of Montreal: *L'Avenir de Brôme-Missisquoi* in Farnham and Cowansville, and the Eastern Townships *Advertiser* in Knowlton. Black began his career as publisher of these newspapers and occasional speech-writer for Daniel Johnson.

While still the mere part-owner of the two weeklies in rural Quebec, Black was rebuked by the local town council for questioning the water quality in Brome lake. He says, "I resolved to show them the power of the press.

"Like Orson Welles in *Citizen Kane* saying 'People will think what I tell them to think,' I launched a violent campaign against the mis-managers of the dying lake," Black recalls in his 1993 autobiography, *A Life in Progress*.[6] Much later, in concluding the book, he writes that "newspapers, especially quality newspapers, remain powerful outlets for advertising and information (and Political influence)."[7] On his purchase of the influential *Jerusalem Post* in 1989, he writes, "We were, for reasons that have already been outlined, buying a good deal of influence relatively cheaply."[8] And as we will see in chapter three, he has also admitted to enjoying such influence in the British context of *The Daily Telegraph*, saying how pleased he is to have been the "beneficiary" of what he considers to be a culture unafraid of ingratiating itself to those in power.[9]

In 1969, Black and his two partners, Peter White and David Radler, bought the Sherbrooke *Record* for $20,000. According to *Financial Post* journalist and Black biographer Richard Siklos, "The new owners merely kept firing people until they reached the threshold under which it was apparent the paper would cease to function in decent form. It was a ruthless exercise, and the staff of forty-eight was soon pared in half."[10]

This soon developed into a pattern as Black and his partners formed the Sterling chain of newspapers in the early 1970s, buying up small dailies across the country. In some cases they would buy papers sight unseen over the phone; in others they would visit the papers for prior inspection. Both methods almost invariably resulted in unemployed journalists.

While Radler unobtrusively acquired small U.S. papers through American Publishing, Black diverted his attention to Argus Corp., Norcen, Hanna Mining, and other takeovers. It wasn't until the latter half of the 1980s that Black turned his attention back to newspapers. With the help of the banks and a $7 million inheritance, Black would eventually turn Hollinger Inc. into the third largest newspaper company in the world, and through Hollinger International Inc., the (Chicago) *Sun-Times* Company, and over 500 American daily, community, and free-distribution papers, the largest publisher in the U.S.

Profits of 35 Percent

In 1996, Hollinger International's profits increased fivefold from a year earlier. The Chicago-based company reported a profit of $31.7 million (U.S.) compared with $6.2 million in 1995. Hollinger Inc. CFO Jack Boultbee told *The Globe and Mail* that cost-cutting at Southam newspapers had helped the Hollinger bottom line. "We've been discovering opportunities to improve business, cut costs and increase revenue at an ever-increasing rate. It's quite astonishing what we've found. It's way beyond what we had imagined," Boultbee said. "These are papers that can get 35 per cent [profits] and even more . . . the majority of them should be in that 35 range."[11] Boultbee said the goal for the Southam newspapers is to get to 25 percent by the end of 1998. Southam's newspaper group had operating profits of about 13 percent of revenue in 1996. This is in keeping with the view, expressed by Boultbee in April 1995, that "Southam's philosophy was that they were in the business of delivering news. We're in the business of selling ads."[12]

By 1997, through Southam alone, Black controlled more than thirty dailies ranging from the *Vancouver Sun* and *Province* to the *Calgary Herald*, *The Edmonton Journal*, *The Windsor Star*, the Montreal *Gazette*, and *The Ottawa Citizen*. In total, he owned sixty out of 105 Canadian daily papers, including a 20 percent interest in *The Financial Post*. Their cumulative circulation was 43 percent of that of all Canadian dailies, and 50 percent of English-language circulation. He owned all of the daily newspapers in three provinces: Saskatchewan, Newfoundland, and Prince Edward Island; 71 percent of the dailies in Ontario and British Columbia; and two-thirds of those in Nova Scotia.

Black's international holdings include the London *Daily Telegraph*, the Chicago *Sun-Times*, and *The Jerusalem Post*. Until late in 1996 he also held a significant interest in the Fairfax chain in Australia, which he sold off to ease the debt burden resulting from his Southam and Thomson purchases. Black's remaining 142 paid-circulation newspapers have a world-wide daily combined circulation of 4,021,000. In addition, the company owns or has an interest in 358 non-daily newspapers, as well as magazines and other publications.[13]

Like American William Randolph Hearst, Black has been quite open about using his newspapers for political influence. Editors who disagree with him have sought employment elsewhere, in keeping with Hollinger president David Radler's dictum that "if editors disagree with us, they should disagree with us when they are no longer in our employ."[14] One example is Claude Gravel, who quit *Le Soleil* after less than two years of Black's ownership. Gravel said Black "did not want news stories that irritated business leaders, certain interest groups and top civil servants . . . He wanted a newspaper that was less critical. I could not bring myself to accept that *Le Soleil*, which was a respected newspaper, be turned into nothing more than a publicity pamphlet."[15]

Black has turned the Montreal *Gazette* from a moderate voice, under former editor Joan Fraser, into a shrill voice of anti-separatism. And by adding columnists such as Barbara Amiel on international affairs, and neoconservatives Andrew Coyne on national affairs, Giles Gherson on economics, and George Jonas on media and politics, Black has shifted the Southam chain sharply to the right.

Special Treatment

Two of Black's Canadian papers have thus far been selected for special treatment: the Montreal *Gazette* and *The Ottawa Citizen*. The editors of both papers resigned in 1996 over differences with the plans of Black and Hollinger. *Citizen* editor James Travers, for example, commented that "there was some room for differences of opinion that would make it difficult to continue in a job like this." He went on to add that "on social policy issues, I think we are quite far to the left of Mr. Black's point of view."[16] Under the editorship of Neil Reynolds, former president of the Libertarian Party of Canada, the *Citizen* was subjected to a thorough makeover early in 1997, from a more moderate right-wing vehicle to a strident champion of neoconservatism. In an understatement, one journalist described the changes as "probably the most dramatic transformation a Canadian newspaper has seen this decade." *The Globe*'s Doug Saunders went on to indicate that "at the same time as [Black] slashes staffs, shuts down departments and demands far higher profit margins from most of Southam's 32 papers . . . Black is shaking up the content of the larger newspapers."[17]

The *Citizen*'s new editorial-page editor, replacing Peter Calamai, who also resigned over differences with Black and Hollinger, is William Watson, former executive member with the right-wing Fraser Institute. He is joined on the editorial board by fellow Fraser Institute alumnus John Robson, conservative writer Dan Gardner, who came directly to the *Citizen* from Ontario Conservative Education Minister John Snobelen's office, and before that premier Mike Harris's office, with no prior journalistic experience. In 1997, managing editor Sharon Burnside resigned from the *Citizen*, along with her colleagues columnist Ken McQueen, editor Rozz Gucci, and health writer Elaine Medline. The latter commented, "I don't want to make any more money for Conrad Black."[18]

As for *The Gazette*, Black's partner David Radler said in August 1996 that from then on the Montreal paper would stand up for the minorities he saw as victimized by Quebec's separatist government.[19] In shifting to a hard-line stance, *The Gazette* risks exacerbating Canadian unity problems. Representing as it does the voice of English Canada to French-speaking Quebeckers, its approach may well further entrench the two solitudes. The first indication was provided when Black hired Mordecai Richler as a columnist for Southam in the spring of 1997. Richler, still on his winter hibernation in London, England, began immediately to write columns attacking the Quebec separatist movement.[20]

Political Influence

Black is also not above using the services of his journalists for partisan purposes. He describes in his autobiography how he spoke at the British Conservative Party annual conference in 1990, and how he "was assisted in preparing the speech by one of [the London *Daily Telegraph*'s] most talented and traditionalist editorial writers, Simon Heffer."[21] (A 1,510-word excerpt of this speech appeared in *The Financial Post*, of which Black owns 20 percent.)[22] Black's autobiography also reveals that he has not hesitated to use his newspapers to promote his political views. During the Conservative caucus revolt against Prime Minister Margaret Thatcher, writes Black, "our editorial support of Mrs. Thatcher was unambiguous." He goes on to describe how, during the revolt, he and editor Max Hastings "worked out our next day's editorial, which concluded that Mrs. Thatcher had been one of the greatest prime ministers of British history, and 'as long as she seeks to retain that office, she may count on the support of this newspaper.'"[23] Subsequently, according to Black, Prime Minister John Major and company went off to the Maastricht conference on European Unity in December 1991 with, "ringing in their ears, an editorial of Max's in which I had had a modest input. (My contribution was prompted in part by Barbara reading aloud to refresh our memories excerpts from Orwell's 'England, Their England.')"[24] (Max Hastings had vowed to contribute 500 pounds Sterling to his church if the Tories were re-elected.)

In the 1992 British election, as Black writes, "the newspapers owned or directed by Murdoch, Rothermere, Stevens, and me consistently warned of the consequences if Labour came in and raised income taxes and National Health Service payments to a total of 59 per cent (from about 45 per cent) as it had promised. The *Sun*, on election day, put a 300-pound topless woman on page three, and headlined: 'If Labour wins, the Page Three Girl will look like this.' They had already used the headline: 'Nightmare on [Labour leader Neil] Kinnock Street.' On election day, the front page of the *Daily Mail* was taken up by the warning: 'Don't Trust Labour!' The corresponding front page on the *Daily Express* was 'Don't Throw It All Away!' The proverbial Tory press, all the London newspapers except the *Guardian*, *Independent*, *Observer*, and *Mirror*, did a much better job of warning the people of the implications of a Labour victory than the government did." Despite this, Black claims there was balance on the news side. "We own serious newspapers and reported fairly but went as far as we could in rational editorial argument in favour of the government. In the last *Sunday Telegraph* before the election, Charles Moore, Paul Johnson, Frank Johnson, Sir Peregrine Worsthorne, Ambrose Evans-Prichard, Christopher Booker, most of our most powerful and elegant writers, fired every cannon we had in promotion of the government's cause."[25]

Black also admits to calling from as far away as Florida to make suggestions to his columnists who were not vociferous enough in their support of the Tories. "I had called Perry Worsthorne from Florida the week before, after he had virtually endorsed Labour, so colourless and convictionless did he find the Tories. I urged him to contemplate the full horror of a Labour win, and he gamely responded in the last pre-election Sunday with an endorsement of the government . . ."[26] Black writes that, after the election, "[Labour leader] Neil Kinnock gave the most ungracious concession speech I have ever heard but uttered the truest words I have heard from him: that the Tory press won the election. Certainly, the government's official campaign was not well-organized." For his role in the unofficial campaign, Black writes, "John Major graciously wrote to thank me for the *Telegraph*'s contribution to the result."[27]

More recently Black's *Daily Telegraph* played a central role in the attack on British Labour leader Tony Blair and his wife, Cherie Booth, during the spring 1997 election. According to Madelaine Drohan of *The Globe and Mail*'s European bureau, "If there is a silly picture to be had of Mrs. Blair it can be found in the news pages of *The Telegraph* . . . These are the awkward out-takes that newspapers usually reject as being needlessly demeaning of the subject or just plain juvenile." Drohan concluded that "the motive for the personal attacks would seem to be to unsettle Mr. Blair and force him into making a mistake in the crucial weeks leading up to a general election."[28]

As the British election wore on and it became increasingly evident that Blair was going to win, a unique poll by one of Black's competitors, the *Guardian* newspaper, indicated that Blair's lead had dropped to about five percentage points. *The Daily Telegraph* liked the *Guardian* poll so much that it ran on the front page, and the *Telegraph*'s own poll by Gallup, which showed Labour with a 21 percentage point lead, was relegated to the inside pages.[29]

Is this just something that takes place on foreign shores? In August 1996, following the consolidation of control over Southam, Hollinger president David Radler told *The Toronto Star* that there would be two distinct areas where Hollinger would impose its corporate will on the editorial content of newspapers. "One, the Montreal Gazette will stand up for the minorities who have been victimized by separatist governments," he said. "Two, any Hollinger paper that wants to support a Bob Rae–type socialist government better have pretty compelling reasons. We're not going to back a political party that seeks our destruction and the destruction of the capitalist system."[30]

A Thirty-Year Tradition

The conscious use of editorial power is not something new for Black and company. He has made his views known through his publications since those days in 1966 when he alternated between writing editorials in the Eastern Townships *Advertiser* and writing speeches for Quebec premier Daniel Johnson. In 1969 he published a long article in the Sherbrooke *Record* in which he paid homage to Lyndon Johnson's Vietnam war efforts. Black writes, "It was a violent assault on Johnson's critics, whom I continued to think had overlooked his efforts on behalf of blacks and the poor, misrepresented his objectives in Vietnam, and engaged in 'vulgar snobbery.'"[31] He fondly recalls writing for *L'Avenir* of Sept-Îles, Quebec, which he owned, during the provincial election of 1973. "Our reporting was fairly balanced for most of the campaign, but we did an editorial sand-bag job on the P.Q., complete with publication of a poll indicating a Liberal victory. There was no indication of the number of people sampled so the fact that I consulted only seven people (including myself) never came to light."[32]

In a 1989 exchange with former publisher Robert Maxwell over Quebec's language laws, Black demonstrated that he is capable of using the front page of his newspapers in his personal campaigns. He recalls that Maxwell "scurrilously attacked me for opposing the prohibition of bilingual commercial signs." Black says, "I replied on page one of *Le Soleil* the next morning that Bob's expressed view was 'hypocrisy and buffoonery.' He faxed me back a rather wan reply, and I published this and another withering response on page one of the following day's *Le Soleil*."[33] Black wrote in October 1991 that "when my associates and I bought that newspaper in 1987 I undertook to Premier [Robert] Bourassa to respect editorial independence at *Le Soleil*. I have occasionally, when I strongly objected to ultra-nationalist comment in *Le Soleil*, published my own, signed, dissenting views and been vituperatively attacked in nationalist circles in Quebec for my trouble."[34]

In October 1996 Black instructed his fifty-nine Canadian daily newspapers to run a column he had written responding to "The Paper King," a CBC-TV documentary which Black termed "a smear job," and "a televised kangaroo court."[35] In fact, the CBC documentary was balanced and — if anything — understated. It was produced by senior correspondent Joe Schlesinger, who confined himself to interviewing mainstream "critics" of Black such as Peter C. Newman, chronicler of the rich and famous, former Conservative MPs, and Black's former drinking buddies. Author Mordecai Richler told the camera, "I don't think [Black] should be dismissed out of hand," and went on to support chains because individual newspaper owners have gone the way of "doctors making house calls." Black's partner David Radler was given equal time to respond to the (mostly) friendly criticisms. Of the Cranbrook *Daily Townsman*, he said, "I think we are producing as good a newspaper as we can, in a market which only warrants a weekly." Radler insisted, "We are not going to change liberal papers into Conservative think-tanks."[36]

Black refused to be interviewed for the documentary, but in his column of rebuttal he denied being "extremely conservative." Margaret Thatcher would disagree, having said she found herself on his left, politically.[37] Black said he seeks "no more than a fair hearing for a range of intelligible views" in his newspapers, and that "we have had our share of controversy, but we have never departed the mainstream of Canadian opinion and our names and views do not frighten reasonable people." In the same column Black wrote that in his thirty years in the industry "we have built up one of the largest and highest-quality newspaper companies in the world," saying he has "strengthened every newspaper franchise [he has] influenced." While this might be the case for Black's flagship paper, *The Daily Telegraph* (nicknamed "the Torygraph") in London, and recently *The Ottawa Citizen*, it's hard to think of a single other example among the 500 titles he owns worldwide. The much-vaunted *Jerusalem Post* has had its reporting staff cut by 50 percent since Black took it over, while its editorial content moved far to the right.

Black went on to claim that "no editors of ours have ever retired because of interference." This, of course, would be cold comfort to Joan Fraser of the Montreal *Gazette* and James Travers and Peter Calamai of *The Ottawa Citizen*.

Black saw the CBC documentary as further evidence of what he calls "the virtual monopoly [of] the soft left" in the Canadian media. By insisting that his column be run and even dictating the headline, he has made it impossible for his own editors to deny his influence, galvanizing opposition even within the journalism ranks. He has also established a nasty precedent. What's next, front page editorials by Black, endorsing Jean Charest's Conservatives?

"Saving" CP

The extent of Black's influence over the Canadian Press may be seen in some significant 1996 events. After Black consolidated his control of Southam in June of that year, the company announced that it was considering pulling out of CP — a move that would effectively decimate the news service — and served notice to CP that it intended to do so by the end of the year. Black used the power of his threat to effect drastic cutbacks at CP, and to extract major concessions, including the resignation of CP president David Jolley. Jolley was replaced by Sterling president Michael Sifton, a Hollinger employee who, several months earlier, had proved his loyalty to Black by selling him his family's (Saskatchewan) Armadale chain and announcing a 25 percent cut in staff.

Yet in the corporate press (largely owned by Black), Black was reported to have disagreed with the Southam plan to withdraw from CP, and was credited with rescuing it from certain demise at the hands of his own company. This was a little like crediting the executioner when a reprieve for the condemned is granted. Black ended up firing Southam CEO William Ardell, who became the scapegoat for allegedly creating the threat of withdrawal in the first place.

"If people are saying we saved CP . . . fair enough," Hollinger president David Radler told *The Ottawa Citizen* in August 1996.[38] With friends like this, who needs enemies?

To provide another example of the potential for abuse of concentrated media ownership, we can turn to the Irving family of New Brunswick. The Irvings own all four English-language dailies in New Brunswick, and many of the broadcasting outlets as well. How could these news media avoid the appearance of bias and be seen to be reporting fairly on the strike by workers at Irving Oil Ltd. in Saint John, a strike which began in the spring of 1994 and lasted almost three years?

In 1997, Black added the Halifax *Daily News* to his collection, and strove (at this writing) to increase his control of Southam to 100 percent. The buyout would cost $923 million and would mean minority shareholders could no longer keep Black from using Southam's cash generated from operations — $111 million in 1996 alone.[39]

Black has become notorious for his draconian cost-cutting measures. For example, when Black purchased the Armadale chain from the Sifton family, within days he laid off about 181 people, or 25 percent of the staff. This reflects his *modus operandi* in newspapering, which entails cutting staff by an average of 30 percent, and sometimes as much as 50 percent, with the resultant boost in profits.

A case in point is the Cambridge (Ontario) *Reporter*. With a circulation of about 10,000, it was purchased by Hollinger from Thomson in the fall of 1995. One reporter with that paper called in to CBC Ontario's *Radio Noon* phone-in program in May 1996 to describe the changes under Hollinger. She spent six years as an editor under Thomson, but was demoted to reporter with the Hollinger cutbacks, which reduced staff levels by 30 percent. Under Thomson, reporters were each expected to write forty stories every month. Under Hollinger, this has doubled, "plus editorials and taking pictures and writing opinion columns," she said. As for local news content, she said, "They have people there who are doing nothing but rewriting press releases and [the owners are] tossing these off as local news."[40]

Is this something new? Back in 1978, when a PWA jet crashed in Cranbrook, B.C., the local Hollinger paper, the *Daily Townsman*, had been cut back to just four employees. As a result, according to Peter C. Newman, "the paper had to cover the tragedy mostly through dispatches from the Toronto-based Canadian Press news agency."[41]

The lesson here is that we must never underestimate Black's

ability for what he calls "demanning" in the interest of profits. The Cambridge *Reporter* example answers the pundits who wonder how it is that Black can actually buy Thomson papers and make more money with them. Thomson is merely notoriously stingy, while Black is ruthless. The irony is that the pundits then go on to heap accolades on Black because of the "commitment" to journalism he shows by his willingness to buy papers that even Ken Thomson is shedding.

Patient Shareholders

Conrad Black made $2.6 million in 1996 as CEO for Hollinger, up 5 percent from 1995. President David Radler made $2.5 million in compensation, while *Daily Telegraph* CEO Daniel Colson made $2 million. Black's personal holding company, Ravelston, has been contracted to act as manager of Hollinger and to carry out head office responsibilities. In 1996 Hollinger paid a management fee of about $11 million for this arrangement, an amount which is set to rise by 17.5 percent to almost $13 million for 1997.[42] The Southam chain cut the equivalent of $20 million in annual expenses in the third quarter of 1996 by eliminating more than 100 jobs at its Toronto head office. Severance payments to a handful of Southam executives, such as Bill Ardell, exceeded $7 million. Southam made a profit of $94 million on $1 billion in revenues in 1996. (Interestingly, Black was asked in early June 1996 whether he planned to make some changes at the senior level at Southam. He replied, "No, not the senior levels. I think they've got a lot of good people there. I think Bill Ardell has assembled a good team. It's more fine-tuning and giving a bit of leadership in places where there has been a necessity by management to tread carefully over eggshells because of the factionalism among the directors."[43])

In the spring of 1997 *The Globe and Mail* reported that Conrad Black handed himself a gift of $70 million, in the form of a special dividend on Hollinger shares. "It really was Conrad's view that it was time that our good and patient shareholders received something," said Jack Boultbee, Hollinger's chief financial officer. Boultbee added that Black has been "a good and patient shareholder, but there's lots of others . . ."[44] The dividend amounted to $2.50 per share, for a total of $140 million: half for Conrad and half for all the other patient shareholders at Hollinger. According to *The Globe and Mail*, the dividend represents some of the proceeds from the $523 million sale of Hollinger's Canadian publications to Hollinger International Inc. of Chicago early in 1997. Perhaps this kind of gift-giving is what Black was referring to when he wrote in his autobiography, regarding his Argus Corp. days in the mid-1980s, "I do not like boastful or overly materialistic people, but I had put myself in a position where I had constantly to justify my record as an executive and could only do so on the basis of enrichment of the shareholders, myself first among them. There is nothing reprehensible in that, but it was not exactly attractive, especially in Canada, where money making comes well behind 'caring and sharing' in general esteem, even in the business community, and the model of a business leader would resemble Alan Alda, if not John Denver . . . There was nothing for it but to finish the reconstruction of the business and capitalize on the antagonism that existed and to do so by continuing to exploit our relatively low share price."[45]

In the Southam Inc. annual report, distributed the week before the announcement of the special Hollinger dividend, Black wrote that the fired Southam executives were "consoled by an astonishingly generous system of golden handshakes." He lamented the fact that "management paid great attention to reinforcement of their own income security."[46] Evidently, what's good for the gander is not good for the geese.

The Southam annual report for 1996 also indicated that new publishers were hired in that year at Southam newspapers in the following cities: Kamloops, Medicine Hat, Calgary, Brantford, St. Catharines, Timmins, Hamilton, Kingston, Cornwall, and Sydney. These hirings coincided with the consolidation of control at Southam by Black. In the spring of 1997, another new publisher was announced at *The Windsor Star*, where accountant Jim McCormack, former director of circulation and marketing for *The Toronto Sun*, was hired to replace publisher Jim Bruce, who accepted "voluntary" early retirement at age fifty-five. Unlike McCormack, Bruce had risen through the reporting ranks to editor and then became publisher when André Préfontaine left to join Quebecor Inc.

Black *is* willing to invest money in some newspapers, his flagship papers such as the London *Daily Telegraph* and *The Ottawa Citizen*. When he is accused of being stingy by the press, he trots out these examples and that's the end of the discussion. But in reality, Black milks the smaller and middle circulation papers in order to feed a few bigger ones. The net result is that most people across this country are receiving a product whose quality has been substantially diminished.

The Windsor Example

When we examine the impact on a local level, it can be devastating. In the city of Windsor, Ontario, for example, the only daily is controlled by Conrad Black. In addition to the CBC, there are four private radio outlets and one private TV outlet. All five of these are owned by CHUM Ltd. under Allan Waters. So, in Windsor, aside from the CBC there is a choice between Hollinger and CHUM. (And of course the fate of the CBC is far from secure.)

Inevitably, the number and range of voices being heard is affected. How can decreasing the number of owners and outlets do anything other than reduce the diversity of views? In cities across the country we have gone from a situation where we had community, family ownership of newspapers to a family compact of chain owners. In Windsor, for example, the Graybiel family owned *The Windsor Star*, and ran it as a family business. It was quite progressive, as newspapers go. They hired Mark Farrell as editor, and in the 1970s the *Star* became the first daily paper in the country to endorse the New Democratic Party in a federal election campaign. The report of the Special Senate Committee on Mass Media, the Davey Committee, classified it as a quality newspaper in 1970. Then the *Star* was bought out by Southam, and it became more conservative and began to deteriorate in quality. In 1992, Hollinger bought into Southam, and as indicated, Conrad Black consolidated his control of that chain in 1996, swallowing it up. The fish have gobbled each other up and all we are left with now are the whales.

And the whales are even worse for journalism than the large fish that preceded them. Under Black's direction, like other members of the Southam chain, *The Windsor Star* has been subjected to drastic cuts. News and editorial staff levels were reduced by 26 percent, from 105 to seventy-eight. According to *Windsor Star* journalist Craig Pearson, Southam has begun citing "an industry standard" which allows one newsroom employee for every one thousand copies the paper sells. Pearson says he only heard of this when new publisher André Préfontaine, a hired gun formerly employed by Hollinger and Power Corp., was brought in in 1993. "They try to make it seem like this standard has been around forever, but from what I can tell this is a new thing that they decided because if they do it that way they can cut more staff."[47]

Research Shows the Impact

The quality of journalism has to be affected. Greater concentration in huge chains means cost-cutting "efficiencies" and an even greater emphasis on the bottom line. You can't make cuts in circulation and advertising because these are your profit centres. So, inevitably, if your focus is on greater profits then you have to make cuts on the news and editorial side.

Because Black's takeover of Canadian journalism has been so recent, the evidence of his negative influence has just begun to surface. One such study was conducted by professor Jim McKenzie of the school of journalism at the University of

Regina. He studied the Regina *Leader-Post* over a three-week period in the fall of 1996, after it had been taken over by Hollinger. In point form, here are some of his conclusions:

1. Advertising made up 54 percent of the content.
2. The news section contained a lot of "filler" material.
3. News content was only 25 percent.
4. Only half the news content was locally produced.
5. Human interest photos filled about one-quarter of news space.
6. Sports news dominated local coverage, at 28 percent.
7. Local news was superficial: meetings, news conferences.
8. There was virtually no investigative reporting.
9. Weekend coverage came from one freelancer, paid $150 for twenty-eight hours of work.
10. Editorials were a bland rehash simply calling for careful reflection and taking no position.
11. Local columnists wrote "feel-good" pieces.[48]

Professor McKenzie then compared these findings to an analysis of the editions published during the corresponding period in 1995, when the *Leader-Post* was owned by the Sifton family. He found that the Hollinger papers had less local news and more wire material. The report concluded as follows: "While the Armadale paper was already noticeably weak in quality and content, under Hollinger the *Leader-Post* deteriorated even further . . . Local news has been largely replaced with cheaper wire material . . . This study has shown that in the case of the *Leader-Post*, big chain ownership has not improved the quality of journalism and the news readers receive, but has in fact had the opposite effect."[49]

These findings are of particular interest considering the public claim by Conrad Black, following his purchase of the Armadale papers, that "We have undertaken that there will be no diminution of the editorial quality of those [Saskatchewan] newspapers."[50]

Another group of studies, commissioned by the Campaign for Press and Broadcasting Freedom,[51] looked at *The Windsor Star*, the Montreal *Gazette*, *The Ottawa Citizen*, *The Vancouver Sun* and the Cambridge *Reporter*. The studies, conducted at the University of Windsor and Simon Fraser University, concluded that "coverage of labour, women's issues and Native Canadian affairs was virtually non-existent" in 1996. *The Windsor Star* saw a dramatic decrease in labour coverage. In 1991, before Black's involvement with Southam, 21 percent of all front page items dealt with labour issues. By 1996, that figure had dropped to 1.8 percent. On the editorial pages of the *Star*, labour coverage in columns, letters, and editorials dropped from 9.2 percent in 1991 to just 2.9 percent in 1996. At *The Vancouver Sun*, labour stories fell from 11 percent in 1991 to 5 percent in 1996. Business coverage increased dramatically. And gender inequality increased, as the ratio of male to female writers on the front page went from 2–1 in 1991 to 3–1 in 1996.

Why We Should Be Concerned

Information is essential to our daily lives. We rely on news and information for mundane reasons such as the weather forecast, but also for awareness and understanding of the events in our community, province, nation, and the world around us. For our information some of us rely on diverse sources such as books, the Internet, the World Wide Web, alternative magazines, and so forth. But most of us continue to rely primarily on the mainstream media — television, newspapers, radio, and magazines — to understand the world.

For example, on average, Canadians spend four hours a day, twenty-eight hours a week, two months of the year, and nine years in a sixty-five-year life span watching television.

The information we receive through television and the other news media is crucial to every aspect of our lives. This information forms the basis on which we decide, for example, our stance on an issue or our support for a political candidate or party. Or who to blame for the fact that we are unemployed, or for the cut-backs to social programs.

Whoever owns and controls the news media in our society has tremendous power. The power to hire and promote editors and journalists with the "right stuff," but also the ability to disperse the views they wish to see disseminated.

Writing in *The Globe and Mail* in the spring of 1996, editor-in-chief William Thorsell stated that "the most powerful force for liberalism and democracy is information." He wrote that "power ultimately depends on assumptions, and assumptions are intimately tied to information." This is a relatively recent take on the reliable old saying that "knowledge is power." What's unusual about this particular quote is that media higher-ups such as Thorsell seldom admit to the power and influence they hold and wield on a daily basis. They prefer to downplay both their function and their responsibility.

In her bestselling book, *Shooting the Hippo*, about the role of the federal government and the Bank of Canada in fostering a debt crisis through high interest rates and a zero inflation policy, all the while blaming social program spending for our problems, journalist Linda McQuaig notes that "we must always remember that virtually all media outlets are owned by rich, powerful members of the elite." McQuaig writes, "To assume that this fact has no influence on the ideas they present would be equivalent to assuming that, should the entire media be owned by, say, labour unions, women's groups or social workers, this would have no impact on the editorial content."[52]

The most direct access to the power and influence of the media is through owning them. Increasingly, the media are owned by those with fabulous wealth. They also happen to be older, white, neoconservative males, with the names: Conrad Black, Ken Thomson, Paul Desmarais, Pierre Péladeau, Douglas Bassett, the Eatons, the Irvings, Ted Rogers, Israel Asper, André Chagnon, James R. Shaw, Allan Waters, and Allan Slaight. These thirteen families control the Canadian media. Through Baton Broadcasting, the Bassett and Eaton families control the CTV network. Israel (Izzy) Asper controls the CanWest Global TV network. Rogers and Shaw have over 50 percent of the Canadian cable audience. And Conrad Black's influence over Canada's newspapers has been well established.

When the late K. C. Irving monopolized all four of the English-language dailies in New Brunswick in the late 1960s, "the rainmaker," Liberal heavyweight Keith Davey, responded by heading up his special senate committee to investigate the mass media. A little more than a decade later, when the Southam and Thomson newspaper chains closed dailies and in effect granted each other monopolies, Tom Kent headed a Royal Commission into news media ownership.

When the Davey Committee reported in 1970, the Sterling chain did not exist. In 1981, when Tom Kent's Royal Commission reported, the Sterling chain consisted of eleven daily newspapers, nine of them in British Columbia, with a combined weekly circulation of only 292,000 readers. Black owned 6 percent of the circulation in B.C. Moreover, the Kent Commission was dismayed to report that three newspaper chains — Southam, Thomson, and the Sun chain — owned 67 percent of all English-language daily circulation, and half of all English titles. Today, Conrad Black alone owns sixty out of ninety-four English-language dailies (63 percent), with about 50 percent of English-language circulation.

If we compare this situation to what exists in the U.S., we find that eleven American corporations control 50 percent of American daily newspapers. The largest chain in the U.S. has about 10 percent of their circulation, whereas one chain has 43 percent here. And in the U.S. there are over 1,700 daily newspapers, while we have only 105.

Canada's small group of homogeneous media owners, the "Family Compact," is further interrelated through shared memberships on boards of directors. For example, Douglas Bassett, of Baton, and Conrad Black are both directors of the T. Eaton

Company Ltd. (Eaton's). Another Eaton's director is Richard Thomson, the CEO of the Toronto Dominion Bank, who also sits on the board at Thomson Corp. Of course, Eaton's filed for bankruptcy protection in February 1997, creating an enormous potential for conflict of interest. At a minimum, this gives the appearance of a conflict of interest for the news organizations owned and/or run by these people. And in its Statement of Principles, the Canadian Newspaper Association indicates that "conflicts of interest, real or apparent, should be declared." It goes on to read that "the newspaper should guard its independence from government, commercial and other interests seeking to subvert content for their own purposes."[53]

Conflicting Interests

Several other examples illustrate how the rich and powerful and their associates move effortlessly between corporations, government, and the media. Peter White is one prominent example, having bounced back and forth between serving as principal secretary in Brian Mulroney's office, while Mulroney was prime minister, and acting as overseer for Conrad Black. White also worked at *Saturday Night* magazine, owned by Black. He was president of Black's Unimedia Inc., and publisher of *Le Soleil* and *Le Droit*. Currently he enjoys an interesting combination of responsibilities, as board member for Hollinger and Southam and chairman of the PC Canada fund. In the fall of 1996 and winter of 1997, White wrote on Hollinger stationery soliciting funding as campaign chairman on behalf of the federal Conservative Party and Jean Charest.[54] This is an unusual move, because newspapers ordinarily want to maintain at least a pretence to objectivity even when they recommend support of various candidates. And here we have a prominent member of what is essentially a newspaper monopoly plunging into politics. When the Council of Canadians attempted to raise the issue publicly in the spring of 1997, just prior to the national election campaign, the news media ignored it, with the exception of one inconsequential article in *The Toronto Star*.

Another recent example of a figure with mixed interests is Norman Spector, former chief of staff for Brian Mulroney, who later appointed him Canada's ambassador to Israel from 1992 to 1995. He subsequently was hired at Imasco Ltd., parent company to Imperial Tobacco, Shoppers Drug Mart, and Canada Trust. Spector was vice-president at Imperial Tobacco. Effective in May 1997, Spector took over as publisher of *The Jerusalem Post*, appointed by none other than Conrad Black.

Allan Gotlieb was appointed Canadian ambassador to the U.S. by Mulroney. Gotlieb subsequently headed up Burson Marsteller in Canada, the giant public relations firm. He also joined the boards of Alcan Aluminum and MacMillan Inc., and then was appointed by Black to the board of Hollinger. Currently, he is also the honorary publisher of Black's *Saturday Night* magazine.

It is a direct conflict of interest for the head of one of the world's largest public relations firms to be on the board of the country's largest newspaper publisher, and publisher of a national magazine. Public relations firms such as Burson Marsteller are engaged in corporate "crisis management," which entails managing public opinion, or "damage control," during company disasters. Some of the best known examples of crisis management in the past decade have involved the following scandals: the Union Carbide chemical leak disaster in Bhopal, India, the Exxon Valdez oil spill, the asbestos and lung disease problems of Johns Manville Corp., the Dalkon Shield I.U.D. produced by A. H. Robins Co., and a connective tissue disease and its relation to silicone-gel breast implants produced by Dow Corning Inc. If any of these disasters were to occur today, and if Burson Marsteller were employed by the company involved to coordinate damage control with the media and the public, Allan Gotlieb would find himself in a serious conflict of interest. It is his job, in his primary occupation with Burson Marsteller, to manipulate press coverage of his clients.

In addition, how can we tell the people who are making policies from the corporate leaders they are making them for, and from those whose companies are reporting on those policies to the public? Black quotes approvingly from (Argus Corp. founder) Bud McDougald in his autobiography. "I asked Bud McDougald if [Claude] Wagner's [trust] fund bothered him. 'Good God no!' he replied. 'It's politicians who won't take a bribe that frighten me.'"[55]

Tools for Power

If anyone, no matter who they are, exercises monopolistic control over one of our resources, then this is cause for the utmost concern. When that resource is the daily newspaper market, which is central to our information, knowledge, and democracy itself, there is particular cause for alarm. The situation in Canada is further exacerbated by the fact that the people in control of our newspapers are Conrad and Barbara Amiel Black. If, for example, sixty out of 105 of our daily newspapers were in the hands of Ken Thomson and his chain, then it would be deplorable. Thomson, who owns *The Globe and Mail* and ten other dailies, certainly has a reputation for penny-pinching, drastic cutbacks, promotional journalism, and relentless profiteering. But aside from this, Thomson is not known for undue interference with his newspapers. As long as they make the profits, he largely leaves them to their own devices.

Because he goes beyond the miserly Thomson in the cost-cutting department, Black's newspapers are, generally speaking, necessarily of lower quality than Thomson's. But in addition to this, as we have seen, not only does Black hold rabidly neoconservative views, but he guides his newspapers in the same direction, using them for propagandistic and political influence. Where Ken Thomson is merely interested in large profits, Conrad Black wants bigger profits, as well as power and influence.

It is this aspect of Black's control that is most disturbing: his desire to use his newspapers for purposes of power and political influence. That is why he got into newspapering in the first place. That is why he has been writing cheques for political campaigns dating back at least to the mid-1970s. In 1983 he paid to bus Quebec delegates to Winnipeg to vote against Joe Clark, "stuffed into buses like sardines, having no idea where they were, what they were doing, or what the Conservative Party was, taught only to vote yes for a convention."[56] That's why he loaned Peter White to work full time on Brian Mulroney's leadership campaigns. Of the 1983 leadership campaign, Black writes, "As the campaign progressed, our companies supported Brian not only with large donations, but also in picking up Peter White's bills as he travelled and worked with the candidate."[57] While he supported Claude Wagner's leadership bid in 1976, he says, "I gave some support to Brian."[58] He notes, "Our companies contributed somewhat generously to John Turner's campaign to succeed Pierre Trudeau in the summer of 1984."[59] And power is the reason why Black has stacked his board of directors at Hollinger with international movers and shakers, from Margaret Thatcher to Henry Kissinger, Peter Bronfman, Paul Reichmann, and Peter Munk.

Academic and broadcaster Laurier LaPierre taught Black when he attended Upper Canada College, a Toronto private school. He also advised Black's master's thesis on Duplessis at McGill University. LaPierre says, "I don't think Conrad wants to be prime minister, but he really *does* want to be the power behind the throne and feels his money will buy him that . . . He is one of the few people I know for whom attaining power is an all-consuming goal."[60]

To a degree, Black endorses this assessment in his autobiography. Writing about his investment in Southam, Black intones, "Our corporate destiny is now disclosed, if not manifest, to even the most sceptical onlooker, (though few audible sceptics remain). Newspapers, especially quality newspapers, remain powerful outlets for advertising and information (and political influence)."[61]

In writing about his beginnings in the newspaper business, with his two small weeklies in rural Quebec, Black remembers, "I had a sense that I had started on a career that could be greatly fulfilling. The combination of information, comment, finance, management, and potential influence was very alluring, even at the mundane levels I had experienced them."[62]

Although concentration of ownership of the news media has been developing throughout this century, it has now reached such alarming proportions that we simply cannot rely on the news to inform us about our society and the world around us. The distortions are evident from reading alternative sources such as Linda McQuaig's books, or those of Noam Chomsky, or others.[63]

In just three decades Conrad Black has evolved from a wealthy law school dropout (he failed most of his law courses at York University, but eventually graduated in law from Laval University) who owned two weekly newspapers in Quebec to the fabulously rich owner of one of the largest media empires in the world. Much of his Canadian influence was achieved in less than four years. He continues to use his newspapers and his wealth to attain and exercise power and influence in North America, Great Britain, the Middle East, and elsewhere. Along the way he has been dubbed the "Establishment Man," the bad boy of Canadian capitalism, with his controversial takeover of holding company Argus Corporation, the sale of Dominion Stores with its pension fund scandal, and the dismantling of Massey-Ferguson, the farm implement manufacturer which was once Canada's largest multinational firm.

Black seeks power and claims he has none. "Most people are corruptible. I agree with Lord Acton, power does tend to corrupt. But I've never perceived that I have much power," he told journalists while promoting his autobiography.[64] Others — including Black himself, no doubt, in more candid moments — would disagree. But the greatest power of all is the power to influence, if not determine, what people think, and this is Black's ultimate pursuit.

2

WANTING TO BE LIKED

"I'm not interested in popularity. I just don't want to be synonymous with something that is a magnet for public hatred."

— CONRAD BLACK

"It's terrible not to be liked."

— BARBARA AMIEL

We can tell a lot about people by whom they choose to admire. Conrad Black's long-time friend, journalist Brian Stewart, has said, "Conrad has always been impressed by the impressive — in the sense that he likes political figures to look impressive, be regal, authoritative in appearance. That's why he likes [Charles] De Gaulle."[1] Daniel Colson, a close friend from Black's law school days at Laval, says, "What I do remember vividly is that Conrad has always had this great fascination with power. Newspapers — quality newspapers, big newspapers — are obviously closely associated with power and influence. The fact that he ultimately became interested in and involved with newspapers to that extent doesn't surprise me in the least."[2]

Three of Conrad Black's most admired heroes are American publisher William Randolph Hearst, Maurice Duplessis, the premier who ruled Quebec with an iron fist, and Napoleon Bonaparte. Biographer Richard Siklos sums it up: "The goal is invincibility, if not immortality."[3]

As a young man travelling in Spain in the 1960s, Conrad Black read a biography of William Randolph Hearst. According to journalist Brian Stewart, Black's travelling companion at the time, Black was transfixed. "He had just read the book *Citizen Hearst*, and it struck me as a very unusual person for Conrad to be fascinated by. He'd go on about Hearst and quote him endlessly."[4] Hearst inherited fabulous wealth from his parents, was expelled from Harvard University, established an influential newspaper chain, was elected to the U.S. Congress, and in the early years of this century, ran unsuccessfully for mayor of New York City, governor of New York, and the U.S. presidency. Hearst, who was given an unflattering depiction in the 1941 Orson Welles film *Citizen Kane*, and subsequently curtailed the film's distribution, is remembered for the grotesque opulence of his castle at San Simeon, California. His outspoken militarism directly influenced the declaration and conduct of the Spanish-American War, and some blame him for starting it. He is renowned for his pursuit of power and prestige, above all else. W. A. Swanberg, the author of *Citizen Hearst*, described Hearst's inner self as, "Caesar, Charlemagne, and Napoleon combined. He was the most megalomaniac of men, supremely sure of his own greatness . . . He revered greatness and felt a kinship with the great."[5]

Black seems to have a deep interest in history's more autocratic and warlike leaders. He has described himself as "an amateur Napoleon buff" who is "partially captivated by his attainments as a military commander, aphorist, swashbuckler, and self-mythologist."[6] Elsewhere, Black is quoted as saying, "[Napoleon's] talents as a military commander are, to say the least, rather impressive . . . How he managed to persuade the French public to become nostalgic about him after all the carnage for which he was largely responsible, is an amazing thing. Selling glory is a little hard when the sole beneficiary of the glory is yourself — I mean, selling it to the people who give up their lives and limbs for you. But all that said, I've never found him an attractive personality, just a great talent . . . He was indifferent, I think, to the misery that arose at least partly in consequence of his policies. In certain areas he was surprisingly unimaginative. As a statesman, he had no policy really except making war."[7] A collector of model battleships, Black's preoccupation with military history is renowned, his fixation revealed through his constant use of military analogies. When Black appeared on the BBC radio program *Desert Island Discs*, where guests play songs they would choose if confined to a desert island, his selections included Beethoven's *Emperor* piano concerto, "The Battle Hymn of the Republic," and General Douglas MacArthur's 1951 farewell address to the United States Congress.[8] He has also expressed his admiration for Abraham Lincoln and his steadfast approach to war, saying, "Now there was a man associated with a terrible war, but whose solicitude for the victims was very real. And yet he made the conscious and no doubt the difficult decision of pursuing the war to absolute victory in the name of a just cause."[9]

Another hero is former Quebec premier Maurice Duplessis. Black became interested in Duplessis during a conversation with the man's disciple, former Quebec premier Daniel Johnson, in the mid-1960s. "I had, until then, the standard English-Canadian view of Duplessis as more or less of a domestic Hitler," Black later wrote.[10] "George C. Scott said of General Patton, whom he so masterfully portrayed in the famous film, and I felt similarly about Duplessis: 'He was a splendid anachronism and I rather enjoyed the old gentleman.'"[11]

Duplessis was rabidly anti-communist and introduced the infamous "Padlock Law" in Quebec in the 1930s. It included draconian measures which prevented people from gathering in groups, and resulted in the jailing of liberals and Jews and others "who were communists even though they didn't know it," as a cabinet minister in his government at the time commented. The law, which was in effect for twenty years, until the late 1950s, allowed the government to padlock businesses and residences, closing them down.

After failing law school in Ontario and later passing the bar exam in Quebec, Black wrote his master's thesis at McGill on Duplessis and in 1977 published a 684-page book on him, with over one thousand footnotes. In Black's view, Duplessis's negative image was the result of an English ("Toronto specialists") and French ("quasi-fascist Jesuit myth makers") conspiracy, a "vast and oppressive orthodoxy."[12] To Black, the man who ruled Quebec so tyrannically for eighteen years, jailing anyone he suspected to be a communist, exemplified the benefits of benevolent dictatorship.

Black went on to defend Duplessis, praising him, ironically, for adopting the very social measures which Black would later come to condemn. "Quebec had made more economic progress, adopted more useful social programs, including some of Canada's most generous pension, day-care, and minimum-wage arrangements, built more roads, schools, hospitals, and universities, all under Duplessis, than ever before or subsequently."[13]

Others have influenced Conrad Black greatly as well, such as his father, George Black, who was president of Canadian Breweries in the 1950s under E. P. Taylor (see chapter five, "News Without Journalists"). Indeed, as Richard Siklos writes, "For Black, a quest [to make money and succeed in business] that may have been fuelled by a sense of destiny coupled with a craving for the approbation of his deceased father has moved far beyond earlier motivations,"[14] to what has become empire building.

Through his newspapers Black has been a staunch defender of the Vietnam policies of Lyndon Johnson and Richard Nixon, and the trickle-down economics of British prime minister Margaret Thatcher and U.S. president Ronald Reagan. Of Johnson, whom he has described as "a great man," Black wrote in one of his newspapers in the 1960s that "a less patient and dedicated man, when taunted incessantly with the chant 'Hey, hey LBJ, how many kids have you killed today?' might have been tempted to reply: 'None, unfortunately.'"[15]

Black has written that Nixon was "a figure of transcendent durability, startlingly intelligent, surpassingly skilful in his analysis of international affairs and domestic politics," describing him as "a considerate, courteous, unselfconscious, humourous even pleasant, or at least generous, man."[16] Earlier, Black had told Peter C. Newman, "Nixon's problem was basically psychological and he deserves the compassion due to sick people. He was sleazy, tasteless, and neurotic, but I thought he had one partially redeeming virtue: he had the mind of a foreigner . . ."[17]

Of Thatcher Black has said, "I have rarely knowingly yielded to anyone in my admiration for Margaret Thatcher." She had, he said, "redeemed her country from vassalage to the thugs of the Labour union leadership."[18]

He introduced Reagan as keynote speaker at the annual Hollinger dinner in 1989 as follows: "He has been judged by his countrymen, to whom alone he was answerable, to have altered for the better the course of American and of world history. No statesman can aspire to more, and few there are who attain so much."[19] Elsewhere he wrote that Reagan's introduction of a top personal income tax rate of 28 percent "qualified him in my estimation for Mount Rushmore," and that "the nation and the world vindicated him. His entire public career was based on the incentive economic system, the superiority and legitimacy of democratic government, and the criminal fraudulence of communism."[20]

What People Think

As we've seen, Black was an important financial backer for Brian Mulroney's two federal Conservative Party leadership bids. He also employed Mulroney for a time when Black controlled and Mulroney was president of the Iron Ore Company of Canada Ltd. Of Mulroney he wrote, "he was in policy terms the best [prime minister] Canada has had since Louis St. Laurent."[21] Earlier, following the 1988 election, Black said: "Brian Mulroney, whatever the electorate's just or unjust reservations about him, emerges as a leader of serious historic proportions . . . The Prime Minister's record of political and legislative accomplishment is impressive by any standards."[22] Black made it clear, however, that his opinion of Mulroney does not even approach the esteem he holds for people like Nixon, Reagan, Thatcher, Henry Kissinger, and so forth. He agrees with the policies Mulroney introduced, and admires his relentless ambition, but feels Mulroney falls short on deep commitment to Black's own paleoconservative ideals.

But there are similarities between Mulroney and Black. Both are preoccupied with external approval. "[Black] was always very curious and anxious to know what people thought of him," says his friend and partner Peter White. "Whenever he met anybody that he looked up to or that he was impressed by, he always wanted to know what they thought of him. He doesn't do that much any more, but he used to do that all the time," White told Richard Siklos. "Mulroney always had the same anxiety. I'm not a psychologist but it's a sort of need for appreciation and recognition that I think Conrad and Mulroney and a lot of other people share."[23] For his part, Black says, "I'm not interested in popularity. I just don't want to be synonymous with something that is a magnet for public hatred."[24] In another interview he was reportedly surprised to learn that "some people see him as an intellectual bully." Black responded, "You cannot possibly be unaware of the fact that it is difficult to know exactly what one's image is. I do not at all have the mind of a bully — in my mind, bullies are intolerant of contrary opinion, domineering and rather cowardly. I would hope that none of those terms could be fairly used in describing me."[25]

"Like stringing fish"

From those beginnings in the fall of 1966 when Black was co-owner and publisher of two small weekly newspapers in the

Eastern Townships of Quebec, he began to acquire other newspapers. After a failed attempt to buy the collapsing Toronto *Telegram* in 1971, Black writes, "Undismayed by our inability to buy one of Canada's largest newspapers, the *Telegram*, I picked up Keith Davey's Special Senate Committee on Mass Media report, consulted the appendix that listed the daily newspaper owners, and telephoned all the independents, offering fairly explicitly to buy their properties."[26]

By 1972, Black owned newspapers in Sherbrooke, Quebec, Prince Rupert and Fort St. John, B.C., and Charlottetown, P.E.I. As he put it, "We now owned newspapers from coast to coast, admittedly with long gaps on the way. It was like stringing fish."[27] In 1977, Black sold the Sherbrooke *Record* to media magnate John Bassett's cousin, George MacLaren, for $865,000, having bought it for $18,000 eight years earlier.

With his newspaper chain underway, Black turned his attention to Argus Corp., E. P. Taylor's former holding company — in what was perhaps an effort to avenge the firing of his father twenty years earlier. Methodically describing his approach to gaining control of the company, then under the leadership of Bud McDougald, Black writes, "I spent 1977 establishing my candidacy as a plausible alternative to Paul Desmarais and Hal Jackman when the McDougald era might end."[28] In 1978, after the death of Bud McDougald, Black achieved control of Argus, and soon began to dismantle two of its major holdings, farm implement giant Massey-Ferguson and Dominion Stores. But this period was laden with lawsuits and corporate machinations, for which Black eventually lost patience. By 1984, he had turned his attention to expanding his little newspaper chain and taking it international, first into the U.S. through American Publishing and then into Britain and Australia.

A Public Transformation

According to Black's first wife Joanna (nee Shirley Walters), "I was attracted to the *real* Conrad Black — the person that is under there. When I first met him I didn't see that real person, I saw this arrogant stuffed shirt. But after a while I realised that underneath that arrogance was a wonderful, vulnerable, very shy man."[29] Biographer Richard Siklos says Joanna saw the private Black increasingly transform into his public persona. "See, Conrad is very quotable because I think he's living in a book," Joanna said. "Conrad had written his life and he'd had it all planned out. And everything he spoke was quotable. Not to me — he would say, 'Let's get a pizza' to me — but if he were being interviewed by somebody or if he were at a dinner party with people there of interest or influence, he would be very quotable, very colourful."[30] The former Mrs. Black married a former priest about a year after their divorce was finalized. Said Black, "What proved to be a mortal blow to our marriage was my wife's almost unquenchable interest in the company of selected members of the Roman Catholic clergy. Our houses were virtually turned into seminaries, where I was not her de facto preferred male company . . . In May 1993, she married one of the clergymen, after he had changed his occupation to environmental studies."[31]

"Power is sexy"

Shortly after Conrad Black acquired the London *Daily Telegraph* in 1986, Barbara Amiel wrote, "I have never noticed how [Conrad] handles knotting his tie or washing behind his ears, because he handles words with such considerable skill . . . I have always been intrigued by the manifestations of Conrad Black. He understands power."[32] Richard Siklos notes that in a 1986 article in *Chatelaine* entitled, "Why Women Marry Up," Amiel wrote that "power is sexy, not simply in its own right, but because it inspires self-confidence in its owner and a shiver of subservience on the part of those who approach it."[33]

Barbara Amiel was born into a comfortable middle-class family in east London in 1940. Her father, a lawyer and a colonel, and her mother, a nurse, divorced when she was nine. In 1952 her mother remarried and emigrated to Hamilton, Ontario. Soon thereafter her father committed suicide. According to Richard Siklos, "relations between Barbara and her mother were tense."[34] When she was fifteen her family moved to St. Catharines, where Barbara enrolled in high school. "I could construct fairly decent sentences and so between after-school jobs I became the St. Catharines *Standard* high school correspondent with my own newspaper column." She was also editor of the school yearbook, which helped her to become "pledged to the best sorority in St. Catharines."[35] She enrolled at the University of Toronto in 1959, studying philosophy and English, meeting her first husband Gary Smith, a political science student from Forest Hill. Their marriage, the first of four for Amiel, lasted less than nine months.

She joined the CBC after graduation as a typist for the *Juliette* show, rising to script assistant and on-air interviewer, a role in which she later described herself as "a lacquered apparition with bouffant hair, glazed smile, and detachment bordering on the unconscious often reinforced by the mandatory dosage of Elavil," an anti-depressant to which she says she was addicted for seven years.[36] In a CBC television interview to promote her book in 1980, Amiel said she remained addicted to codeine, but was down to "eight to ten" 222s a day, from twenty.[37]

An Ideological Mentor

With her second husband, George Jonas, Amiel co-authored her first book, *By Persons Unknown*, about a Canadian businessman who contracted his wife's murder. Her relationship with Jonas lasted seven years until 1979, when she left him for travel agent Sam Blyth, who was thirteen years her junior. Siklos comments, "The relationship with Blyth didn't endure, but Amiel and Jonas remained close friends and Amiel considered him her ideological mentor."[38] Jonas has remained an important influence. When she was editor of *The Toronto Sun* early in the 1980s, she ran his columns in the paper. Early in 1997, as vice-president editorial for Hollinger, Amiel hired Jonas as a columnist for Southam News.

Writing in *Maclean's* in 1987, Amiel paid homage to her mentor, whom she described as "a best friend." "Jonas and I had no grand design, only a need to write. Gradually we came to be perceived as 'neoconservative' writers, and later on we were branded as even extreme right-wing by the mainstream media that remain almost universally left-of-centre in its [sic] leanings. We did begin to see ourselves, I think, as slightly beleaguered, although I was probably more sensitive to this than Jonas. It disturbed me that we were never asked to contribute even guest columns to mainstream newspapers like *The Globe and Mail* or *The Toronto Star*, even as they were bringing more and more left-wing columnists on board."[39]

Amiel reserves high praise for Jonas. "I think in all the years of writing, reading and travelling, I never met as fine a mind as that of Jonas. We were together for seven years, then divorced, but my estimation of him has never wavered."[40] And, she is not in the least offended by suggestions that Jonas has influenced her own thinking. "One Canadian writer, I forget whom, said in a book that I had 'the finest secondhand mind in Canada,' referring to the influence on me of George Jonas. Perhaps the remark was meant to hurt, but it didn't."[41]

Writing earlier in her autobiography, Amiel described an incident on the Sparks Street Mall in Ottawa in 1972, when she and Jonas came upon some Vietnam war protestors. Her account is interesting for what it reveals of Jonas's (and her own) views. "By now I loathed the sight of pretend-moralists of all placards and no brains latching on to second-hand causes," she wrote. Her fiancé Jonas confronted the protestors. "His face bright with enthusiasm, he stood in the middle of their path." The protestors avoided him. "Jonas, who came from Budapest in 1956, always dreamed of finding a left-winger in North America who would be willing to live up to the militancy of his words, not when mobbing a lone liberal school administrator, but in a hand-to-hand encounter with a large, unpleasant Hungarian. 'It's a little guerrilla theatre they need,' he'd say. He was forever out of luck."[42]

Making reference to Jonas's work, Amiel says he "takes on every sacred cow grazing on the uncultivated Canadian landscape of ideas," that he "illustrates the absurdities of Canada's feminist no-fault divorce and community property laws . . . " She then quotes at length from his work and goes on to conclude, "Oh, Canada! What monstrous ideas we have legislated in the name of progressivism. Thank God we have one writer [Jonas] who can see them so clearly. And thank God that unlike Barbra Streisand, who wept over the phone to Robert Redford in *The Way We Were* that her divorce meant she had lost her best friend, I managed to keep mine."[43]

Southam introduced Jonas as its new columnist in 1997 as, simply, "a Toronto broadcaster and author." In one of his first columns he wrote about the "two sides to any environmental issue." He quoted one scientist's data which he said showed "that global warming is a trivial problem, and climate changes are part of nature's ebb and flow." Jonas wrote that beginning in the late 1960s we "were being overtaken by ecological hysteria," as journalists became "propagandists for environmental causes . . . For 20 years, the environment was placed on the media's own 'protected species' list, there to join certain other issues (feminism, for one)."[44]

"Always a right-winger"

In 1980, aged thirty-nine, Amiel published her autobiography, *Confessions*, ostensibly about her transformation from a naive young ideological Marxist to a much wiser neoconservative. The change may have been more obvious to her than to observers. She quoted Rosemary Speirs, now a journalist with *The Toronto Star*, but then a review editor for *The Varsity*, the student paper at the University of Toronto, as telling her, "You always were a right-winger, even at university." Amiel responds, "Whatever the perception of others, I saw myself clearly as a left-winger. It was also clear to me that, welcome though such views were on the campus, I was not talented enough for an academically distinguished life. This was crystal clear to the University, who regretfully informed me in a discreet note that I was debarred from the School of Graduate Studies on this, the occasion of my second failure in Anglo-Saxon grammar."[45]

Amiel acknowledges that she was given her start by Peter C. Newman at *Maclean's*, where she still writes a monthly column. "How many journalists of any persuasion get such an opportunity?" she has mused.[46] In 1981 she was hired as a columnist by *The Toronto Sun*, and within two years became its editor, the first woman editor of a Canadian daily. One of the things she did as editor was to cut back her former school chum, columnist James Fleming, from three to two columns weekly, with a commensurate reduction in the pay he earlier negotiated with publisher Donald Creighton. As Minister of Multiculturalism in the cabinet of Pierre Trudeau, Fleming introduced a draft Canada Newspaper Act in 1983, in a vain attempt to limit corporate influence on the news. (The act was ultimately killed by political pressure exerted by the newspaper chains.) For his part, Fleming described Amiel, in an interview in 1996, as "extremely right wing."[47]

Along the way, Amiel has dropped hints that she is insecure about her own worth. In 1980 she lamented in a column in *Chatelaine* magazine: "I so loathe the permissive promiscuous society and so long for fidelity, stability and monogamy, but it is always just out of my reach. There is a thing called discipline. I have tried to inflict it on my work. I've tried to inflict it on me. But all that emerges is self-indulgence."[48]

In 1984 Amiel married cable television magnate David Graham, and gave up the *Toronto Sun* editorship to accompany him to England, where she was hired as a columnist by the prestigious *Times* of London. Three years later, this third marriage had ended. Siklos writes, "Joanna Black recalled running into Amiel in a shop on Sloane Street a few months after the Blacks had taken up residence in London in 1990. Amiel congratulated Joanna on how well she was doing in London and how she must have done the right thing to become so popular. 'Everybody likes you,' she recalled Amiel telling her. 'It's terrible not to be liked.'"[49] Elsewhere, in 1980, Amiel had commented, "Really, I won't talk about my personal life because I am ashamed of it."[50] And, in an interview promoting her autobiography, *Confessions*, Amiel said, "I wish I were a better person." Asked whether she liked herself, Amiel replied, "If you ask do I like me, this person sitting here, on a very personal level? No. Not particularly."[51]

By 1991 Amiel was a political columnist with the London *Sunday Times*, and rumoured to be involved with its publisher Lord Weidenfeld,[52] although she later maintained the relationship was purely platonic. Her marriage to Black occurred in 1992. By 1994, Amiel had given up her column with the *Sunday Times*, after undergoing surgery. She relinquished the column, in part due to the difficulties of working for her husband's competitor, Rupert Murdoch, during a time of intense competition and a price war in London. Amiel continues to write for *Maclean's* magazine, and Black's sixty Canadian dailies, including *The Financial Post*.

3

TO THE MANNER BORN

"I have always had the twin ambitions to have at least $100 million and to get away from Canadian winters."

— CONRAD BLACK[1]

Canada is a nation in social transition. In the last decade, 60 percent of families with children lost ground: Campaign 2000, a national coalition of social welfare groups, reports that since 1989, the number of poor children has risen 46 percent, those living in poor single parent families by 58 percent, and those living in families needing social assistance by 68 percent. Canadian society is creating an entrenched underclass and a new elite.

The wealthiest 10 percent of Canadian families now hold as much of the income pie as the bottom 60 percent. Corporate profits hit a twenty-year high in 1996. Since 1975, executive pay has jumped over 100 percent; some CEOs now earn 1,000 times more than their workers. While ordinary Canadians pay 22 percent more income taxes than they did a decade ago, corporations get away with paying less every year; they now account for around 10 percent of all tax revenues collected in Canada.[2]

Conrad and Barbara Amiel Black have clear and emphatic views on the issues of wealth, privilege, and class. They are themselves very wealthy and move in a rarefied global circle that includes corporate barons and royalty. Black views his station as earned and he defends the growing class system in Canada and elsewhere as the inevitable and natural consequence of liberty. He writes, "It has always seemed to me that the real establishment in this country should be a handful of owners and a group of extremely capable managers so self-assured as to *behave* like owners, plus a battery of some lawyers and heads of large accounting firms and discreet stockbrokers who serve them well and with whom they are comfortable. The core of the actual establishment ought to be this relatively small number of actual proprietors whose companies are on the move."[3]

Another time Black wrote, "My natural sympathies are with the proprietors, whose own money is at stake . . . The buck literally stops with him. It has been a particular pleasure to see some of Canada's leading financial families renew and multiply their fortunes in a way that the usual leftist caricature of the hereditary rich doesn't provide for. Less satisfying, but no less an affront to the leftist conviction that the rich (inevitably) get richer (as if there were anything wrong with that), has been the evaporation of many recently accumulated fortunes . . .

"That the fact of having successful antecedents doesn't deprive people of all possible merit brightens the horizons for all those aspiring to continuity and seeking to avoid the treadmill of clogs to clogs in three generations. Nor does this durability of deserving families imply any inaccessibility to newcomers. Paul Desmarais, the Reichmanns, Ted Rogers, Jimmy Pattison, and many others assumed their rightful positions as successful and respected leaders in their fields without being constrained for an instant by the presence of 'established' socio-economic families.

"It is a myth of the left and one of the well-springs of the pervasive Canadian spirit of envy that the success of a person implies the failure or exploitation of someone else. Our economic system is not based on single-combat war or a zero-sum game. It is a dynamic process where the greater the number and effort of economic participants, the greater the transactional velocity of money, the greater the general prosperity, given a reasonable legislative and regulatory framework."[4]

"I had not been uninfluenced by my father's laudations of capitalism and had enjoyed my limited experiences of its benefits. I had always found most of the redistributive left phoney, envious, and mediocre bleeding hearts whining and snivelling about meritocratic Darwinism, almost as boring as and much more dangerous than the Establishment drones who aroused their resentment."[5]

Black grew up with wealth and in the presence of the establishment elite. His father was a "pervasive capitalist." "Toronto in the fifties and much of the sixties was, as has been described, a dreadfully drab and unstylish place and much of what little flair there was was provided by these men. They served wine at dinner and were driven about in cars that usually had some high-quality coach work on them. Their rites of the Establishment helped to give the city a patina of taste and refinement: Phillips at the University of Toronto, McDougald at the Toronto Club, and Taylor at the Jockey Club, where almost every year, he accompanied the Queen Mother or some other Royal to the winner's circle at Woodbine, which he built and where, in effect, he, as chairman of the Jockey Club, gave the trophy to himself as winning owner."[6]

"When [Taylor], to whom the horse-racing enthusiasts of Ontario owed so much, including the existence of the splendid racetrack in which we were then assembled, accompanied the annual visitor from the Royal Family to the winner's circle the boos and brickbats were thunderous. This was not a good-natured, sporting Bronx cheer; it was the full-throated roar of Canadian spite and envy, a voice I have heard many times since."[7]

"Membership in the Toronto Club, the supreme seat of the Toronto Establishment, was very useful. My father had bought the building next to it on Wellington Street for a headquarters for the United Appeal. When the organization determined that it couldn't use it, he offered it at his cost, despite a sharp increase in value, to the Toronto Club to be turned into a parking lot. The longtime chairman of the management committee, John A. (Bud) McDougald, whose control of access to the membership was legendary and real, demonstrated his gratitude by having delivered to my parents' house on my twenty-first birthday a letter welcoming me as a member of the Toronto Club. My brother was admitted the same day. I don't believe that either of us had ever made out an application."[8]

(Of McDougald, Black said, "Behind this imposing facade there still existed the seamy and meanly cynical Bud of old whom his acquaintances of youth had never forgotten. 'I like depressions; I always make a lot of money from them,' he boasted.")[9]

A trip to Cuba in his youth "was all so depressing, that there was nothing for it but to go, via Mexico, New Orleans, and Miami, to Palm Beach, to take up the invitation of my father's business partner, John A. (Bud) McDougald. It was an efficient antidote to the Cuban sojourn. The huge, splendidly maintained mansions, the swarms of Rolls-Royces and Ferraris and Mercedes-Benzes and Aston Martins, the violently rich winterers in the Everglades, and Bath and Tennis Clubs, even the demented Birchite social prattle of the idle rich, all, even that, seemed to have more of a future than the Spartan, Newspoken, tropical Stalinism of Fidel."[10]

The young Black also visited France, where he got very drunk one night. "One evening in Biarritz, after pausing for dinner in the Pyrenees near Pau, my companions and I settled into an ambitious night of fiery Armagnac and nostalgic reflection. We were staying in the Hôtel du Palais, built as Napoleon III and Eugenie's summer palace, which I had first visited in 1963, when the Duke of Windsor and the Emperor of Ethiopia were staying there . . .

"I expressed measured awareness to my friend M. Lafarge, the chief concierge, of the excesses of the previous evening and the hope that his attentive colleagues were not 'scandalized.' He professed not to know what I was talking about, and he assured me he had seen the 'crowned heads of Europe pass out in the fountain and crawl through this lobby on their hands and knees. I respectfully urge you, sir, not to utilize the word 'scandal' lightly.'"[11]

Black's father's funeral was a who's who of the Canadian Establishment. "We thought of a private funeral, but at the very welcome suggestion of my sister-in-law, we resolved to try to recreate the days of his prominence. As honorary pallbearers, I recruited Bud McDougald, E. P. Taylor, Nelson Davis (an old friend, who fervently avoided publicity but had just been revealed by Peter Newman to be one of Canada's wealthiest men), even John Bassett, who, when Douglas asked him, replied that he hadn't 'seen George Black in ten years,' but accepted . . . It was a moving tribute and a poignant hour, capped by the industrialists' prayer at the graveside that I had first heard when my mother and I attended the memorial services for Neil McKinnon in 1975, the former chairman of the Bank of Commerce. 'May God's mercy come to those who serve him, by expanding the commerce of the nation.'"[12]

The "violently rich"

So Conrad Black, the adult, took his place with Canada's royalty. "The first step was to establish credibility in the Establishment manner, become known, pick up a few directorships, especially a bank."[13]

His days were spent with his kind, like Nelson Davis — "a shy and private man, but a tasteful owner of classic boats and private golf courses"[14] — whom he picked to be chairman of Argus, and from whom his family had always bought their Cadillacs — banker David Montagu — "I had met him once, at a race track, when I was in Britain on Massey-Ferguson business in 1979. David had been a very active race-horse owner and once, when queried by telex from Merrill Lynch in New York why he had flown first class from London (to watch one of his horses at Longchamps), telexed back, informatively, 'Chartered jet not available.'"[15] — and Walter Annenberg — "whom my father might have described as 'down to his last four billion dollars.'"[16]

He describes a dinner party an "arch-conservative, violently rich community" in Palm Beach had given for then governor Ronald Reagan, attended by, among others, "a retired air force general, advertising head and friend of Alexander Woolcotts, who, in the mad fashion of Palm Beach, actually believed that General Dwight D. Eisenhower was a 'card-carrying communist' . . .

"At the end of it all, a mighty procession of Palm Beach's most ostentatious automobiles awaited at the front of the Breakers Hotel. As far as the eye could see were Mercedes Benz 600s and 900s, Rolls-Royce Phantoms, Silver Clouds, Corniches, Shadows, and Spurs, many elongated or transformed from saloons to drop-heads in proof of their owners' ingenuity at devising methods of spending an additional $100,000 on a $200,000 automobile."[17]

Black also recalls with amusement an incident with Hal Jackman, a director of Argus. "It was at about this time that Fred Eaton asked our commissionaires to remove a jalopy from our parking lot on Toronto Street during a board meeting he arrived at while it was in progress. He couldn't imagine that such a vehicle could be driven by an Argus or Hollinger director. It was a wreck of Jackman's that was one of his many send-ups to the conventional attitudes of the Toronto Establishment."[18]

In 1987 Black set up an international advisory board for Hollinger that has included former British prime minister Margaret Thatcher, former U.S. secretary of state Henry Kissinger, past secretary-general of NATO Lord Carrington, financier Lord Rothschild, American conservative columnist George F. Will, former chairman of the U.S. Federal Reserve Paul Volcker, industrialist and European parliamentarian Sir James Goldsmith, and *National Review* editor William F. Buckley, Jr.

And in surrounding himself with the illustrious, he has come to have some interesting and powerful allies. When he was being publicly shunned by some during the Ontario Securities Commission hearings on Norcen, Black was "more than compensated for by the presence of Henry Kissinger, David Rockefeller, Jack Heinz and Tony O'Reilly, chairman and president of the H. J. Heinz Company, who dropped by on the way to the Bilderberg meeting at Montebello, Quebec."[19]

The Royal Sterling

Conrad Black sees himself as a kind of Canadian royalty; he explained how he and his partners came up with the name for his newspaper chain in 1971. "We requested a name for our expanding company from Alex Konigsberg, Peter White's very agreeable law partner, and asked for something with 'Royal' in it . . . 'Sterling' was the closest he could get, so oversubscribed was 'Royal' in British Columbia and Prince Edward Island."[20]

Destiny has conferred on his shoulders the burden of ruling. And all natural-born rulers have an opposition. "I was able to monitor the rising antagonism of the forces of envy, both the disgruntled yuppies suffering the frustration of obscene ambitions and the trunkless bull walruses in lairs of the geriatric establishment, as well as those whose hostility was, intellectually at least, more consistent . . . Those who simply didn't like me for legitimate reasons of ideology or taste I always embraced virtually as a loyal opposition."[21]

Hankering After the Goods

Barbara Amiel, unlike her husband, was not born to wealth, but she certainly knew what to do with it when she found it. "My journey to the land of salmon mousse had not been as difficult or spectacular as that of many, but it had been a journey that had taught me a few things. And along the way I had decided that I was prepared to fight, modestly, for the survival of salmon mousse and the opportunity for it to be sampled by the greatest possible number of people."[22]

While working on a film, a young Amiel got a taste of the

good life in London. "I knew what I wanted. To be dropped at Selfridge's or Harrods to pick up fresh salmon, and search for quail's eggs . . . The masseur came every Thursday, in between pounding the exquisite back of Nureyev and the wealthy one of Lady Weidenfeld. Walking from room to room in the luxurious apartments overlooking a small square with stone balconies off the master bedroom and the drawing room, I took to heart my Uncle Bernard's dictum: 'It is not a question of giving up what we have. We simply want everyone to enjoy our standard.' Uncle, I thought, I'm on my way."[23]

"I wanted to pontificate on the world — when not hankering after its goods. And by now I no longer had the excuse of naivety or ignorance," she said of her decision to be a writer on current affairs,[24] and now admits that she lives on a "velvet treadmill . . . To whine about a job that gives you a very nice expense account, all kinds of perks, the best seats in restaurants, the ability to go wherever you want, secretaries picking up your dry cleaning and libraries doing your research, to whine about that would be absurd."[25]

Now the same person who calls for the destruction of the "nanny state" and writes endlessly about individual liberty and the need to get government out of our lives is willing to make an exception for government funding for high art, like opera. In a column entitled, "In defence of elitism: benefits for everyone," Amiel denounces the "egalitarian screeds of the NDP" and calls for an opera house for Toronto. "Opera, throughout the English-speaking world at least, is elitist, but this elitism is not based on social or intellectual class. Instead, opera is elitist in the sense that it is enjoyed by a narrow band of people. This is the difference between art and pop culture . . .

"But in the same way that physical beauty, agility or power have a narrower distribution among all classes of human beings, so the love of fine arts is guided by a narrower development in the human brain . . . It is silly to deny that opera is a narrow taste, and it would be silly to deny that there is anything wrong with cultivating human qualities that are only accessible to a narrower band of human beings in any human endeavour."[26]

"A decent manicure"

Both Amiel and Black speak disparagingly of Canada. "There is nothing that so offends public consciousness in this country as an unbroken series of successes," says Black. "The Canadian mentality simply can't abide it." Canada, he says, breeds mediocrity and requires "the highest, happiest, most agile flyers be laid low, as a cat, [which] faced with a garden of birds, pursued the most swiftly flying and brightly feathered, the one whose destruction would most frighten the others. It was, I suggested, a sadistic desire, corroded by soul-destroying envy, to intimidate all those who might aspire to anything in the slightest exceptional."[27]

Writes Amiel, "The minute I got off my London–Toronto flight, I headed for my hairdresser. I'm sure someone like the Duchess of Windsor said that she could face anything with a good cut and a decent manicure, which is pretty much how I feel whenever I hit Bob Rae's Ontario."[28]

And both prefer the high life in England, where success and wealth are admired. Amiel saw it early: "For an English girl, Canada, even in the fifties, appeared to be a truly classless society. Alas, that also meant that it had no class."[29]

So did Black, who first saw London as a child. "As we drove into London from Southampton, my father purported to quote Bismarck: 'God, what a city to loot!' The majestic facades, splendid palaces (especially Apsley House), the great hotels and clubs (we stayed for a time in Claridge's before moving on to Connaught Square), the endless colonnaded porches of the West End, the many categories of richly liveried support people . . . all was magnificent. London did not seem as powerful, of as mighty a scale, as assertively energetic as New York, nor was it or is it, but it was great and fascinating and, in any case, the comparison with Toronto, by the end of the trip, the only city in the world I knew better, was invidious."[30]

He never changed that view. "As a Canadian, I wish I could sit here, hand over heart, and tell you otherwise. But the fact is, London is more interesting than Toronto. It's an endless sequence of sumptuous lunches and dinners with terribly interesting people from all over the world."[31] "It is part of the British culture that owners of the great newspapers are greatly deferred to, more, undoubtedly than their own merit justifies. I was a beneficiary of this and there is no one, in my experience, more agreeable than the British upper echelons setting out to be ingratiating to those whom they consider can be of use or importance to them."[32] (In fact, when Black addressed a British Conservative convention on the issue of the European Union, he clearly included himself as a citizen of England. "In Britain, we are seeing the crucial debate over the future of the European Community and our participation in it develop in these terms." If the House of Commons agreed to monetary union, he thundered, "that ratification would be the last properly sovereign act of our Parliament."[33]) Notes Ewa Lewis, social editor of the British glossy, *Tatler*, in England, "They are power and glamour. They are not perceived as Canadians at all."[34]

Says Black, "The only circumstances I think in which (Canada) would become more interesting and stimulating a place than London would be more or less as I described at the end of my book: If I really thought that through some great act of Canada taking hold of itself and reshaping its future and so on."[35]

Title Doesn't Matter

Interviewed in 1989 by *The Toronto Star*, Amiel said, "Being a newspaper owner in England makes one a very significant political figure . . . Conrad has played England very well." She was asked about his chances of getting a peerage, knighted membership in the House of Lords (to date, every publisher of the London *Daily Telegraph* has been). "Personally I don't think he gives a damn about it. But the fact is that he's going to have to get one. He's the most credible, intellectual and erudite publisher in England. And he is a Thatcher supporter of considerable enthusiasm. There's just no way Mrs. Thatcher can leave office without giving it to him," Amiel said.[36] In 1994, Black was quoted in *The Financial Post* as saying, "The one thing I learned from [China's] Deng Xiao Peng is that title doesn't matter that much."[37] However, in his biography of Black, Richard Siklos says that while "Black has always publicly played down the notion of a peerage," privately he "ran through various titles he might like to be called if one were ever bestowed. He had not particularly liked his name to begin with, he joked, and did not wish to be called Lord Black. Perhaps 'Lord Ravelston', after his private holding company."[38] Black still awaits his appointment with the Queen.

It was hard for him to return part time to conduct his business in Canada: "I was prepared to divide my time more equally between London and Toronto. I was not enthusiastic about trading altogether the life I had earned as a London newspaper owner to immerse myself in the suburban life of Bob Rae's Ontario. All my life I had sought a more distinguished, varied, and eventful life than could be provided by the milieu in which I was brought up."[39] Besides, "In my position, I move around not exactly according to what municipality I most like the public parks in, the theatres or the skyline. I go where my essential economic interests lead. I like London and I like New York. So I'll be a good deal in both of them."[40]

Black and Amiel speak for the wealthy and hold that any constraints upon them are the result of small, envious, Canadian minds. On criticism of Ontario's appointment of Toronto socialite Hilary Weston to the post of lieutenant-governor, Amiel is in full rhetorical flight: "I can't remember an appointment that has brought out the smelly side of journalism more than this . . . Perhaps from now on, the only people eligible to become lieutenant-governor should be social workers who can swear they wouldn't recognize Prince Charles from a tree and have had no association with any community effort except a shelter for AIDS victims . . .

"Taking potshots at the rich in a modern democracy is the ultimate fish-in-a-barrel sport. You simply can't go wrong. The theme taps into that great pool of universal envy that allows writers to count on acquiescence to any nasty remark from a huge variety of readers."[41] Black has said, "Wealth accumulation is not considered heroic by most people though, in fact, it often is."[42] And, "While some people are offended by extreme opulence, I find it entertaining."[43]

On a "wretched" article by a fellow *Maclean's* columnist decrying excessive and ostentatious spending by the wealthy, calling on them to give back to society in some way, Amiel says, "You don't entitle yourself to freedom by giving to charity. Surely, we have not reached the point that before people can spend their own money however they want, it is not only necessary for them to pay taxes, but they must also further entitle themselves by charity work. You either live in a free society or you don't . . . Mind you, this is the great thrust of our age, isn't it — the institutionalization of envy. Envy used to be one of the seven deadly sins, always regarded (rightly, in my view) as a vice or a sickness. Now it has been turned into an honorable emotion."[44]

Even the conservative-minded *Globe and Mail* came under attack when it published an editorial that dared to suggest that real corporate philanthropy comes from giving to charity over and above what can be written off as a tax deduction. Amiel responded: "By allowing a tax deduction for certain contributions, the government is saying two things: it encourages you to spend your money on the arts or hospitals or various other designated areas so government can spend less on them and, second and as important, it is saying that it will also allow citizens some say in how their tax dollars will be spent."

Amiel went on to promote the right of the monied to have more individual say in the spending of their tax dollars and said that an important side-benefit of charitable deductions is less money, and therefore, reduced power for the state: "If a principle of this society is that a person's private property and income belong to him, then the more say he has in how the government spends his money, the better." She said that if corporate giving becomes an obligation, she would recommend to "any potential donor, large or small, that they pack up their piggy banks and paintings and move to a more hospitable country where their charity is not scrutinized to make sure it is free of 'self-interest.'"[45]

Wealth and Influence

Amiel and Black deny the political power of their class even as they wield it. On the courts, Amiel claims that "Justice wears a blind. She does not peek to see if a man is black or white, rich or poor," but that nevertheless, "in this day and age one might go as far as to say that to be rich and powerful is more a disadvantage in court than an advantage. While few judges or prosecutors would be afraid to exercise their perfectly legitimate discretion in favour of an ordinary man, not to mention a minority-group member, most would be terrified to exercise the same discretion for someone politically, financially or socially powerful."[46]

Black agrees: "This influence is largely a fiction. Wealthy individuals and corporations are public-relations sitting ducks and they are, in my experience, practically the last people whose advice the political leadership of this country seeks or takes seriously."[47] And yet he contradicts himself when he boasts that big business delivered the 1988 election on free trade to Brian Mulroney "because business leaders such as Paul Reichmann, Galen Weston, David Culver (Alcan), and Alf Powis took a public position and pulled more votes than Stephen Lewis, June Callwood, and Margaret Atwood."[48] Further, he wrote in opposition to proposed conflict of interest legislation for members of Parliament, saying that they would "banish all those whose success is measurable in financial terms from our public life," forcing the wealthy to make their voices heard "in surreptitious ways."[49]

Black also used his influential *Financial Post* column to help defeat proposed amendments to the Bank Act that would have prohibited a bank loaning more than $50,000 to a corporation whose CEO is also a director of the bank in question, a perfectly reasonable limit to corporate power in most people's eyes. "It proposes a Dickensianly hair-shirted definition of the point at which bank directors might supposedly lose their independence of judgment by being beholden borrowers . . . Failure to amend significantly would be a clear signal that our lawmakers are dominated by a spirit of unworldly, fear-stricken, and morbidly suspicious pauperism."[50]

And Black openly acknowledges the advantage of his powerful international connections. Black is the co-leader of the Canadian arm of the influential Bilderberg group, set up in the mid-1950s by the Crown Prince of the Netherlands to "strengthen understanding" between prominent political, military, academic, and corporate leaders of the "non-communist" North Atlantic community. The meetings are held in remote places, without spouses or prepared texts, and discussion is confined "as much as possible to English."[51]

Camaraderie

Although Black had met Henry Kissinger before, it was at Bilderberg that he got to really know him, along with "Gianni Agnelli of Fiat, Dwayne Andreas (controlling shareholder of the giant agri-business Archer-Daniels, Midland), Zbigniew Brzezinski (former national security adviser in the Carter Administration), Lord Carrington (former British foreign and defense secretary and secretary-general of NATO), Andrew Knight (editor of the Economist), Richard Perle (former U.S. assistant secretary of National Defense and one of the champions of the Strategic Defense Initiative ['Star Wars'] and Euro-missile deployment), Paul Volcker (former Federal Reserve chairman), and George Will (U.S. conservative columnist and commentator), as well as many other interesting people . . .

"Not having very satisfactory recollections of school days, nor being a very enthusiastic or observant university alumnus,

Bilderberg has been the closest I have known to that sort of camaraderie."[52]

(Amiel writes about another forum of this kind, the World Economic Forum at Davos, Switzerland, where "the theme was the same: could Western businessmen please come to the disaster areas of the world and make them work?" The site of this conference is "usually wildly inappropriate, tempting the less committed to lie on their tummies in the sun or wander about mountains yodelling." One year, South African president Nelson Mandela — "a little past things" — came to court private business in his country. But "the old Marxist-Leninist language peppered the speech — all that nonsense about 'the liberation of women' and the 'equitable distribution of wealth.'")[53]

The Blacks also have no shortage of opinions on what Amiel calls "the underclass that menaces our street"[54] and Black calls "unworthy economic groups, such as strikers and voluntary welfare addicts . . . unruly scum."[55]

Black wrote a speech for Michael Meighen when he was nominated to run for the Progressive Conservatives in the federal election of 1974. "My leitmotif in Michael's acceptance speech was welfare bums, and [Tory leader Robert] Stanfield was visibly horrified when Michael attacked 'the 137,000 unemployment insurance recipients who didn't bother to pick up their cheques during the recent Post Office strike.'"[56]

Unsatisfied that he would get protection from the Toronto police during his high-profile battle over Norcen, Black bought into a security company "to ensure that I wasn't totally reliant on the palookas that were oppressing and defaming us to guarantee the safety of my home and family. ([The security guards] were, with only a few exceptions, rented meatballs who spent most of their watch at our home sleeping or, as my wife said, 'staring at their feet.' I was delighted when Dick Chant skilfully sold us out of this, as he correctly described it, 'pissy business,' at a modest profit in 1986.)"[57]

Spraying DDT

Amiel dismisses self-help books for the masses. "The best of these books contain nothing that successful people have not known all their lives, and what is true in them usually relates to attitude and discipline. Insofar as these points are true, unsuccessful or powerless people are incapable of learning them."[58]

When she worked on a CBC film on Toronto's skid-row derelicts, it was Amiel's job to find a "star." She discovered "Charlie . . . the blight of my life." Charlie stole from Amiel and drank her cooking wine; Amiel had to take him back to his shelter. "'Put him back where he wants to be,' I was told. 'We'll be filming there anyway.' Armed with DDT and wearing Saran Wrap inside my underwear, I marched Charlie off to his favourite flophouse. Even without close inspection it was clear that the bed sheets were alive. I sprayed the DDT vigorously about, much to the loud dismay of the occupants, and refused to sit down."[59]

Black had a similar encounter with the great unwashed while at home in Toronto. "I was in my dressing room wearing a dressing gown when a persistent ringing and banging at the front door began. I eventually absented myself from all the Rothschild and Cazenove parties I was talking to and discovered on my doorstep an urchin selling stuffed animals in favour of a children's charity he was rather vague about when I questioned him closely.

"I said, 'This is obviously a scam and I'm rather busy right now but I respect the commercial enterprise of any unannounced young person who comes on foot on a Sunday all the way down this long driveway to sell stuffed animals for a bogus cause' . . . I said I'd give him $10 for a golden bear for my daughter, but when he asked for sales tax I told him I was insulted, that charities needn't pay GST, and that he obviously wasn't remitting tax or anything else. 'I don't mind helping to sharpen up a young merchant, but I'm not going to be made a chump of while underdressed on the doorstep of my own house on a Sunday morning. Take it or leave it.'"[60]

Amiel dismisses those who bring a class analysis to the issues of poverty and equality of opportunity: "If people from poor homes couldn't spell, correct spelling became a class-conspiracy on the part of the affluent."[61] "Certain disparities, of course, are neither unearned nor unjust. Some disparities naturally occur, such as those between the beautiful and ugly, the agile and clumsy, the clever and foolish."[62]

Nor do either have time for those in the Catholic Church who side with the poor and marginalized and seek a role for the church in promoting social justice. Amiel brands them all Marxists and says their role took "a far more malevolent turn in the Church proper during the late nineteen-sixties as it embraced the gospel of social justice in order to ensure its piece of real estate in the Marxist-Kingdom-to-Come."[63] She also believes that "between Christianity and Marxism there can be no reconciliation . . . it would be quite charming to become a Marxist-socialist or a progressive church person, comfy in the idea that one knew unshakably what was best for everyone in a highly organized society run by its own elite of socialist intellectuals."[64]

Black, who converted to Roman Catholicism and counts the conservative former archbishop of Toronto, Cardinal Emmett Carter, a close friend, condemned "their muddled excellencies" of the Social Affairs Commission of the Canadian Conference of Catholic Bishops for political statements — "naive, sophomoric mishmash" — they made on poverty and social inequality in Canada. The bishops, "desperate for attention" and given to "reckless guilt-mongering," have launched a "luddite assault" on capital, a "great liberal death-wish" that would lead to "economic suicide."[65] "And who is it that calls the Church to this banal and possibly heretical destiny? The answer was a few silly and contemptible Canadian bishops, but the problem of trendy clerics mouthing socialist platitudes and depicting God as our pal jogging along beside us is quite widespread. Obviously, if this sort of bunkum had to be taken seriously rather than as incandescently fallible, neither I nor any other serious person could continue in the Faith."[66]

Black practises his own brand of Catholicism. "You don't have to believe in papal infallibility or any of that nonsense."[67] When he decided to marry the thrice-divorced Amiel, Cardinal Carter gave his blessing, "toasting us with affecting graciousness."[68]

He admits Jesus' admonition that "it is easier for a camel to go through the eye of a needle than for a rich man to enter the kingdom of God," gave him pause. "But on examination, a number of things emerge. In those days, most wealthy people were exploitative employers so the statement can be read as a comment on economic practice in 1st-century Palestine. Christ himself had no particular prejudice against the rich — indeed, he dressed rather richly."[69] When the workers at the Vatican certified a union under Pope John Paul II, Black was dismissive: "Vatican clerical and janitorial jobs are so sought after in Rome that there is always a herniating mass of applications for any vacancy in the city state's bloated work force. The Pope should have learned from his own experience the disastrous consequences of giving the store away to the unions or of accepting unions as infallible engines of social reform."[70] This Pope was at least better than Paul VI, who questioned unregulated market liberalism and called for the wealthy to pay taxes; Black is glad to report Paul VI's thinking has been consigned to "a well-earned purgatorial dustbin" to protect Third World "economic innocents . . . more likely to take such ill-considered suggestions seriously."[71]

"Third World ineptitude"

Indeed, any economic or social analysis of the global economy that suggests Western exploitation of the developing world comes in for particular scorn. Amiel calls it "unrelieved tripe about the exploitation of the third world by the rich first world (us)"[72] and says it stems from "a pathological sense of guilt about being white or non–Third World citizens."[73]

"To Toronto they all came, carrying with them schemes and scenarios for global income redistribution. Behind the schemes lies the belief that it is morally right, practically desirable and possible to transfer the resources of the industrialized nations to the underdeveloped countries," says Amiel. But "they" — international aid workers — find themselves up against the Marxist-based ideologies that have rendered the economies of these nations disastrous. "Surely by now it must be evident to our foreign aid lobby that it is not the gluttony of our citizens that has any bearing on world poverty or hunger. No profligate playboy of the Western World could begin to match the squander that takes place when corrupt governments commit themselves to Marxist policies of wasting resources."[74]

Black's travels have taken him to the developing world. "Our trip to Istanbul had to be scrapped because of the utter incompetence of the personnel in our roach warren of a hotel and at the airport. It was a classic case of Third World ineptitude, worthy of Evelyn Waugh's famous trip up the Amazon — elaborate plans breaking down, each initiative starting out attended by much hopeful pomp and ceremonious leave-taking, but gradually crumbling in a ludicrous debacle . . .

"In desperation, we finally crowded onto an Air France plane taking pilgrims back from Jeddah and Mecca to the Maghreb via Paris. Never did I admire French sang-froid more. The passengers (we were almost the only Westerners) filled the plane to a depth of half a foot from the floor with litter; the lavatories were quickly rendered unusable. The little man next to me had the disconcerting habit of continually removing and reinserting his artificial left eye . . .

"I had the pleasant sensation of having crossed the great cultural divide to more familiar and welcoming terrain when, in the currency-exchange line at Charles de Gaulle airport, my erstwhile neighbour with the artificial eye, ignoring the queue, bustled ahead of me, burrowing into the flank of a giant of a man from the southern United States, who looked amusedly down at this commotion and said, 'Where are you going, little stud?'"[75]

Amiel visits Kenya. She muses on Western superiority. "Our party was made up of three Americans and myself, with

11 Kenyans cooking and cleaning for us as we 'roughed' it." A leopard kills a young Kenyan boy. "[The leopard] hadn't read the small print about game parks being places where tribes, species, predators and cows exist in an oyster of jolly multiculturalism. Alas, now one protected leopard and a bright-eyed boy of 16 is gone. There isn't much to say about it, I suppose, except to muse on the irony . . .

"The Masai are a pastoral nomadic people of a Neolithic culture. They seem rather happy, and speaking as a member of the Western technological society, nothing could be more astonishing than to see these tribes perfectly content to live in their huts made of cow dung surrounded by an eight-foot-high thornbush fence. Reasonably clean, members of the tribe bathe in the river once a day or so and defecate on the ground a good number of yards away from their dwellings. The flies that crawl over them come from the cattle they own and are proudly worn as a mark of wealth — more flies, more cows . . .

"Getting the Masai into the 20th century is part of what is crucial, I suppose, to turning Kenya into a grown-up, modern democracy. If Africa is to come out of the Dark Ages, it will have to transplant some of the fundamental institutions of the West which do not root easily, especially among illiterate nomads."[76]

4

BUSINESS IS WAR

"This would be the jungles of Guadalcanal, the beaches of Tarawa, the sands of Iwo Jima, the caves of Saipan; hand-to-hand combat ending only with the incineration of the enemy by flame-throwers."

— CONRAD BLACK

Conrad Black approaches the world of business as a general approaches war. The key to understanding Black the corporate mogul is to understand Black the war-history student. He views corporate acquisitions as a military manoeuvre and delights in outwitting his enemies. Like a professional military strategist, Black is a calculating adversary who lies in wait for the right moment to strike. Like a powerful general, Black hones in on the weakness and moral ambiguity of his opponents: "Most people are corruptible."[1] And like a mercenary, Black feels little personal animosity toward his rivals, no matter how bitter the fight, particularly if they have been vanquished.

Black was fascinated by war and the great battles of the world as a young person. At the age of nineteen, he travelled to Europe with his brother, seeing "the home base of the French navy at Toulon (where the splendid battleship *Jean Bart*, which had seen action at Casablanca in 1942 and Suez in 1956, was in the road-stead) to the beaches of Normandy and Dunkirk, from the German submarine pens at St. Nazaire to Napoleon's palace at Fontainbleau. His tomb at the Invalides was as uplifting a place to me as it had been to the young de Gaulle, as described in the opening pages of the general's memoirs . . .

"The most memorable sight of all was the battle of Verdun, with the statue of Maginot, the little monument *Ici fut Fleury*, the *tranchée des baïonnettes* where a column of French soldiers had been buried alive, only their bayonets protruding above the ground. We walked around the great fort of Douaumont, where de Gaulle had been wounded and captured, March 2, 1916, and the ossuary containing in its walls the bones of 130,000 French killed soldiers in the great hecatomb around Verdun."[2]

The adult Conrad Black is no less excited by these images. On the wall of Black's London office at Canary Wharf hang paintings of Napoleon and Admiral Nelson. "You see there's Napoleon after Waterloo and behind him is Nelson before Trafalgar. Napoleon lost and survived and Nelson won and died," he says, explaining his instincts as a military survivor.[3]

Military Metaphors

Black uses military metaphors to describe a corporate strategy that might otherwise seem incomprehensible to most ordinary business observers. Alexander Ross, a director of Key Publishing, in which Hollinger owns an interest, says that one implication of Black's military approach to business is that a lot of "huffing, puffing and to-and-fro churning can often serve as a substitute for genuine strength."[4]

Black explains a major reorganization of his newspaper chain: "So I got out General Fuller's life of Julius Caesar and I opened it to a map of the Battle of Alesia. This was in the suppression of the revolt of the Gauls, you see, and Caesar chased his enemies into town and laid siege to them. But then a much larger enemy force came and laid siege to him. So you had two lines, a line of *circumvallation* and a line of *contravallation*, and I said, 'There he was — he was between those two lines. He was keeping the inner group in and the outer group out, but it was making for an awful lot of fighting all the time . . . It always struck me as the most astonishing military map I had ever seen, along with its description of Caesar himself charging around in his red cape for weeks on end. He'd be in the east and he'd be in the west . . . I'm not saying I'm in that kind of position. It's just that there's a lot going on at once.'"[5]

But Black takes offence at the notion that he is out of control in his corporate acquisitions. "I am amazed by the number of so called financial experts luxuriating in the view that I am some sort of punch-drunk prizefighter on the ropes. Well, screw them," he once told Peter C. Newman.[6] More recently, he explained that he keeps advancing "like a platoon of men through a forest, parallel lines moving in various directions. Wherever there is a breakthrough, I try to exploit it."[7]

Of his ferocious battle over Argus, told in painstaking detail in Black's autobiography and also in Peter Newman's *The Establishment Man*, Black says his adversaries were "like generals fighting a war by the methods of the last one. They could not conceive of any corporate alternatives to trench warfare, attrition, and promotion by seniority . . .

"Tactical surprise was total and the first inkling they had that they were in combat, and in very unfavourable circumstances, was when Dick Chant and I handed Max Meighen the call on his shares. He was thus like the 'unhappy General Mack' at Ulm, the Austrian commander in the Austerlitz Campaign, who suddenly found that Napoleon had surrounded him. The ant-like movements of my corporate equivalent to armoured reconnaissance were so stealthy and insidious that their position had been completely eroded, riddled and honeycombed before a shot was fired in anger."[8]

He compared the executive vice-president to a housefly to whom he had just delivered a lethal blast of insecticide and declared, "If my associates were screaming for the financial death penalty, and for Max Meighen to be delivered trussed up like a partridge to their guillotine, I would not fidget and fumble with the blade levers . . . Off with his head."[9]

Black loves to cite Napoleon's "expanding torrent offence" — attacking in so many directions that the enemy can't guess what you'll do next. On capturing control of Argus he said, "If we accept Napoleon's definition of force as mass times velocity, our strength would have to reside for the foreseeable future in a high-multiple equation: we had no mass but I was determined that we would develop considerable velocity. Our commercial position was slightly analogous to Napoleon's when he took command of the army in Italy in 1795. It was a shabby, demoralized, largely unarmed and wholly undisciplined rabble, but he moved it about the river valleys of Northern Italy with such dexterity that he bundled the far superior Austrian forces right out of Italy while giving battle only in the minor engagements of Rivoli and Castiglione . . .

"In Acquisitions, our strategy would be Captain Liddell Hart's inter-war theory of the expanding torrent of air and mechanized offence. We would go where resistance was least as, in Liddell Hart's preferred analogy, water poured onto the top of a hillock makes its way to the bottom but by an unpredictable course. We couldn't be confidently precise in advance of our investment targets when we would be in a position to have any, but as in Liddell Hart's championship of modern warfare, logical objectives would commend themselves at the appropriate time."[10]

Black even extended the battle analogy to his first wedding, which he squeezed in the day after the coup at Argus. He vowed to set the newly reformed company on a "corporate Long March . . . but before taking the first step there was the pleasant leitmotif of my marriage, Bastille Day, the day after the elevation of the new slate at Argus Corporation." So exhausted was he from this fight that he went to bed early on his wedding night, leaving his bride and his guests to celebrate without him. He was back into battle "on the first business day after these festivities."[11]

Black considered entering into a private-public partnership with the Quebec government agency, the Caisse de dépôts et de placements, in a takeover bid for Noranda. He thought of seeking an order-in-council from the Quebec government enabling him to waive the normal notice period for a takeover bid and go straight to the floor of the Montreal Stock Exchange. Black makes it clear he expected the government to bend the rules for him. "Such a move would not have been the apogee of fair play, but what was the point of having a government as a partner if its powers were not applied to the support of defined public policy?"[12]

But, in the end, Noranda proved too troublesome. "Noranda was . . . potentially a corporate Vietnam into which we might pour more and more resources and never win."[13] With its sale and the settling of problems at Dominion, Argus, and Massey, "the first phase of the 'campaign of manoeuvre' was successfully concluded . . . We had graduated to a corporate combat potential: from the penurious General Bonaparte in Italy, we were now MacArthur setting out from Guadalcanal, with an amphibious assault capability, provided we island-hopped with agility."[14]

"Napoleon's precepts"

Even when a war analogy is not intended, Black comments using military imagery. When he called a stock-market floor bid for the mining company, Norcen, Operation Catapult, he felt compelled to add, "The World War II action of that name, the British smashing-up of the French fleet at Mers-el-Kebir in July 1949, was not an inspiration."[15] On bailing out of Massey-Ferguson, he said he was not "abandoning the fight, merely 'transferring my flag to a more seaworthy vessel, like the American Admiral Fletcher at Midway.'"[16]

Similarly, his takeover of Argus was approached as a military operation. "In taking over Argus Corporation in 1978, I had sought tactical inspiration from the blitzkrieg methods and swarming infiltrations of the German tank commanders of 1940. In the sequence of sales and shuffles with Crown Trust, Power Corporation, Domtar, and Noranda, a successful war of manoeuvre was conducted to acquire some critical mass. This series of actions, though hardly worthy of a great strategist like Napoleon, aspired, at least pallidly, to apply some of his precepts. Force was achieved through transactional velocity and was translated into advantageous acquisition of an excellent asset, Norcen.

"The next phase, which I had ambitiously hoped would be a MacArthur-like island-hopping sequence of selective inexpensive amphibious assaults, had got off to an unimpressive start. [*The Financial Post*] had failed, but no one had been lost on the beach. In that sense it wasn't even a Dieppe . . . We had escaped from Massey as painlessly and with as much dignity as possible, but, as Churchill said after Dunkirk, 'Wars are not won by evacuations' . . . The reorganization had been cumbersome and had more of the tactical qualities of the disastrous Japanese plan for Leyte Gulf than the luminous simplicity of some of MacArthur's actions."[17]

Over his *Daily Telegraph* price war with Rupert Murdoch's London *Times*, Black said in 1994, "If you speak of military history, it is always useful to get your opponent to commit as much resources as he can before you have to fire any live ammunition yourself . . . We are dealing with a formidable adversary; Rupert is a bold man. He is like — and I make this comparison in one sense and one sense only — the *early* Hitler, always wanting a *ruse de guerre* because he always thought his opponents were ninnies who would react too late and indecisively."[18]

Of John Major's 1992 campaign, he wrote to his *Telegraph* editor and military historian, Max Hastings, "Is it the French Army of 1914, preparing for victory at the Marne, or of 1940, preparing for cowardice and rout?"[19]

In describing his celebrated 1981 dust-up over control of the Hanna mining company, Black is a man at war. Executive committee minutes calling Black a criminal, a racketeer, and a recidivistic fraud specialist are "like a grenade with the pin pulled . . . As someone who revelled in somewhat glib references to Napoleon, it was doubly humiliating to be implicated in such an appallingly amateurish launch . . . We had a grenade to throw back if we could survive the opening barrage.

"This would not be any conventional notion of 'island hopping,' by which I had meant the avoidance of unpromising obstacles (as MacArthur bypassed the 250,000 Japanese soldiers at Rabaul) and advance by swift and inexpensive assaults on unsuspecting targets. This would not be Attu and Kiska. This would be the jungles of Guadalcanal, the beaches of Tarawa, the sands of Iwo Jima, the caves of Saipan; hand-to-hand combat ending only with the incineration of the enemy by flame-throwers.

"I rationalized that constant manoeuvre, to be effective, must be punctuated from time to time with real combat. Sometimes, to defeat the enemy, you have to inflict casualties as well as inconvenience."[20]

About this battle, Black told Peter C. Newman, "I told him the Hanna case was like the Yom Kippur War of 1973. We were Israel and had got off to a bad start but had crossed the Suez Canal and enveloped one of the enemy's armies."[21]

"Low-lives at the warehouse"

Black's treatment of Dominion Stores, which he had acquired in the mid-1970s with the Argus holdings, was similarly hostile. By 1984, Black was working "fiercely" to "disassemble and liquidate" Dominion Stores, "preferably to foreigners."[22] He sold stores a chunk at a time, and was aggressive and unapologetic in dealing with all who questioned his methods or treatment of Dominion workers.

He brought David Radler in to deal with the sticky problem of contractual obligations: "He explicitly threatened shopping centre owners who wouldn't release us from our covenant to operate with a reasonable penalty with the bankruptcy of the lessee and in a couple of cases had employees put rotting vegetables out in front of the stores to reduce the general ambience of the shopping centres and to encourage a greater desire by the landlords to see us off as tenants."[23]

A high-profile controversy over a large surplus in the Dominion Stores' pension plan led to a confrontation with the government of Bob Rae, then premier of Ontario. Black publicly took on "the yuppie-ridden lumpen proletariat" of the "Ontario wimpocracy" for its criticism of his treatment of the workers, saying it was "the symbol of swinish socialist demagogy at its worst."[24]

But his strongest warlike language was saved for the "shiftless union" at Dominion. "The war to the (commercial) death between the union and Dominion had one violent exchange left . . . I recommended that a scythe be taken through the ranks of the low-lives at the warehouse, and it was."[25] He sold the last stores as franchises to Mr. Grocer. "My hope was that, as our old union was being subsumed into A & P's union, and the continuing Dominion workers were being relentlessly laid off as the stores were closed or franchised, the union leaders, to preserve their own nepotistic sinecures as much as their members' jobs, would be disposed to compromise and that the compromise could be extended to the pension surplus as well."[26]

Black came by his feelings of hostility toward unions naturally. "I have never had much regard for organized labour, other than when it has taken on heroic proportions as in Poland . . . [My father] George Black had never ceased to revile labour leaders as self-seeking frauds who cared little for the workers and often were gangsters or communists . . . most unions became enemies of productivity increases through automation, advocates of feather-bedding, and a mortal threat to any sense of community in an enterprise."[27] "Unions perform little useful role. They are a dead hand in virtually every land except Poland."[28]

He did admit to some discomfort in the very public Dominion battle. "Even I became rather uncomfortable tearing companies down and cutting and pasting unrelated assets." However, the warrior would not give in: "But the more vitriolic the financial press and general business community group-think became, the more determined I was to carry it through to the natural end of its utility."[29]

"Through 1986, if a military inspiration were required for our company, it was a defensive war on interior lines, such as Frederick the Great's in the latter phase of the Seven Years War, Napoleon crossing the Berezina in 1812 in the face of three Russian armies on both banks of the river, with a combined strength triple his own, or, more upliftingly, the Battle of Britain."[30]

"Dominion's war to the death with the Retail, Wholesale and Department Store Union had resulted in the death of both, a fate they both deserved as mismanaged, anachronistic, and useless organizations."[31]

Helicopters versus Women's Groups

Barbara Amiel, not having been a businessperson before assuming the vice-presidency of Hollinger, does not write about corporate battles and conquests. But she does have plenty to say about the role of the military, the meaning of war, and the moral supremacy of the West: "We consider peaceful coexistence a part of civilization."[32] Her views on the role of military might in the political world are similar to his and also mirror Black's take-no-prisoners views on the use of sheer force to advance one's position in business.

"I honour the military. And I do not believe that honour is a temporary quality found only during the pressure cooker of war. The military is the single calling in the world with job specs that include a commitment to die for your nation. What could be more honourable?"[33]

A woman with little good to say about Canada, Amiel approved of our face-off with Spain in the turbot war. "Which is why, just for a moment, to be from Canada is no longer a poor literary address." The literary reference is to a poem written by her ex-husband, George Jonas, in which he says a great navy is a great agent for a great nation. Adds Amiel, "I've always thought that was a brilliant insight: if you want to promote a country's literature internationally, you can do more by giving to the defence budget than to agencies like the Canada Council . . .

"One might also muse on the fact that all the Nobel Peace Prizes in the world cannot do as much for Canada's image or be as great an agent for a great literature as the perception of national power . . . Putting your foot down, of course, requires two qualities: the political will and the foot. Without gunboats, we couldn't have done a thing."[34]

She adds, making an astonishing comparison between the proposal during the Mulroney years to buy billions of dollars worth of helicopters with the small amounts of money spent on women's groups, "At times like this, I rather wish we had not virtually dismantled our armed forces and had purchased the few helicopters that the coast guard and navy so desperately wanted instead of funding more statutory women's councils."[35]

"Send in the CF-18s"

Amiel was also approving of Canada's participation in the Gulf War. Let the peacekeepers "drone on," she says. "Peacekeeping is an admirable pursuit, one that I fully admire, and it works very well provided you send in the CF-18s first. The UN peacekeeping forces aren't much use in the Middle East where they can't shoot guns and tend to run or withdraw at the first sign of trouble, but we love those blue berets they wear." The U.S., according to Amiel, should lose any compunction about what has to be done in Iraq and other trouble spots in the world. "America seems to be the only country in the world that wants to win a war and have the people it is bombing love it. Events seem to suggest that the Arab world respects victory and that their minds understand success. When it comes to their hearts, well, they are unpredictable and in this case there isn't much point in attempting to win them."[36]

Worrying about civilian casualties is "one of the qualities I prefer in the West to the Arab world, where targeting civilians is virtually normal behaviour . . . We had no trouble understanding civilian deaths when they occurred during the Second World War in Hamburg or Berlin because we were threatened in London and Paris. One's squeamishness decreases in direct proportion to the perceived closeness of war."[37] Perhaps in praising the West for its more ethical wartime behaviour, Amiel wasn't paying attention to reports coming back from the Gulf. In 1991, Ramsey Clark, former attorney general of the U.S., obtained permission to go into Iraq with a camera crew. His group travelled 2,000 miles across Iraq, from February 2 to 8, examining civil damage in Baghdad, Basra, and Diwaniya. "There was no 'collateral' military damage; all the destruction was to civilians . . . We saw no evidence of military presence in any of the bombed areas we visited." Clark concluded that "the air assault deliberately targeting the civilian population of Iraq is a war crime."[38]

Amiel fretted that George Bush was "on the verge of creating a dreadful fiasco in the Middle East" when he seemed to be studying proposals for a resolution to the Gulf crisis in the days before the war. "The cause is the virus endemic to the American psyche in postwar years — a failure of will . . . Now [Bush's] co-ed army sits in the Saudi sands while the commander-in-chief in Washington talks softly about the need to find a diplomatic solution and avert a war. This is a fine way to lose everything . . . The stench of appeasement is in the air . . . I am not pacified or encouraged by the new American buildup of soldiers announced last week. Nor by the talk of stockpiling of nuclear weapons in the Gulf."[39]

Amiel says that the U.S. should have done in Central America what they did to Saddam Hussein: "What has kept a relative peace in the world is swift, decisive action against terrorist states . . . Had the United States managed to carry out something more effective in Cuba than the Bay of Pigs fiasco, we might have avoided the export of terrorism to Nicaragua and El Salvador, not to mention Angola."[40]

Amiel has little time for peace activists, and describes being "happily free" of John Lennon's famous song, "Give Peace a Chance." During the Cold War, she lectured these activists, saying that only the use of raw power by a morally superior West could deter war: "[The Soviets] understand, most of all, that the fear of brute power, alas, is all that prevents the use of brute power. And what all westerners should understand is that a universal longing for peace may live in the hearts of all the peoples of the world, but it is only in the free world that 'peoples' influence policy."[41]

Amiel trivializes the campaign to ban landmines that kill and maim thousands of innocent children around the world every year (a campaign that has been taken up by Lloyd Axworthy and Princess Diana, among others), saying it will misfire. "No one can deny that the Red Cross is doing saintly work in looking after people who have been brutally maimed by landmines in (mainly) Third World countries. But the International Committee of the Red Cross is also 'committed to a worldwide ban on the production, stockpiling, transfer and use of all anti-personnel mines.' This is more dodgy."

Amiel argues that such a ban will be honoured only by the more "advanced" countries and that only after the developing world is "democratized" would such a ban be possible. Meanwhile, "the only way to stop APMs [anti-personnel mines] is to end conflict . . . The trouble is that APMs are helpful in war. An advancing enemy that has to clear mines is slowed down . . . The Allied Forces out-flanked the Iraqi mines in the Gulf War. But do we want to hamper our troops in actual combat?" Amiel generously allows that the Red Cross's "woolly thinking" on landmines may have a place in history. "So, even if the princess's travels only encourage the Chinese to make more mines . . . If today we don't tear out the hearts of our enemies and eat them as once we used to, it is to some extent because of those well-meaning do-gooders among us who made us look at things in a different light."[42]

Moral Superiority

Both she and Black believe in the moral superiority of the U.S. Says Amiel, "America ought to act as a great power and play out its role as policeman of the world — at the very least on its own block."[43] Black strongly supported aggressive American military intervention in the Vietnam War and had no time for those in the West who opposed the war. "My desire to see the Americans win and the communists and their specious, faddish, loathsome, cheering section in the salons, campuses, and media of the West, mercilessly routed, caused me . . . to believe in the victory of America and Vietnamization."[44]

Black was very unhappy with the American loss of face in Southeast Asia. "The fall of Saigon in May 1975, and the military subjugation of the whole of South Vietnam by the Hanoi regime, was a depressing event. The international forces of anti-Americanism had their greatest victory of all. The joyous shrieks of the left were deafening. The Communist powers and committed fellow-travellers had somehow earned their hour of brutish triumph. More annoying were the numberless legions of complacent trendies, and they were pandemic in such a place as Toronto. I could take it from the cadaverous and intense left, but corpulent hedonists flashing V-signs from their Mercedeses and BMWs and embracing with look-alikes in their Yorkville wine bars and trattorias were very trying."[45]

But U.S. might would prevail, to his satisfaction. "I never doubted that the forces of political repression would fail or that the strength of the United States and particularly of its presidency would be re-established. No one could foresee then that the Communist alternative would collapse early, as it has, though I never worried about the ultimate outcome of the Cold War. Yet, in the spring of 1975, the forces of good sense and good taste, as I perceived [the U.S. military], were passing through the valley of humiliation."[46]

"I never doubted that Ronald Reagan would rout the hapless Jimmy Carter, that his tax cuts would reinvigorate and ultimately reindustrialize the U.S. economy, that his defence build-up would ultimately bring the Russians to heel, and that he would restore the presidency's place in the U.S. political system and America's place in the world."[47]

"Open bomb sights"

As a young man, Black visited Cuba — a "horribly depressing" place for which he had no sympathy. "When I left Cuba, the passport control official asked me whether I would be back to see Havana again. I replied, 'Yes,' and whispered to a British businessman standing next to me, 'Through open bomb-sights.'"[48]

Amiel also came down in favour of Ronald Reagan's Strategic Defense Initiative, then known as Star Wars: "Weakness never deters bullies; it only incites them."[49] In 1981, she indicated her support of then U.S. secretary of state Alexander Haig's "reasonable statement" that the defence of Europe could best be achieved by the deployment of a new generation of nuclear weapons. Amiel could not understand why hundreds of thousands of Europeans marched against nuclear weapons on their soil, as they were "the people who would be most helped" from this strategy. She lamented that she had to "document the obvious once again" for them, suffering as they were from an "irrational fear" that made them "impervious to reason."[50]

It must be the fear of nuclear death that causes the problem, she mused. "It is puzzling to rational thought why other forms of death — a hail of bullets, slow starvation in a labour camp or being garroted with both arms fractured — seem preferable to so many to the swift obliteration of a nuclear explosion . . . as to the scale of destruction — the total number of victims — there is every reason to believe that in an all-out Third World War of a nonnuclear kind, the havoc would merely be spread over a longer period of time. Nuclear war, alas, would claim the same number of victims — although in a shorter period of time . . .

"Since nuclear *war*, as opposed to one-sided nuclear slaughter, could come about only if the West continues to maintain and update its own nuclear defences, the only way to avoid nuclear war is by doing precisely that."[51]

And in the end, it is quite simple. "Simply put," she has said, "the United States did not arm itself with weapons of mass destruction in order to enslave and murder millions of people. There was an evil empire and that was the Soviet Union, and it was bent on conquering as much of the world as it could and establishing the most inhumane systems wherever it had influence . . . The West, on the other hand, armed itself in order to slow down, contain, and prevent the spread of this terrible virus."[52]

"You *can* tell the good guys from the bad guys. Our side is more humane than their side. And you must, alas, always put bullets in your guns because you can't ward off evil by whistling Mozart in the dark."[53]

"Do lunch or you are lunch"

For Conrad Black and Barbara Amiel, life is so competitive, it must be approached as a battle; business is a theatre of war. Opponents are enemies to destroy. Nation states are judged by their military strength. The language of compromise and cooperation are not part of their vocabulary. In the 1996 Hollinger Inc. annual report, Black wrote: "The war is not over, but we are winning it and can conduct it fairly effortlessly and very profitably. Shareholders should not be disconcerted by the stertorous bellicosity of our adversaries. On the ground, to improvise military parlance, our position has proved very formidable."[54] This from a man who has triumphed in his takeover bid of Canadian journalism.

The implications for Canada are troubling. Our history in war, while always valiant — our military has fought with distinction in every conflict in which Canada has been involved — has not been one of aggression. Essentially, we are a peaceful people. When the war is over, we put away our weapons. Our Capital is filled with symbols of peace, not war, and perhaps the largest distinction between our society and U.S. society is our approach to gun ownership.

The Americanization of Canada means the imposition of a more aggressive business style. As one American CEO said, "You do lunch or you are lunch in this business." Will our approach to business, to guns, to capital punishment, to war itself be affected by Black's opinions and behaviour in his own media empire?

For Black, war games are deadly serious. When the Queen inspected the Governor General's Foot Guards during her trip to Canada in the summer of 1997, she was followed by a very sombre-looking Conrad Black in full military uniform. For an "undisclosed sum of money,"[55] Black was allowed to dress up as an honorary colonel to attend the Queen. It seems money can buy just about anything in Conrad Black's Canada — including a little boy's dreams of military power.

5

NEWS WITHOUT JOURNALISTS

"One of the greatest myths of the industry [is] that journalists are essential to producing a newspaper."

— Conrad Black

The Roots of an Anti-Worker Mentality

A few weeks before the birth of Conrad Moffat Black, in August 1944, his parents received a visit from Edward Plunkett (E. P.) Taylor, the famous Canadian beer baron and racehorse owner. Taylor was recruiting Conrad's father, George Montegu Black Jr., who would eventually come to work for Taylor, quickly rising to become president of Canadian Breweries Ltd. (CBL).

When the Brewers' Union went on strike in the summer of 1959, Black resisted settling, over E. P. Taylor's objections. The seven-week strike cost CBL $100,000 per day. By October of that year, Taylor effectively fired George Black. "I think it's time we had a new president of Canadian Breweries Ltd.," Taylor said. "Well, that's fine with me, Eddie," Black replied. Embittered, he accepted early retirement at forty-eight.[1] In his memoirs Conrad recollects, "[George Black's] idleness was not serene and it was a difficult time for him."[2]

His father's attitudes and early retirement may help to explain the younger Black's animosity toward unions, journalists, and workers in general. In his book about the press lords, *Paper Tigers*, British author Nicholas Coleridge repeats the advice given to him by friends of Black. He writes, "To understand Conrad Black, you must examine his relationship with his father; the talents and disappointments of George Black have more to do with Conrad's motivation than any single factor."[3]

"I've fired so many people in my life that it's sort of an art," the elder Black once explained. "I can do it without bitterness."[4] And it's no wonder, for he had nothing but contempt for his employees and their representatives. For example, as Conrad explains in his autobiography, his father didn't like labour leaders' poor grammar; he "was also irritated by their syntactical inelegance." As Black recounts it, one head of a brewery union accused the elder Black "during negotiations of 'deviating pretty low,' seeking to have him 'rooneyed' (i.e. ruined), and of living in luxury in a 'suit of rooms' in the Royal York Hotel."[5] Black goes on to explain in his own words that, "once laws existed to protect workers against capricious or exploitive employers, most unions became enemies of productivity increases through automation, advocates of feather-bedding, and a mortal threat to any sense of community in an enterprise." Union leaders were "corrupt Luddites" who were "less concerned with the welfare of their membership than I was,"[6] he writes. Not surprisingly, given their shared views, "Conrad was the apple of his father's eye," says Black's partner Peter White.[7]

Unions and Socialist Hordes

Black's own animosity and hostility toward unions comes through quite clearly in his autobiography. In 1986, he withdrew a $38 million surplus from a pension fund for unionized employees of Dominion Stores, prompting Ontario NDP leader Bob Rae to describe Black, in the Ontario Legislature, as "bloated capitalism at its worst." The Ontario Supreme Court eventually ordered Hollinger to return the money to the fund with interest, and he repaid $44 million. Writing about Dominion Stores, which was owned by Argus Corp. when he first took over the holding company, Black describes a visit to a Knob Hill Farms store in Etobicoke in 1984, which he compares with the Dominion stores he owned. Marvelling at the "huge-volume, low-price, thinly-manned store," he observes, "How were we to compete with this, with [our own] smaller stores feather-bedded by clock-watchers paid $40,000 per year for stacking bags of frozen peas?"[8]

These are a few of the numerous derogatory references to labour and the working class in Black's autobiography. Earlier we mentioned his comment about British prime minister Margaret Thatcher, in which he says he "felt passionately that she had redeemed her country from vassalage to the thugs of the labour union leadership."[9] Later he describes the poll tax riots in London in the spring of 1990, "where the unruly scum of London's mobs vandalized the area in and around Trafalgar Square."[10]

Of course, labour, unions, and the New Democratic Party are all lumped in together in Black's view. On the topic of the labour legislation brought in by Bob Rae's NDP government in Ontario in 1992, Black writes, "As the Rae government handed over all industrial power to the labour unions, as it had pledged to do, private-sector capital investment and job creation were sure to dry up . . . No one in his right mind would invest a cent in Ontario under this regime . . ."[11] Especially, it turned out, himself. In response to the legislation, Black shifted the Hollinger headquarters from Toronto to Vancouver.

According to Black, the enactment of the rather mild labour reforms introduced by the NDP "was, as I wrote in *The Financial Post*, the seizure of the commanding heights of the private sector and the elimination of the shareholders' interest in favour of the employees'. The employers would lose all ability to withhold profit from the workers and remit it to the investors."[12] To Black, this "socialist" NDP government represented roughly half of the problem faced by the country. The other half comprised the "craven ethno-narcissists in Quebec."[13]

Black's move from Toronto to Vancouver was, he said, in protest, "while Ontario is under the hobnailed fiscal jackboot of Bob Rae." Black implied that the only reason he invested abroad was the existence of the "socialist" Rae government. "Thus, in our company, Hollinger Inc., jobs are created, payrolls expanded and dividends paid in the United Kingdom, in 28 of the United States, in several other Canadian provinces and even in Israel, rather than in Ontario, because of the government of Ontario's implacable bias in favor of labor union bosses and against the shareholder."[14]

According to Black, Rae's policies compared unfavourably even to those of other "labour" governments. "The labour party in power [in Australia] is to the right of our Conservatives. Bob Hawke cheerfully broke an airline strike. He would have no use for Bob Rae at all. He would consider him an insolent, impudent, reckless, dangerous little upstart who needed a good kick in the ah, derriere. Labour leaders like that I get on fabulously with."[15] This was in 1991, but by 1994 Bob Hawke told an Australian parliamentary inquiry into foreign ownership of the media that "the simple fact is that Conrad Black does not tell the truth. He has the habit of distorting events through the prism of his own perceived self-interest."[16] Ultimately, the two men issued a joint press release to the effect that they agreed to disagree over their remembrances.

Journalists as Leftists

According to Black, the problem with workers in general is that they have a nasty penchant for wanting to share in the profits which should rightfully be reserved for owners alone. This mentality is part of a broader problem, which Black sums up scornfully as an attitude of "caring and compassion." He sees this attitude as held and promoted by certain influential elements in our society, including journalists and labour leaders. In his view, the crux of the problem, symbolized by the "caring and compassion" of our social programs, is socialism. And the reason socialism is rampant in our society, says Black, is that influential people such as journalists are leftist in persuasion.

In a column in *The Financial Post* in 1992, Black elaborated on his theory. He traced "the birth of official 'caring and compassion'" back to the government of Louis St. Laurent, in the mid-1950s, when "the bureaucrats, journalists, academics, left-wing clergy, labor leadership and trendies in business and the learned professions clambered spontaneously, unquestioningly and almost unanimously, on to this new bandwagon." For a whole generation, wrote Black, this became a mantra. But, he said, "'caring and compassion' really meant socialism, wealth confiscation and redistribution, taking money from people who had earned it and giving it to people who had not earned it in exchange for their votes and in the name of fairness. Here, truly, Canada has vastly exceeded the United States . . . 'Caring and compassion,' however well-intentioned, would more accurately be called plundering and bribery . . . For decades, too many of our business leaders mouthed self-reliant and ruggedly individualistic platitudes while lining up for government preferments like the locusts of feminism and multiculturalism, and the kleptocracy of organized labor . . . Of course, we must always care for the disadvantaged, but 'compassion' is not a fair description of the wholesale purchase of the people's affections with the people's own money."[17]

Time and again in his writings, Black has accused the "academic, bureaucratic, and journalistic elites of this country"[18] of selling Canadians on this redistributive policy which, according to Black "has saddled a fundamentally rich country with a back-breaking debt."[19] And he believes that the "compassionate" ideology these journalists have sold to North Americans produced a dangerously soft approach to communism and foreign policy during the Cold War. Black illustrated his attitude toward liberal Cold War behaviour in a 1988 column about the "ghastly" spectre of "Democratic congressmen [who] were openly cavorting with the Nicaraguan Communist leader, Daniel Ortega." Black saw this as "illustrative of the aggressive re-emergence of the great liberal death wish. After seven years of Reagan achieving peace through strength instead of Carteresque groveling, and prosperity through incentive rather than high taxes, bracket creep, and the purchase of minority votes in the name of 'caring and compassion,' the evocators of the old liberal American guilt complex are oozing out of their closets."[20]

Black was not without his own ideological weapons during the Cold War. For several years late in the 1980s, he writes, "Hollinger effectively owned the right-wing intellectual magazine *Encounter*. It had been founded at the height of the Cold War, in part, by the C.I.A., and among its editors were Malcolm Muggeridge, Stephen Spender, and Irving Kristol. *Encounter* played a splendid role in defeating the early post-war communist attempt and was also an eminent literary magazine, publishing, *inter alia*, Nancy Mitford's famous essay on what was 'U and non-U.' For these historic reasons and as a long-time subscriber, I was happy to help *Encounter*."[21]

While of late Black has begun to use his own journalistic holdings in this way to promote his views, he has spent a great deal of energy over the years claiming that the media is lamentably leftist. As far back as 1969 Black wrote in his Davey Committee submission that "the majority of working journalists" are what he described as "reflex ultra-liberals."[22] More recently he has come to see this leftward bias as somewhat moderated, but not eradicated altogether. In 1994, he toned down his earlier comments in a speech to the annual convention of the Canadian Association of Journalists. He said, "Since the collapse in shambles of the international left, this attitude tends happily to take less predictable and monolithic forms than in the Vietnam era when almost all journalists in Canada seemed to me to want to replicate Sweden."[23] But pockets of this sort of thing seem to remain, in Black's view. Take, for example, the Vancouver papers. In an interview with *The Globe and Mail* in 1997, Black said, "Let's face it, the Vancouver *Sun*, for a time, if you read it you'd conclude it was a paper written chiefly for the benefit of the gay community, the militant gays and the militant native people."[24] Presumably he has been able to rectify this situation since his initial investment in Southam, which owns the *Sun*, in 1992. But this is not a phenomenon restricted to the Vancouver papers, says Black. Writing about the negative Canadian media coverage resulting from his marriage to Barbara Amiel in 1992, Black alleges that Canadian journalists displayed "lesbian antagonism," while "the British press was much more able to accept her editorial gifts."[25]

Evidently, the problem exists as far away as Australia. Black writes, "The premier of Victoria called the *Melbourne Sunday Age* 'the morning star in drag,' while a prominent political clergyman wrote to me complaining of the 'Sydney Morning Homosexual.'" According to Black, however, "both exaggerate."[26] The media, in his view, pander to gays and lesbians, but also to innumerable other special interest groups. What he finds objectionable is "the process begun by Trudeau of using the federal treasury and parliament to identify and appease ethnic, regional, behavioural, sexual, and physiological complainant groups [which] has become both dangerous and absurd. Virtually everyone except Anglo-Saxon, able-bodied, middle-aged, heterosexual, male, middle-class Ontarians is now the officially recognized bearer of a subventionable grievance. Organizing society into clamouring categories of self-pitiers is scarcely distinguishable from and just as dangerous as Quebec's old practice, much despised in English Canada, of putting collective rights ahead of individual rights. This is, and has always been, recognized as a matrix for dictatorship, whether we are purporting to protect society from Communists, Jehovah's Witnesses, assorted bigots, wife beaters, gay bashers, office voyeurs, or discriminatory hirers."[27] So, for Black, putting collective rights ahead of individual rights is a matrix for dictatorship, by which he means communism. To him, the news media promote gays, lesbians, and multiculturalism —

but more importantly collective rights — for an audience which includes policy makers as well as citizens.

On his first visit to the Regina *Leader-Post*, about a year after buying it and its sister paper, the Saskatoon *StarPhoenix*, and laying off 170 employees, Black described the *Calgary Herald* under Southam's ownership as an "anti-oil industry, anti–Ralph Klein, basically NDP newspaper, in what has got to be the city in Canada least sympathetic to the NDP perspective. It's a recipe for self-destruction."[28]

When Black bought out the Power Corp. shares in Southam in 1996, the Council of Canadians and other groups challenged the Hollinger takeover in court, arguing that Black's control of Southam would mean a decline in the diversity of opinions in those newspapers. In response, Black told *The Globe and Mail*, "I've never met [Maude Barlow of the Council of Canadians] but to judge from her public efforts it's not hard to impute to her the motive of regret that the Southam papers may henceforth be less absolutely reliable and predictable mouthpieces of her feminist, socialist, envious, anti-American views than they have been."[29]

In his Chairman's Statement in the 1996 Southam Annual Report, Black described how single newspaper monopolies had led to "complacency" and the attraction of "second-rate" Southam journalists, prior to his consolidation of control over the company in 1996. He pulled no punches, saying that "the Southam newspapers tended to . . . produce blandly written material echoing the political faddishness of the time. A politically correct pursuit and championship of many rather esoteric and unrepresentative causes often took the place of style, balance and accuracy."

Black pointed to the *Calgary Herald* and Montreal *Gazette* as examples of this political correctness. He wrote, "Many Southam newspapers profoundly alienated their natural readerships and in many cases the goodwill attaching to the trademarks eroded with their circulations. Calgarians, for example, tired of attacks on the petroleum industry and the provincial government, and English-reading Montrealers wearied of apologia for Quebec's mistreatment of the non-French cultural minority."[30]

Amiel, too, is concerned about this "left-lib journalism." In a *Maclean's* column in 1992, she responded to the "nasty remarks" and "screeching" peppering the Canadian press about her new-found relationship with Black, her elusive bluebird of happiness, as she put it. "All the same, I can't help musing on some of the natterings about me. I am, for example, rather bemused by the internal contradictions of Canadian left-lib journalism faced with my situation. I have been portrayed as a cross between a screaming Jezebel (Rosemary Sexton in the Toronto *Globe and Mail* had me 'chewing men up and spitting them out') and a parasitic harlot (as in *The Toronto Star*'s Aislin cartoon)."[31] Amiel is no doubt the first person to identify former *Globe* gossip columnist Rosemary Sexton as an example of "left-lib journalism." Earlier, in her autobiography, Amiel summed up all of Canadian journalism as leftist. "This is not the United States, where William F. Buckley sails and holidays with John Kenneth Galbraith. This is Canada, where no magazine or television network departs more than Very Occasionally from a sentimental socialist's look at the issues — whether it is our own venerable *Saturday Night* magazine or the trashy weekend newspaper supplements."[32]

In a speech to the right-wing, corporate-sponsored Fraser Institute in 1988, Black discussed how he coined his own version of the expression "military-industrial complex," seemingly attributing the latter expression to "the left," when in fact it was coined by General Dwight D. Eisenhower, former U.S. president. "I must add that this cumbrous phrase, academic-bureaucratic-journalistic complex, is one I invented 15 years ago out of vengeance for the left's then incessant prattling about the military-industrial complex," he said. Black went on to say that he had hopes for some alternative to the left-wing press. "In Canada, there is no intellectually presentable conservative media outlet, though I and others are determined to make the *Financial*

Post a candidate for such a distinction."[33] Although Black has identified *The Globe and Mail*'s editor-in-chief William Thorsell as "something of an ideological soulmate," he evidently thinks *The Globe* is still too "leftist."[34]

In January 1984, *Maclean's* columnist Fred Bruning, who works for *Newsday* on Long Island, wrote a column criticizing the way in which the Reagan administration kept out the press during the U.S. invasion of Grenada in November 1983. (*Maclean's* has managed to find two women columnists, in Barbara Amiel and Diane Francis, who make their male counterparts seem absolutely progressive by comparison.) Barbara Amiel responded with a column the next month, calling the invasion a "mission," and defending Reagan. "The exclusion of the press from Grenada may not have been wise in a political sense. But it was most assuredly deserved," she wrote. Amiel asked, "What if the media is [sic] in the grip of a fashion in which the press confuses . . . the victim with the enemy?" It is up to leaders such as Reagan to help the media avoid such pitfalls.

The problem, according to Amiel, is that the media have taken up leftist causes such as the environment, and adopted an anti-corporate perspective, to the point where they have ruined their own credibility. "For 20 years the mainstream press has spewed out the message that Western society was rotten. And the American people listened and looked around and found that that message did not coincide with either their internal or external feelings about their homeland. Understandably, they started not to believe the press. Furthermore, they started looking at the press as one that was gratuitously opposed to their hopes, their values and their traditions," she wrote. According to Amiel, the danger here is that "members of the press have been crying wolf for so long when there was no wolf that we now face the hellishly dangerous position that, when the wolf really comes, no one will believe them."[35]

At the Southam annual meeting in May 1997, Peter Murdoch of the Communications, Energy and Paperworkers Union suggested that the chain's newspapers are lacking in opinion that is either "middle of the road" or left-of-centre. Black responded, "It is a bit rich for a person of your views to come in asking for that, having wallowed quite comfortably in a state where for many years it was practically impossible to find in these newspapers or virtually throughout the Canadian media the slightest derogation from the most rigorous adherence to a politically correct, left-wing, anti-American, socialistic, feminist and, in respect to anybody who actually achieved anything, envious viewpoint, and that's what we've buried."[36]

Journalistic "Demanning"

Although Black has had dalliances in other areas of the economy, from Argus to Dominion Stores and Massey-Ferguson, his primary involvement over the past thirty years has been in the newspaper industry. As such, for Black, workers are journalists and journalists are employees, and the fewer of them the better. Since in Black's (and Amiel's) view, the vast majority of journalists are unrepentant leftists, it has been relatively easy to do the right thing with respect to the bottom line, and fire them.

The extreme nature of Black's position surfaced in 1989 at the London *Daily Telegraph*, when management put out two editions of the paper during a thirty-six-hour strike by journalists. Black writes in his autobiography that the two newspapers produced by management exposed what he calls "one of the greatest myths of the industry: that journalists are essential to producing a newspaper."[37]

Black's thirty years of newspaper ownership has been characterized by layoffs. He describes how, at the Sherbrooke *Record*, he "instituted frugalities that vastly transcended anything I have seen unearthed in the [Ken] Thomson organization or elsewhere." Since the *Record* had lost $180,000 in the previous twenty-two months, Black says, "over 40 percent of the work force had to go." The three partners (Black, Peter White, and David Radler) divided the firing responsibilities. "Peter [White] became so zealous he reached one targeted employee in a cabin at Niagara Falls. Unfortunately it was subsequently discovered to have been her honeymoon and Peter managed an awkward partial recantation; she worked half-days."[38]

There was considerable wrangling over compensation for the staff who remained. "I eventually devised what I described as the elastic compensation system for the reporters and debated with them at the end of each week what they 'deserved' on the basis of the volume and quality of their journalistic production." Black confesses that the system was "outrageous," but rationalizes that he was giving the journalists valuable journalistic experience. "It was an outrageous system, of course, but many of our reporters went on to considerable distinction at larger newspapers, and few of them would deny that the *Record*, despite the oppressions of our management, did give them a firm grounding in the journalistic craft."[39]

Black describes other innovative cost-cutting measures at the *Record*. "One scheme I struck upon for reducing salaries with an impeccable cover of good intentions was to hire a convict under a federal government bonded rehabilitation service, at a modest salary . . . After two weeks he started writing forged cheques and fled to New Brunswick."[40] These measures paid off in spades for him and his two partners. He knew then that he had found the mother lode. "The *Sherbrooke Record* was a tight ship, and a year after we bought it, it was making ten to fifteen thousand dollars a month, having lost nearly $10,000 per month in the two years before we bought it."[41] The *Record*, purchased for $18,000 in 1969, sold in 1977 for $865,000, after making annual profits of over $150,000. Black says the sale price was "forty-eight times what we paid for it eight years before, and [we had] stripped out about a million dollars of profit with which we built our newspaper company."[42]

Black justified his cost efficiencies on the basis that they were necessary for the survival of the newspaper. "Chronically minority, marginal, with tenacious but elderly and not very prosperous readers scattered across a hundred miles along the U.S. border, all within the circulation area of the Montreal *Gazette* and *Star*, the *Record* would not have survived with any management significantly less purposeful than ourselves."[43]

As for what would become of the journalists he fired, Black felt that there were ample opportunities for them elsewhere. He told the Davey Committee in 1969, "Finally, it should be remembered that journalists enjoy a high degree of job mobility; they are freer than most corporate employees to seek employment elsewhere if they feel that their talents are being misused."[44] If it was true then, of course, it is no longer.

In 1992, Black's partner David Radler told *Maclean's* columnist Peter C. Newman how he went about finding newspaper bargains. "I visit the office of each prospective property at night and count the desks. That tells me how many people work there. If the place has, say, 42 desks, I know I can put that paper out with 30 people, and that means a dozen people will be leaving the payroll even though I haven't seen their faces yet."[45] In 1994, Radler's advance man for the American newspaper purchases, Arthur Weeks, told journalist Jennifer Wells that: "Radler would turn to Weeks, as he did at the time of their first U.S. purchase, of the *Wapakoneta Daily News* in Ohio, and say, 'Arthur, count the chairs.' Radler distrusted vendor body counts, wary as he was of part-time workers, corporate America's zebra mussels — subsurface and astonishingly plentiful."[46] By 1995, a more savvy Mr. Radler was quoted by *The Globe and Mail* as follows: "Mr. Radler said Hollinger intends to continue to maintain salaries and benefits at the current level for employees at the newspapers, *and he doesn't expect there to be layoffs.* 'It's a local publisher's decision on how many people work at the place, and it may surprise you *there may actually be some additions,*' he said."[47] (Emphasis added) Yet we have already seen what happened at some of those newspapers, such as the Cambridge *Reporter*, where about one-third of the staff was laid off subsequent to the Hollinger takeover. This type of behaviour also contradicts statements Radler made to journalists shortly after buying *The Jerusalem Post*. According to one editor, Radler said, "We don't buy newspapers for the physical plant. What I'm really interested in is the people."[48] And Radler himself says, of the *Post* takeover, "I never fired anyone. No one was fired. Thirty-two resigned. Now, it was convenient for me, because there were thirty-two too many people, if not more, in the editorial department at that time."[49]

According to Richard Siklos, "Staffing levels [at the *Post*] were pared virtually in half, from 130 journalists on the payroll in 1989 to sixty-two in 1993; overall headcount was slashed to 210 from 450."[50] Said Black, "obviously, we thought, economies could be effected, no matter how difficult Israel's labour laws were." He saw a confrontation with the managing editor at the *Post* as "an opportunity for relatively inexpensive demanning so we peremptorily rejected [their] demands and happily received the uncompensated resignations of fifteen journalists."[51]

Labour-Management Disputes

Disputes between labour and management are an inevitable byproduct of a situation where ownership is fixated on layoffs as a means to the end of a more profitable bottom line. In his 1993 autobiography, Black looks back affectionately on the field experiment of his first daily paper from the cold comfort of his hundreds of millions of dollars in personal assets. He describes how he and his partners "fiercely overmanaged" the Sherbrooke *Record*, where "some of the economies we effected must have set records." Black brags about some of their more draconian measures. "Employees were monitored, more or less good-naturedly, but with superhuman persistence. We had a Montreal telephone directory by sequence of telephone numbers and relentlessly hunted down any personal calls from Sherbrooke to Montreal. When one reporter marched into David's office to present a petition of grievances, David fined him two cents, deducted from his weekly pay cheque, for wasting a sheet of paper. When, on the night of NDP leader Allan Blakeney's first victory in Saskatchewan in 1971, the same reporter raised the two-finger V for victory sign, then current among the left, to David, he too raised up two victorious fingers and said, 'That just cost you two,' and deducted two dollars from his next pay cheque, 'for provoking the owners.'"[52] Black describes the underlying philosophy of the owners. "David [Radler] kept a copy of William Taylor's famous early-19th-century manual on industrial relations and regularly recited the opening sentence, which asserted that any such study must start from the premise that all employees are slothful, incompetent, and dishonest."[53]

In 1991, when faced with the changes to the Ontario Labour Relations Act being contemplated (and eventually implemented) by Bob Rae's NDP government, Black offered up the workings of Richard Nixon and Ronald Reagan as examples of how to best deal with labour. "The only postal strike in the history of the United States collapsed after two hours when President Richard Nixon instructed the National Guard to deliver the mail. Ten years ago Ronald Reagan gave a well-remembered cram-course in how to deal with striking air-controllers . . . There is nothing sacred about the right to strike, in the public or the private sector. All have a right not to be exploited, abused, or capriciously treated by their employers. All have the right to quit their jobs."[54]

In 1972, Black purchased *L'Avenir* newspaper in Sept-Îles, Quebec, and by the next year had what he called "a labor problem." "We moved into a new building, bought our own press, and were contemplating going daily, but our publisher lost control of events and the journalists announced they were forming a union . . . I fired the entire editorial department of four people, purportedly for cause (professional incompetence). Naturally, in the parlance of labour law, they grieved, i.e. took out a grievance against me. The publisher and I did the reporting for a while and then gradually scabbed it." Black was hauled before the Quebec Labour Board. "One evening, after the fourth day of the trial, I bought a case of beer to distribute among loyal employees, but [lawyer Philip Matthews] and I stopped at our hotel, drank the beer ourselves, sinking into armchairs in front of my hotel window and watching the northern sunset descend on Sept-Iles."[55] According to Black, the matter was resolved as follows: "We eventually wore down the [Confédération des syndicats nationaux], paid one and a half times normal severance to the dismissed reporters, and carried on uncertified."[56]

On a strike in 1992 at *Le Soleil*, his daily in Quebec City, Black writes, "Having endured a good deal of Marxist agitation and anglophobic provocation from elements of the French-Quebec press over many years, I was proud of the performance of our Quebec management . . . They skilfully divided all the rest of the work force from the journalists, who finally struck us after working two years without a contract. They refused to be assigned and demanded a sharp increase in average pay to $60,500 for a three-day work week in the midst of the most severe recession in sixty years. Their pickets were ignored: freelancers working and faxing from home and editors produced an improved paper, as polls that we steadily published on page one showed, and we turned the historic tide of industrial relations in the newspaper industry in Quebec."[57]

According to the Montreal *Gazette*, polls by both management and the union at *Le Soleil* did not demonstrate "an improved paper"; rather, they showed that readers "didn't think the quality of the paper had declined" as a result of the strike, and with the use of wire services, freelancers, and management-written stories. The management poll found 73 percent in agreement with this, while the union poll about a week later found 56 percent in agreement.[58]

Black comments, "The whole episode was well executed by our Quebec management and culminated in a Christmas Eve vote to accept management terms causing the union executive to resign. It was one of my more pleasant career experiences."[59] Gambling with the level of his profits while the journalists gambled with their livelihood, Black concluded, tongue firmly planted in cheek, "I would never, even in my most combative moments, have gone quite as far as Jimmie Goldsmith, who broke a strike at the Paris magazine *l'express*, when he owned it, by haranguing the journalists that 'Instead of blood, you have only pus in your veins.'"[60]

When he failed in his 1992 attempt to buy the New York *Daily News*, Black explained that he lost interest because of the concessions given to the unions by a fellow bidder. "Once Mr. [Mort] Zuckerman decided to give the most militant unions, the pressmen and the drivers, everything that they asked for, and return effectively to pre–[Robert] Maxwell manning levels, and to forgo any progress at all in work rules or what I described as the culture of the workplace, we had no interest in it at all."[61]

When Peter Murdoch of the Communications, Energy and Paperworkers Union had the temerity, at the 1997 Southam annual meeting to question Black about the rightward shift and homogeneity of his papers, Black responded with a lecture on unions. The "fact is unions contributed importantly to all of the problems that the newspaper industry has had in this country," Black said. He went on to blame unions as directly complicit in the closing of the Montreal *Star*, the Toronto *Telegram*, and the Ottawa *Tribune*. "The movement you represent, which has a huge number of good people in it and has an important role to play in the country, has a great deal to answer for in this country," he said.[62]

On Job Prospects

Earlier, we indicated Black's opinion, dating back to the Davey Committee in 1969, that "journalists enjoy a high degree of job mobility" because they are free "to seek employment elsewhere."[63] When two journalism students, Dawn and Heather on their name tags, approached Black after his address to the Canadian Association of Journalists convention in Ottawa in 1994, they asked what they could do to get jobs when they graduated. "We're in journalism school and there's no jobs out there," they said. According to biographer Richard Siklos, Black told them to travel to Europe as he had done, and said that a journalism degree is "better than no degree." He added, studying their name tags, "all work and no play makes Dawn a dull girl." Then, leaving the hall, he raised his fist toward them and yelled, "Don't be demoralized, girls!"[64]

On Working Journalists

In 1987, a controversy erupted between Conrad Black and journalist Linda McQuaig. In a column in *The Toronto Sun* in 1987, Black wrote that she was a "weedy . . . not very bright, left-wing reporter," when commenting on her coverage of a bribery scandal involving the Ontario Liberal government of David Peterson and developer Elvio Del Zotto. (Black's wife later defined "weedy," after declaring that the "weedy look of English men has been a national characteristic for eons." She said that weediness "suggests a lack of mental robustness coupled with a certain physical limpness."[65]) Black went on in the same article to label investigative journalists in general as "swarming, grunting jackals." In his autobiography Black puffs that McQuaig "would have had trouble successfully suing me [for libel] even if I had written that she was a vampire bat specializing in child molestation."[66] But in an interview with Peter Gzowski, promoting his book on *Morningside*, Black surpassed himself, saying, "I thought McQuaig should have been horsewhipped, but I don't do those things myself and the statutes don't provide for it."[67]

(Like her husband, Mrs. Amiel Black is not opposed to the use of the whip. When Black was embroiled in a controversy with former Australian prime minister Bob Hawke in 1994, Barbara Amiel was interviewed on Australian television and said Hawke's performance made a convincing argument in favour of public flogging. This was the highlight of the whole matter for Black, who commented, "I thought that was a scream."[68])

In 1996, Linda McQuaig gave a widely promoted speech to an audience of about 600 people in Peterborough, Ontario. The local Black-owned paper, the Peterborough *Examiner*, chose not to cover the event. Reportedly, when challenged by irate readers, the paper's editor falsely claimed that McQuaig had denied his paper an interview,[69] a claim which McQuaig subsequently refuted in a letter to the editor.

When Black was gobbling up some of the Thomson papers in 1996, Gail Lem of the Communications, Energy and Paperworkers Union said that this was "a frightening and dangerous development." She said that "Canadians should be put on alert that one man, Conrad Black, is making a relentless bid to control the press in Canada." These comments were reported in *The Globe and Mail*, where Lem was a reporter, and were accompanied by Black's denial. "Black said the union's statements were 'a complete load of rubbish,' and argued that many of his deals had increased the diversity of newspaper ownership in Canada," the paper reported.[70] Just how, neither Black nor *The Globe* explained. Not content with this, in May 1996 Black penned a letter to the editor in which he bashed the unions and recommended therapy for the unemployed journalists. "It is even more galling," he wrote, "to endure the alarmist claims of spokesmen for organized labour who by their feather-bedding greed and irresponsibility have done more than any other group or interest to imperil the newspaper industry . . . Those who practice or profess print journalism should seek whatever therapy is necessary to overcome the trauma of past abrasions and learn to distinguish the friends of the craft from its enemies."[71]

This was returning to an old theme for Black, who confides in his autobiography that "many" of the journalists who have worked for him "had neurotic and familial problems that David [Radler] and I were always happy to help with if asked (including recruiting a psychoanalyst for one of them), and even I was able to teach many of them something about the English language and how to give an employer value for money."[72] Elsewhere Black admitted, however, that he and his partners played a role in some of the emotional problems experienced by employees. "One of the advertising salesmen came in one of those early days to say he could work only half weeks because of illness and, when pressed, said that his psychiatrist had identified 'the new owners of the *Record*' as the source of the illness. We imposed draconian cost controls and turned our first profit after a couple of months."[73]

Barbara Amiel recommended therapy for fellow *Maclean's* columnist Fred Bruning, when he decried excessive and ostentatious spending by the wealthy, calling on them to give back to society in some way. Amiel described his column as "wretched." She wrote, "Could envy have actually reached such pathological proportions, even among normally well-tempered souls like Fred Bruning? Is it possible that such people genuinely feel like 'chumps' because another person spends money in a frivolous and profligate way? Surely, I thought, this is not the matter for a column but something to be quietly discussed with his therapist."[74]

According to Richard Siklos, "Invariably, Black's staunchest critics hail from the group he has disparaged since the age of twenty-five: the media. It is more than a love-hate relationship. His wife is a journalist, so too is his good friend Brian Stewart; so are other friends. Despite what some might think, Black says he likes most journalists, and indeed, most people he meets."[75]

6

VAMPIRE JOURNALISM

"Why, I ask myself, does someone stay in a wretched occupation like journalism?"

— Barbara Amiel

Chain Ownership and Monopolies

In his autobiography, Conrad Black writes that Hollinger is "one of the world's greatest newspaper companies," with a total daily circulation of nearly 4.5 million. He notes that his company ranks third "in the Western world," behind "Ganett [sic] a middle-brow supplier of newspapers," (correctly spelled Gannett), and Rupert Murdoch's News Corporation, which he said is "essentially a purveyor of down-market tabloids."[1]

In his submission to Keith Davey's Special Senate Committee investigation into the mass media, in 1969, Conrad Black wrote as the co-owner of a single small daily newspaper, the Sherbrooke *Record*. At the time Black and his partners also owned one English-language weekly and one French-language weekly. Black began his submission by indicating that "expensive printing equipment" required a pooling of facilities with other publications or "a profitable satellite printing business."[2] As a result, his daily was initially printed thirty miles away in Granby, by a competitor, Paul Desmarais's Power Corp.

As an independent newspaper owner surrounded and indeed dependent upon a "media colossus," Black felt well placed to comment on the topic of media concentration. "We accordingly have a useful vantage point from which to assess the effects of the high concentration of ownership which now characterizes the printed media in Quebec," Black wrote.[3]

Black went on to argue that where chains exist, there should be local editorial initiative and control. "In the best of circumstances, [newspaper] chains are public companies, generally confined to one medium, spread over a wide geographic area, and strongly committed to the concept of local editorial motivation and control." Even under the best of circumstances, Black said, chains tend to restrict the diversity of opinion by sharing correspondents and centralizing administration. "Even in such instances as these, there is a tendency to combine feature services, such as parliamentary correspondents, and to centralize administration, necessarily reducing the diversity and particularism of press opinion."[4]

Black singled out what he called "the Power Corporation-Trans Canada Publications-Gelco-Gesca group," which he criticized for the extent of its control and the fact that it could offer advertisers package deals with which he could not compete. Black said, "Apart from four daily newspapers, each the largest in its area, and one radio station which operates in our circulation area," Power Corp. also "controls a large number of week-end and weekly newspapers with a combined circulation that approaches one million, all in the province of Quebec . . . There has also been a heavy concentration of newspaper production [sic] and editorial facilities; and package deals have been offered to advertisers that could not be matched by independent publishers."[5]

Black criticized the Power Corp. "colossus" specifically, but also the general development of such monopolistic chains. "The situation that has been created is uncompetitive and in some areas monopolistic. Our relationship with this media colossus, on whose good will our very survival to some extent depends, has not been very satisfactory, and we consider the existence of such a group to be a bad augury for the future of an independent press in Quebec." Black argued that the development of such huge chains is not inevitable. Although businesses might naturally tend toward such concentration, it is something to be resisted. "The present degree of concentration in the ownership of the Canadian media was not inevitable and reflects only the natural but not irresistible tendency of business to concentrate," he wrote. Black went on to suggest that part of the problem is the inadequacy of government legislation regarding estate tax structures. "The purchase last year of newspapers in Owen Sound and Prince George by the Southam Press may presage a greater concentration of medium and smaller newspapers, whose passage from individual and family ownership is in any event encouraged by present gift and estate tax structures."[6]

Black then indicated that the tendency toward monopolization is "reprehensible," and should be discouraged as "undesirable." He said such monopolies should only exist where they are an economic necessity, and even then they should be strictly regulated. "However, further consolidation toward monopolistic situations in markets sufficiently large to support competition is reprehensible and should be discouraged at least as vigorously as monopolistic developments in other industries. It is a widely held social proposition that where they are not an economic necessity or at least subject to strict regulation, monopolies are undesirable. The establishment of large industrial enterprises with multimedia appendages in uncompetitively favourable positions of dominance is economically unjust and socially harmful." With the lack of competition brought on by chains and monopolies according to Black, "diversity of opinion and aggressive news-gathering tend to disappear, . . . and public opinion could thereby become more of a hostage to private interests than a master to public policy."[7]

In March 1997, on his first visit to the Regina *Leader-Post*, purchased from the Sifton family a year earlier, Black admitted that owning half of the newspapers in the country is "odd," but he said the view that such control gives Hollinger monopoly power is obsolete. "The idea that 42 per cent of the circulation of Canada's daily newspapers constitutes an ability to dominate, or in any way abuse our position, is simply preposterous," he said. The proliferation of media voices, including broadcasting, cable and satellite TV channels, foreign newspapers, and the Internet makes monopoly control a virtual impossibility.[8]

A Day in Court

In concluding his comments to the Davey Committee about twenty-five years earlier, Black had made these recommendations: "The anti-monopoly provisions of the Combines Investigations Act should be applied to the media as zealously as they have been to other industries. It is high time the media divisions of the Power Corporation group, and perhaps the Irving media interests also, had their day in court."[9]

Later, in his autobiography and elsewhere, Black would espouse a different view of the Southam chain, Power Corp., and newspaper monopolies. Instead of being "undesirable," monopolies had become "splendid," and now could be categorized according to their returns as either "broadsheet," or "English-language," or "absolute." The fact that they were "awash with money" was good. Their only shortcoming was that they were only wringing out about half of the potential profits. For example, commenting in 1993 on the condition of the Southam chain in the mid-1980s, he wrote, "[The Southam] franchises were splendid — broadsheet monopolies in Calgary, Edmonton, and English-language Ottawa; English-language monopoly in Montreal; and absolute monopolies in Vancouver, Windsor, Sault Ste. Marie, Kitchener-Waterloo, North Bay, Moose Jaw, Medicine Hat, Prince George, Owen Sound, Barrie, and Kamloops — all good towns . . . [the] properties were accordingly awash with money; in almost every

Southam town, the newspaper building loomed up on the horizon like a Taj Mahal, a monument to the feckless lack of imagination of its owners in the art of reinvesting earnings. Nor were the earnings adequate, never more than 12 per cent pre-tax cash flow on daily newspaper revenues, less than half what we wrung from very mediocre franchises such as Sherbrooke, Quebec, and Prince Rupert, British Columbia. Nor, contrary to fervently propagated mythology, were they very distinguished newspapers."[10] Elsewhere, Black made the revealing comment that "the Southam newspapers in 1988 made their all-time high percentage of gross income of 15 per cent, against 26 per cent and 27 per cent at the vastly inferior franchises of Sterling Newspapers and American Publishing."[11]

Need for Editorial Conformity

In a speech to the annual Canadian Press dinner in Toronto in 1988, Black looked at the newspaper owners and publishers and said that the successors to some of the "greatest figures in the history of Canadian newspapers" have not measured up. He said "this renders especially implausible the organized consternation in this country about concentration of media ownership. Neither Thomson, nor Southam, nor Maclean-Hunter has ever attempted in my memory to impose any editorial conformity on their newspapers."[12]

In April 1993 Black was defending his initial purchase of a 22.5 percent stake in Southam to a reporter from *Maclean's*. On this occasion he described concern about concentration of ownership as "paranoia." He said, "What's in the shareholder's best interest is turning the company around, not continued paranoia about takeovers."[13] Also, at the May 1996 Hollinger annual meeting, which followed closely on Black's announcement that he was consolidating his control of Southam by buying out the Power Corp. shares, Black told journalists: "You may not like it, but I appear to be the only game in town. If we're the only people buying, where am I a menace to the public interest?"[14] Gone was the notion that a single game in town might be contrary to the public interest. Asked at the meeting whether corporate concentration of newspaper ownership is limiting expression in Canada, Black said no. "Go to a hotel and turn on your TV set and you get sixty channels courtesy of Ted Rogers. What are [the critics] talking about?" Black now wondered. He said, "I don't think there's been much criticism [of Hollinger's corporate concentration]. There's the predictable people from schools of journalism that they dredge out on these occasions and a few union leaders."[15] He might have added that the voices of independent publishers, such as he was in 1969, have all but been extinguished, thanks to the monopolization which he once decried but in which he was now the key player. In his forty-minute speech to shareholders Black added that "our grand total of newspaper copies sold is only 7.2 per cent of the Canadian population. No serious assertion can be made that this constitutes a threat to free or varied opinion."[16]

As for Power Corp., Black changed his mind considerably about the threat it poses. Soon after he entered into a controlling partnership at Southam with Power CEO Paul Desmarais Sr. in 1993, he wrote, "I expressed happiness to work with [Desmarais] in a structured, agreed way — against any lingering culture of inefficiency that might exist at Southam, not against each other . . . We would effectively become co-controlling shareholders without either of us paying a control premium."[17] In 1996, the two parted company, apparently amicably, as Black bought out Desmarais and consolidated his control over Southam.

On Government Subsidies
In his submission to the Davey Committee, Black lamented "recent postal rate increases," which he said "necessitated a doubling of the [Sherbrooke *Record*'s] subscription price," leading in turn to a 20 percent decrease in rural circulation. Black went on to argue that postal delivery trucks are making their rounds anyway, so they might as well carry his newspapers. He suggested as

an alternative that corporate taxes should be raised. "[The] postal rate increase is wholly unjustifiable as an elimination of a 'subsidy', which is how it has been presented," Black argued. "Foregoing the small shortfall in the case of the *Record* and the many Canadian publications in a similar position would not, we believe, have seriously strained the federal treasury." Instead, wrote Black, the monies could be obtained "through the corporate income tax."[18]

Freedom of the Press and Free Expression

At the Southam Inc. annual meeting in May 1997, Black talked about his investment and his purposes. "Our associates and I have put an awful lot of money — a lot of it our own money — into this business because we believe in the whole project of trying to inform this country, entertain it in a responsible way, enlighten it, promote diversity of view and resist precisely the kind of conformity that we felt was the bane of the newspaper industry in the past in this country."[19] One could argue whether or not Black has been trying to inform and enlighten this country and promote a diversity of views. However, in terms of his investment, this statement directly contradicts what Black had earlier written in his autobiography. "We had started nearly twenty years before, with $18,000, which came from the *Knowlton Advertiser* (the enterprise in which I purchased a 50 per cent interest in 1967 for $500 less a cheap rug, ultimately my only investment in Sterling or Hollinger)."[20]

In his submission to the Davey Committee, Black defended the right of reply for what he termed "our ideological opponents." Black wrote, "We have consistently offered our ideological opponents a full right of reply in our own pages, and this is our principal outlet for pressure groups that feel themselves aggrieved by our treatment of them."[21] It is interesting that even at this early stage Black appears to define "pressure groups," by which he presumably meant what are currently called special interest groups, as his adversaries. That aside, one wonders whether his offer of a full right of reply still stands.

Barbara Amiel too is a defender of freedom of speech. Writing in 1985, about a month after Ernst Zundel was found guilty of harming social and racial harmony by claiming that the Holocaust was a hoax, Amiel argued, "It is a popular assumption that the prosecution of Zundel and the upcoming prosecution of Alberta teacher James Keegstra on similar charges are necessary in order to prevent the development of a climate that could lead to a new Third Reich . . . Hitler was right, alas. You either have free speech for everyone or you do not have free speech. You cannot have a little free speech or free speech 'except for . . .'" Amiel wrote. "What all the people who support the prosecutions of the Zundels and Keegstras don't understand is that limiting free speech creates the conditions for the rise of Hitler or his equivalent. The problem with freedom is that it is indivisible."[22]

In 1969 Black defined freedom of the press as the ability to report without interference. He related the threat posed by media conglomerates such as Power Corp. to the issue of freedom of speech. He saw the Achilles heel as advertising. "Any group capable of asserting genuine pressure on the media poses a threat to impartiality and complete liberty of expression, and the place of maximum vulnerability to pressure is in the area of advertising revenues." When faced with this type of pressure, scrupulous publishers should avoid tailoring the paper's policy and expose it as "attempted blackmail," Black wrote.[23]

Language Police

For Amiel, writing in 1980, the threat to freedom of expression is posed not by advertisers or conglomerates, but by "commissars" among feminists and those in government who would attempt to constrain those very advertisers and conglomerates. "We recently had Secretary of State David MacDonald preparing to monitor television commercials to prevent the 'stereotyping' of women. We have already had feminist Laura Sabia complaining about the tellers in bank commercials always being women. Well, most tellers in banks *are* women. What David MacDonald and Laura Sabia and all the other would-be-commissars want *is to depict reality not as it is but as they would like it to be.* This is the definition of 'socialist realism' or propaganda. But forcing artists or advertisers to lie will not build a better society."[24]

Writing in 1984, Amiel castigated these "commissars" as zealots and language police who were critical of stereotyping. She dismissed "those people who discovered all sorts of nonexistent connections between language and value systems."[25] Later, in a column on "the frightening tyranny of language," which turned out to be about the stylebook used at *The Globe and Mail*, Amiel took issue with the fact that the stylebook dares to go beyond such matters as spelling and punctuation. "By using euphemisms for disapproved ideas, the *Globe* believes that you can make the bad idea disappear. A perfect example of this is the use of the word 'crippled.' This word, as the *Globe* explains, is now in disfavor. Since the days of 'crippled,' we have substituted 'handicapped,' which the *Globe* tells us is now also a no-no. The preferred word is 'disabled.' Crippled, handicapped, disabled: it will all give off the same negativism since human beings have a natural fear and aversion to the state of being less than whole in body."[26] No subtle differences here for the able-bodied Amiel.

Amiel's conclusions were typically extreme. She wrote that "having such a stylebook makes a mockery of a free press. This is a stylebook that goes far beyond the legitimate areas of spelling or policies on obscenity: this book seeks to put its ideological stamp on reporting. This is profoundly anti-intellectual and would be even if I agreed with every entry . . . A stylebook that goes beyond spelling or punctuation or notions of that kind is antithetical to both good and free journalism. *The Globe and Mail* — and Canada — can ill-afford this nonsense."[27]

Much as Amiel might sympathize with the Royals — Charles, Diana, Sarah — on the behaviour of the paparazzi in violating their privacy, she wrote in 1993 that there should be no commensurate restrictions on the press to prevent violations of privacy or even writing about the lives of others. "What intrigues me is the attitude of others to freedom of the press. Many European countries, such as France, Spain, and Germany, give people copyright to their 'image.' That means newspapers can't use photos or details of a person's life, without their permission . . . No one should have copyright on their life. We do not own our images and life stories the way we own a bicycle or a house."[28]

Public Opinion and Media Bias

In his Davey Committee submission Black argued on behalf of objectivity, fairness, and balance, as opposed to opinionated journalism. "Instead of leading public opinion by a faithful presentation of facts and events, some members of the [news] profession apparently believe that it is their right and obligation to create public opinion by reflecting the same facts and events through the distorting prism of their own opinions," he wrote. This latter predilection undermines the credibility of the press, Black said. Some would say he was criticizing what he has gone on to become. Certainly his current role may be recognized in the following: "There is a growing [public] distrust of those members of the fourth estate who claim a privileged status as the intellectual and moral arbiters of society."[29]

The CBC and the NFB

One consistent complaint from Black over the past thirty years has been in regard to the CBC. In 1969, for example, he wrote, "Almost surely, Canada's most obnoxious press establishment is that whose suffocating omnipresence is the principal characteristic of the CBC."[30] If Barbara Amiel and Conrad Black had nothing else in common whatsoever, their shared abhorrence of the CBC and public broadcasting generally would give them a sound basis for a strong relationship. The CBC is publicly rather than privately owned, and this is reason enough for Black and Amiel to dislike it, on principle. Even when cuts were made to the CBC in the mid-1980s by Brian Mulroney's Tory government, Amiel felt this just exacerbated the problems. "It is a small irony that the well-founded suspicion of Tories that the CBC was a bastion for Liberal support is now being aided by these cuts: people with the wrong ideas were kept out of the news and public affairs, which is virtually untouched. The few Tory supporters in the CBC have now been axed. At the same time the CBC brass are [sic] trying desperately to mobilize opinion against the Tories for these terrible cuts — because they are all worried that at one point they will actually have to start cutting themselves." Unlike private broadcasting, Amiel says, the CBC has too much administrative fat, "the ever-expanding bureaucracy . . . But administrators in private broadcasting have a great check on arbitrary action: that check is the marketplace. If a program is successful, a producer is not fired. The CBC, on the other hand, has no such constraint."[31]

Two of the major reasons for Black's hatred of the CBC are what he sees as the anti-Americanism of the English-language network and the separatism of the French-language one. "Historically," Black wrote in 1969, "the three principal bases for the Canadian nationality, as distinct from the American, have been the British connection (monarchism, Empire loyalty, etc.), French-Canadian nationalism, and anti-Americanism. The CBC promotes French-Canadian nationalism on its French network (as no less an authority than Prime Minister Trudeau has noted), and anti-Americanism on its English Network . . . Unless the majority of French-Canadians are at least cryptoseparatists, and the majority of English-speaking Canadians Americophobes, the Corporation is attempting to subvert public judgment."[32]

A Televised Kangaroo Court

Black returned to this theme more than twenty-five years later, in his column responding to the 1996 CBC documentary, "The Paper King." "Our federalist and patriotic credentials are unquestionable, (especially by the CBC, whose French language network is often a Quebec separatist propaganda agency, most of whose costs are involuntarily borne by federalist Canadians)." Black went on to add that, "unlike our febrile adversaries in the CBC and the dreary procession of tired and authoritarian leftists trotted through their program, we see no contradiction between quality and profitability. Unlike them and the agitating special interest groups with whom they are holding hands (again at great expense to the unconsulted taxpayers), we seek no more than a fair hearing for a range of intelligible views."[33]

To Black, the documentary was evidence that the same old problems continued to plague the CBC, now manifested in an attack on him personally. He proposed that rather than being frightened by his name and his track record, "I suggest that of greater concern is the factional hijacking of the state-owned national television service so that reputable citizens may be arraigned before a televised kangaroo court over their implied lack of patriotic and socialist fervor."[34]

So, late in 1996, here were the same old charges from Black about separatists, leftists, socialism, and anti-Americanism at the CBC. Similar, in Black's view, is *The Toronto Star*, the daily with the largest circulation in the country. In 1995, Black complained of an instance where the *Star* refused to publish his rebuttal to a rebuttal. He eventually responded in his column in *The Financial Post*. Black had initially written in response to a column by Dalton Camp. "Five days later," says Black, "the second fiddle in the *Star*'s endless repertoire of nostalgic leftist columnists, Richard Gwyn, accused me of 'heroic naivete' . . . Richard invited me to reply. When I did so, 10 days elapsed and an inquiry about my solicited letter produced the lofty assertion that the *Star* would not publish 'a rebuttal to a rebuttal.' The *Star* must always have the last word, no matter how fatuous or mendacious its defence of the beleaguered socialist battlements from which it has poured down bile almost uninterruptedly since before the First World War . . . This is the Canadian economic debate pursued by that newspaper: mythmakers writing tendentious drivel under false pretences invite a debate in which only one side is printed and the other is suppressed with all the liberality endemic to the Canadian left."[35]

We've already seen how Black views the CBC as a hotbed of anti-Americanism. In 1969, he wrote: "Canada is not strengthened by malicious media attacks on the United States, and mindless and misdirected bigotry does not contribute to Canada's esteem . . . The [CBC] network's constant harpings against the USA, if taken seriously, could poison US-Canadian relations . . . The CBC manages to give almost all major international occasions a peculiar anti-American twist."[36] But just what is it that Black finds so admirable about the United States? In a column in 1991 about how Brian Mulroney was afraid to introduce U.S. president George Bush at a Toronto Blue Jays baseball game at Skydome, Black quoted from the British magazine, *The Economist*, which opined that it was "too bad" that Canadians would one day become American. "It is not so bad, nor so inevitable. But it will happen unless we can devise for ourselves what the Americans already have: a country where freedom of expression is inviolable; taxes are reasonable; the social safety net has not become a hammock; people are proud of their country and of their fellow citizens for reasons that transcend mere economics, but shopping in our own country is not an act of economic self-punishment; everyone knows from one year to the next that they will have a country; and the unique act of public officials does not consist in raising a moistened finger to the winds."[37] Black summed up his views succinctly (for a change) in an otherwise and typically long-winded column (his columns regularly run to 1,400 words, more than twice the norm), when he wrote, "I suspect that most Canadians would prefer an American Canada to a socialist one."[38]

For Black and Amiel, the CBC is the worst offender among Canada's left-lib journalism. Amiel describes how there was "a left-wing bias" when she began working there in the 1960s, a bias which she says remains. "Back then, we selected program topics and participants with an eye to confirming our prejudices . . . We were anti-American, anti-big business and pro-feminist and accepted uncritically certain assumptions about the existence of racism and sexism in Canadian society."[39]

According to Amiel, left-wing bias at the CBC is endemic, pervasive, and irrefutable. "When it comes to news and public affairs broadcasting," Amiel wrote in 1988, "the CBC left-lib bias remains in force."[40] In 1991, she wrote, "Political bias in the Canadian Broadcasting Corp. is rather like police brutality: everyone knows it exists, but all employees and supporters close ranks to deny it. The only difference may be that whereas a lot of policemen think brutality is an abomination, a lot of CBC employees I know think that the left-wing bias of the CBC is morally correct." Up against this "CBC Syndrome," the right-wing has little chance of fair representation, according to Amiel. "In the post-war years, some of our 'great' Canadian journalists played footsie or detente with communism and the Soviet Union — one of the most awful ideologies and tyrannies the world has ever seen. Only Lubor Zink and a couple of other columnists were writing accurately about events in Eastern Europe . . . Myself, I'd be content if once in a while CBC programs would just question received wisdom and stop selecting the most idiotic representative of right-wing views in order to pretend that they are giving balanced programming."[41]

Amiel went on to deliver a backhanded compliment to Ivan Fecan, then the director of CBC programming. "Fecan," she wrote, "has eliminated some of the little fiefdoms of inefficiency that have merrily spawned in the ponds of the CBC." However, in what one must assume is the worst tradition of statism, "his method has been to centralize power and gather more authority to himself."[42]

The socialist tendencies that have such a "stranglehold" on the CBC are not present in public broadcasting in other countries, according to Amiel. "I have yet to see any time devoted to any one of a whole range of subjects in the national press or the CBC, ranging from South Africa to multinationals, that gave serious consideration to any side of the problem but the standard left-lib line. This problem does not exist in the U.S. to the same extent. The U.S. offers comprehensive coverage on most issues, as does England. But in Canada there is a stranglehold on the media, no less absolute for being unconscious."[43]

This left-lib proclivity dates back at least as far as the 1960s, according to Amiel, and the phenomenon of Trudeaumania. "It is doubtful . . . whether [Trudeau] would have been nominated without the universal endorsement of the media. He gained this universal support because the left-libbers — that is, the near-absolute majority at the CBC and the considerable majority at all the other networks, newspapers, and magazines — considered him to be one of them."[44] Black too takes a swipe at Trudeau, whom he considers a "leftie." Reviewing Trudeau's memoirs in his *Financial Post* column in 1994, Black begins with the *de rigueur* personal attack. "Pierre Trudeau's book *Memoirs* is a monument to human vanity that refreshes the reader's memory about all Trudeau's tendencies to glibness, faddishness, pretension, and the affected posturing of the inherited-money limousine liberal." Black himself inherited $7 million from his parents, but would no doubt argue that it doesn't count because he has magnified that figure many times since then. He continued, "Almost the only merit of this book is that Trudeau throws down the mask and reveals himself as a leftist of no great moderation." Then it's back to the personal attacks again. "In short, this is a nauseating book. By its superficiality, myth-making, and self-importance, it grossly insults the poor voters who remained so faithful to him for so long. Their disillusionment must now be complete."[45]

According to Amiel, it is not so much a "conspiracy," which would be more limited, as it is a socialist "syndrome" at the CBC. "But I do not wish to suggest — as Trudeau himself was moved to do later — that there is some deep and dark left-wing conspiracy afoot at the CBC. The problem is far worse than any conspiracy, which, being something conscious, would be limited by its nature to a number of conspirators. What afflicts the CBC, and to an only slightly lesser extent the entire

Canadian media, is a *syndrome*. The syndrome can be identified quite easily as soon as a viewer or a reader of the Canadian media tries to find any coverage of an issue that departs from the basic premises of democratic socialism."[46]

After Amiel married George Jonas in 1972 and joined the CBC as a typist on the *Juliette* show, she worked her way up to being a script assistant on *Take 30*, featuring host Adrienne Clarkson. "I soon discovered that what was actually said in an interview seemed to count for less than what the story format planned the interview to say . . . we were liberal arts graduates with solid backgrounds in sociology, anthropology, political science, and graduate English. We had, therefore, unshakable opinions on the chemical effects of pollution (bad), the physical and mental effects of intoxicants (harmless), and the effectiveness of the free market (vicious). Our television experts on these subjects were chosen to coincide with our opinions. We were always frantically busy writing up treatments on the deficiencies of society's social service programs or the abuse of the blackfly." Amiel wrote that, "male or female, in this we were all alike — what we lacked in hard knowledge we made up for in soft sciences and soft thinking."[47]

Soft left thinking, she might have added. For the CBC was a bastion of political correctness long before the term was coined. "Soon I came to understand that in CBC Public Affairs television we muck-rakers (a decent and honourable occupation) had to have a definite point of view. We did stories on union busting, welfare mothers, skid row derelicts, and native peoples. We did battered wives/battered children/battered animals and battered environment. We were fearless critics of government (provided it was not an NDP government) and of business and America."[48]

And the thing about the leftists at the CBC, according to Amiel, is that they are absolutely pervasive. "In Canada, the entire CBC hasn't a single conservative/neo-conservative/classical liberal — call them what you will, the CBC doesn't have one — producer on its public affairs staff. If they do have any, they're tucked away in farm programming or serious music, where they have neither the budget nor air time to do any harm."[49]

In the first chapter we discussed how Black "did an editorial sand-bag job on the P.Q.," during the Quebec provincial election of 1973, by publishing a poll indicating a Liberal victory. He failed to disclose that the poll consulted just seven people, including himself. For her part Amiel tells how she was working on a public affairs program with the CBC in 1968, under producer Peter Herrndorf, when she was assigned to poll delegates to the federal Liberal leadership convention, to determine the front runner. The assignment resulted in what she called her "little fraudulent poll."

"I was put in charge of a massive project to contact every one of the delegates to the Liberal leadership nominating convention and ask them how they planned to vote," Amiel writes. "It was an impossible job. Delegates were difficult to contact; if reached, they hadn't the slightest intention of telling us their choice . . . I appraised the situation. There was no way I was going to continue this madness. I simply couldn't get enough answers from enough delegates to establish a trend."

Amiel arrived at a solution: she would fabricate the results. "The only solution was to select the winner off the top of my head, but which one was I to select? Just about everybody at the CBC, indeed all the media, preferred Trudeau. I knew that if I chose anybody else my prediction would go against the grain. My figures would be checked and double-checked, and of course found to be wanting. But I thought, if I went for Trudeau, there would be no questions asked. I was right. My 'results' were greeted with ringing cries of enthusiasm even as I was filling out the charts. Eventually I gave up on the charts and began typing out summaries instead: a strong margin in favour of Trudeau." Amiel says that complaints from other candidates sparked an investigation, but by then Trudeau's victory had saved her. She felt remorse for "inflicting PET on the country," but rationalized, "my little fraudulent poll had no such significance. Trudeau would no doubt have been nominated without it."[50]

Not all of the Blacks' venom for public broadcasting has been directed at the CBC, as they have managed to reserve some for the National Film Board of Canada (NFB), where the problems are seen to be similar in nature. For example, in April 1986, Amiel wrote, "Although the NFB makes hundreds of films about apolitical subjects, insofar as it tackles issues, it does so from a particular bias. Thus the NFB catalogue will list films about the dangers of nuclear power rather than its advantages, techniques of union busting rather than the abuses of union power, pursuit of peace through disarmament or neutrality rather than strength or alliances."[51] She went on to list five examples of films which illustrated her point. When a representative of the NFB wrote to *Maclean's* to object that three of the five films cited were neither produced nor distributed by the NFB, Amiel responded in her June column, "This is a technicality. The films I listed are catalogued, published and promoted by the NFB."[52]

Amiel summed up her own arguments. "When [the NFB] tackles sociopolitical issues it does so almost exclusively from a left-wing point of view. I suggested that the NFB bias — on such topics as defence, unions, nuclear power, the church, and the role of women — was unrepresentative of the opinions and values of a large number of Canadian taxpayers . . . [D]oes it fairly represent all trends in Canada or is it over-representing those trends that are in awe of statism, totalitarianism and all the left-lib causes in society? From my viewing chair, the NFB's 'left-glib' stance is a blend of statist-socialist-Marxist-feminist-environmentalist views." Unlike the NFB, wrote Amiel, "I don't claim to speak for all Canadians. It is not my mandate to represent all Canadians. I do not take a single tax dollar to pay for my work. If the NFB were honest, it would follow suit."[53] Amiel should hire a new accountant.

At this juncture, Amiel concluded that the NFB still merited saving. "The solution to this problem is not to abolish the NFB but to rescue it. A commission of inquiry could determine whether the charges listed here are accurate and, if so, could also be given a mandate to take the steps necessary . . ." She admitted fallibility on the matter. "It's always possible, of course, that I am totally wrong and most Canadians want an NFB for the purpose of propagating the views of militant lesbians and liberation theologists."[54]

The Barbara Amiel of ten years later had not mellowed considerably. Despite holding the view that "public broadcasting is of genuine value," because, she said in 1996, "a country must look after the health of both its body and its mind," Amiel wrote that "Canada's public communications industries lost their way some time ago . . . much of public broadcasting was captured by silly politically correct special-interest groups — such as the Women's Studio D unit of the NFB." While Amiel now sees some merit in the (drastically cut and besieged) CBC, saying that "the CBC is a great national institution. There are people of real talent and tremendous dedication still there in radio and hanging on by their fingernails in TV news and current affairs, drama and day-time programming," she now considers the NFB not worth the "rescue" she was recommending a decade earlier. Her 1996 conclusion: "The NFB should be totally scrapped. While it has done some very fine work and Canadians excel in the documentary genre, we don't need two government organizations to look after that." Instead, Amiel proposed that a branch of Telefilm Canada could fund the best documentary makers, while the CBC could provide an outlet.[55]

The Role of Newspapers

In his 1969 submission to the Davey Committee Black humbly reported on a ground-breaking scientific experiment he and his partners had conducted at the Sherbrooke *Record* — an experiment which would contradict claims that the newspaper medium would soon go the way of the dinosaur. "A scientifically conducted experiment undertaken by the [Sherbrooke] *Record* has proven to our satisfaction that even now by reliance on the electronic media an individual can replace the printed media in national and international news and comment, though not in local, financial, or sports news, nor in entertainment features," Black wrote.[56] On the topic of press regulation, Black came down somewhat surprisingly in favour of a national press council with the power to accredit journalists. Black was lobbying for a journalism profession. "The much-bruited idea of a national press council with regional divisions has considerable merit . . . Without being endowed with the disciplinary powers of a bar association (at least initially), the council should have a composition capable of calling members to account for their conduct when necessary, and should be vested with genuine powers of moral suasion . . . Eventually, the council should give serious consideration to examining and accrediting journalists on a professional basis."[57]

Using Influence

Conrad Black has used his influence with the press to protect his own public image. One example dates to 1977, when Black was dating his first wife, Shirley Walters. She became pregnant with their son Jonathan prior to her divorce from her first marriage. According to Richard Siklos, "The pregnancy presented other complications for Black. He wanted to keep it quiet, for fear the press would find out. And when their son Jonathan Black was born in November 1977, his father's name was purposely left off the registration. Until the child was roughly a year old, several months after their marriage, Jonathan's existence remained a well-guarded secret — even some close friends and relatives did not know about him until two weeks before the wedding."[58]

Black's attempt to hide his son's existence nearly came a-cropper when a *Globe and Mail* writer checked out the rumours with Black's new mother-in-law. Siklos quotes Black as saying, "When they phoned my mother-in-law she phoned my wife and my wife raised it with me, and I spoke to [*Globe* editor-in-chief] Dick Doyle. And he said, 'That's fine, quite right, what do we want to get into that for?'"[59]

When historian Ramsay Cook wrote an unfavourable review

of Black's book on Duplessis in *The Globe and Mail*, Black, who had earlier asked *Globe* publisher Richard Malone to have someone other than Cook review the book (Malone refused), wrote back that "the *Globe and Mail* is not to be commended for departing from [the rule of peer review] and entrusting the review of a serious work on an important subject to a slanted, supercilious, little twit."[60] Black tells us how he woke up on a Saturday morning, read the review in the *Globe*, wrote his response, and hand-carried it over to the publisher's house. "When I started up the walk in front of his house, he flung open his front door and said, 'I've been expecting you.' He sent me down to the newspaper office to see the assistant to the editor, Cameron Smith, to avoid any possibility of defamation."[61] Black's letter was printed on the following Monday.

Ramsay Cook need not feel singled out. When Black was taking over *The Daily Telegraph* in London, author John Ralston Saul (winner of the 1996 Governor General's Award for Nonfiction) wrote what Black described as "an extremely hostile piece" in *The Spectator* magazine. Black writes, "I produced a comprehensive and caustic refutation, concluding that he 'should confine himself to subjects better suited than this one was to his peevish, puerile, sniggering . . . talents." Black recollects that "Saul's response a few weeks later was as damp a squib as Ramsay Cook's in similar circumstances nine years before and was written, as *Punch* magazine used to put it in Victorian times, 'in a voice grown mighty small' . . . Press attention was more careful and balanced thereafter and has been generally benign in London ever since."[62] Later, Black would refer to the matter as "my demolition of Ralston Saul."[63]

In 1993 Tom Kent, who had chaired the 1981 Royal Commission on Newspapers, wrote what might be described as a measured and charitable assessment of Black's newspaper career in a column in the Montreal *Gazette*. Kent wrote, in part, that "the relatively long part of Mr. Black's record is limited to the Sterling newspapers, mostly in interior British Columbia communities. They are small papers distinguished by the poverty of their journalistic content and the penny-pinching style of their management."[64] Black's response displayed his typical reliance on personal attack. "I am disappointed, but not particularly surprised, by the pompous farrago of nonsense that Tom Kent presents in support of his theory . . . [S]ince Mr. Kent has long inflicted himself on the Canadian public as a pontifical judge of the media, I see it as a modest public service to point out how little he really knows . . .

"Mr. Kent's charges that I am prone to 'milk' newspapers and 'to bind them to (my) ideology' are false and scurrilous. His attempt to substantiate them is contemptible. I do not consider myself an 'ideologue,' though I suspect that he is; and I am not particularly impressed with the many expressions of his dreary leftish ideology that I have read over the years. It may be that Mr. Kent does 'not want to be unfair,' but obviously he cannot help himself. I am afraid that his rather fatuous piece is a representative example of his chronic lack of intellectual rigour. I leave it to others more intimately acquainted with his work to judge whether his habitual shortcoming is dishonesty or merely incompetence."[65]

Journalistic Scum

But Black has never held *most* journalists in high regard. In 1969, when he and his partners Peter White and David Radler made their submission to the Davey Committee, Black stated, "We must express the view, based on our empirical observations, that a substantial number of journalists are ignorant, lazy, opinionated, and intellectually dishonest. The profession is heavily cluttered with aged hacks toiling through a miasma of mounting decrepitude and often alcoholism, and even more so with arrogant and abrasive youngsters who substitute 'commitment' for insight. The product of their impassioned intervention in public affairs is more often confusion than lucidity."[66] A decade later Black reiterated these views, edited only slightly for stylistic purposes, in an article in the *Carleton Journalism Review*.[67]

In his autobiography, Black refers back to these comments and explains, "My view was, and remains, that although most journalists, like most people, are conscientious men and women doing their jobs as well as they can, many are possessed by envious frustration that they are chroniclers condemned forever to report on the sayings and doings of others." He then goes on to reiterate his earlier quotes, slightly embellished, adding for example that journalists are "inadequately supervised," and that "alcoholism is endemic" among both the abrasive youngsters and aged hacks. After summarizing his earlier comments, Black concludes, "My reflections on the Fourth Estate were based on extensive experience of [sic] the Canadian media, socially, professionally, and as consumer-observer. They stirred up strenuous media objections but have never been and, at the time they were made, could not be authoritatively refuted."[68]

In his speech to the Canadian Association of Journalists in April 1994, Black said that although his Davey submission remarks "are used to rouse journalistic faculties throughout Canada to a febrile state of hostility," they were written "mainly about biased separatist journalists in Quebec." He added, "When I wrote these words it was not entirely without admiration." What's more, he said, "most of the people I described, or their successors, are now monogamous and doting, moderate, suburban people who eat quiche all the time."[69]

But one wonders whether Black tempered his comments to reassure his audience of journalists, many of whom were directly or indirectly in his employ. For example, the word "separatist" is only used once in his twenty-eight-page submission to the Davey Committee, and it is in reference to the Quebec City legislative press gallery. There is no indication that any of his other comments are directed at separatists, or even Quebec journalists, in particular. Indeed, his descriptions of "functions of the media," and "credibility of the media" (the latter containing his controversial remarks), are explicitly broad, encompassing American as well as Canadian media and journalists.

As recently as 1989 Black wrote as follows in a letter to *The Financial Post*: "For 20 years I have intermittently described large sections of the Canadian media as irresponsible, narcissistic, self-righteously biased, unqualified to exercise the power they have, over-indulged by complacent public opinion and by owners afraid to offer any ethical direction, and inadequately literate. I do so again, and Allan Fotheringham's effort to trivialize the issue by comparing me to George Bell and Harold Ballard is no response. I would be delighted, though somewhat astonished, if Allan or some other plausible media figures would engage in serious professional self-examination, and if some of those who have written supportively to me, and whose encouragement I appreciate, would come out from under their tables at the parliamentary restaurants and the Toronto Club and take a public position. I don't much care about being mis-type cast, but I'm getting a little tired of wrestling with the entire Canadian left-wing media myself while thousands of publicity-shy well-wishers offer to hold my coat."[70]

In 1993, Vicki Woods, editor of Britain's *Harpers & Queen* magazine, deceptively turned a photo shoot with Margaret Thatcher into an article about her comments and actions during the photo shoot. Amiel wrote a column condemning Woods. "[Emperor Franz Joseph] hit the nail on the head when he described journalists as canailles. Today that means rogues, but as I understand it he used it in the sense of scum or sewers."[71] She went on, "I am a journalist myself and I think we are all made of merde and the craft is merde . . . Why, I ask myself, does someone stay in a wretched occupation like journalism? Anything other than straight news reporting often forces us to become courtiers of people we dislike or resort to little ruses even with those we admire to get our copy — a host of smarm and iffy relationships that brings me out in spots half the time. After each profile I write I vow never to play the game again. And then the vow is broken. Why?"[72]

In June 1994, when journalist Barbara Amiel joined

Hollinger's board of directors, Black said, "you were the one who wrote [journalists] were canailles."

"Yes," replied Amiel, "they are canailles, but they're necessary too."

"Barbara, if I didn't think journalists were necessary I wouldn't employ them. And indeed, our relationship might be quite different," Black said.[73]

Writing in her 1980 memoirs about her first job in journalism as high school correspondent for the St. Catharines *Standard*, Amiel says, "Trading on a minor knack for writing sentences to get by in life doesn't reveal an especially admirable character."[74] On her seven-year addiction to Elavil, she writes, "My mind felt as if it were on vacation . . . like a cow . . . chewing cud . . ." But, she writes, "perhaps having a state of mind somewhat akin to that of a turnip is the best way to begin a media career in Canada."[75]

Journalistic Quality

In the 1996 Southam annual report, Black bemoaned the mediocrity and low levels of profitability at Canadian newspapers, when they are compared to those in the U.S. and the U.K. Few Canadian papers, he said, "have attained the average for journalistic professionalism of leading newspapers in either of those countries. Southam has, even by Canadian standards, been an underachiever and has contributed to a widespread Canadian problem of mediocritization in many ways," he wrote.[76]

Following his consolidation of control over Southam in 1996, Black indicated that he wanted to see changes. "We're going to try and recruit the very best people we can and produce the best papers we can, and publish them to the highest standards we can. And that means separating news from comment, and not just [having] the overwhelming avalanche of soft, left, bland, envious pap which has poured like sludge through the centre pages of most of the Southam papers for some time."[77]

Globe and Mail journalist Doug Saunders asked Black about

the events described in Richard Siklos's biography, *Shades of Black*, in which Black "commanded editors to take specific positions at the [London *Daily*] *Telegraph*." Black denied that these were instances of meddling. "These are straight questions of the maintenance of high professional standards. They aren't censorship or doctoring the news."[78] End of discussion.

According to Black, he is the competent journalist's best friend. "We are, as far as I can see, practically the only buyers in Canada of daily newspapers," Black said in 1996.[79] "Hollinger is the greatest corporate friend working print journalists have."[80] He told the 1996 Southam annual meeting, "No competent journalist or reasonable reader need have any fear of our impact on Southam. In nearly 30 years of newspaper ownership, we have rarely sold and never closed a daily newspaper."[81]

As we have seen, for Black, envy is a Canadian trait. It's also naturally occurring among journalists. Black says the profession can be divided up into happy chroniclers and the envious. "Many journalists and most of the more talented ones are happy to chronicle the doings and sayings of others, but a significant number, including many of the most acidulous and misanthropic are, in my experience, inexpressibly envious of many of the subjects of their attention."[82] Here, Black was returning to a theme from his autobiography, where he indicated, "The vintage Canadian spirit of envy was at its most sulphurous with the young journalists. Their discomfort at being chroniclers rather than the chronicled was energized by a self-righteous awareness that I had made lateral financial movement, especially related party transactions and licit asset stripping, work to my considerable profit."[83]

Libel Chill
Black launched a libel lawsuit against *The Globe and Mail* in 1987. *The Globe*, according to Black, "alleged that my habitually unnamed critics considered that I had 'milked' corporations and institutions, oppressed minority shareholders, pocketed other

people's pensions, 'destroyed' public companies, and had been caught with my 'hand too close to the cookie jar.'" In deciding whether to sue, Black writes, "[lawyer] Peter Atkinson told me there would never be another opportunity so inviting as this one to give Canada's financial journalists a powerful disincentive from defaming me."[84] A little later he would tell the Canadian Association of Journalists, "On the subject of the spurious but once burning question of libel chill, I want to reassure you that almost all my defamation actions were designed to knock out of journalist computer queues the malicious falsehood confected and propagated by that great guardian of the reputations and welfare of us all, Bob Rae, that I had stolen pension surplus from the widows and orphans of Dominion store employees. The only way to emancipate myself from that slur was to sue for a retraction and an apology whenever it occurred. I never asked for money, and I always got the retractions and apologies."[85]

Elsewhere, however, he said libel suits are "a profit centre for me."[86] Biographer Siklos writes, "Black maintains that in each of the fifteen times he has either sued or threatened to sue for libel, it was only because he was being accused of dishonest or grossly unethical conduct. All he ever wants is a retraction, which, without a single case going to trial, he has received every time, often with costs and sometimes a cash settlement on top."[87] Quite unrelated to any statements by Bob Rae are Black's comments on the continent down under. "In Australia," he writes in his memoirs, "as elsewhere, it was necessary to make the point that defaming me had its risks."[88]

In a speech in 1988, Black said, "Anyone who has witnessed, as I have, both as a media owner and employer and as a litigant, the pitiful spectacle of reckless journalists, trying to defend under oath negligent or malicious libels with spurious apologia or glazed prevarication, will not soon forget the illustration of how much better the working press often is at dishing out abuse than at answering for its own conduct."[89] On his lawsuit against *The Globe and Mail*, Black writes, "We gradually went through the ROB newsroom like a blotting paper, taking contradictory evidence from journalists, sweating them under oath, exposing malice, and adding defendants."[90] As for why he did this, it was in part the same socialist syndrome rearing its ugly head again, this time at *The Globe and Mail*. Black said, "Some of the most convinced leftists infested the ROB, attacking not only dishonest and incompetent businessmen as they should, but the system in general. This was an unconventional method of building business readership. I believed that the *Globe and Mail*'s traditional constituencies had been sorely tried by [managing editor Geoffrey] Stevens's toadying to the left . . . The irony was obvious when Roy Megarry suddenly figured out in late 1988 that habitual readers had been thoroughly alienated by the *Globe and Mail*'s Stevens-inspired editorial posture of NDP wolf in the moth-eaten clothing of a spavined old Toronto Tory sheep and fired both Webster and Stevens."[91]

The new editor, William Thorsell, Black's "ideological soul-mate," oversaw what Black said was "one of Canada's most extensive litigated libel retractions," published on June 30, 1989. "The newspaper apologized unreservedly, and generously referred to a poll that had found me to be 'Canada's most respected businessman' (though the sample was small and the survey was hardly scientific)."[92] Thus ended the first part of what Black described as his revenge on *The Globe and Mail*. "The lawsuit was only half of my strategy to return the *Globe and Mail*'s antagonism. The second front was to push for a daily *Financial Post*."[93]

The Role of Publishers

Richard Siklos notes that "Black speaks of gathering and packaging information and entertainment in an appealing way for readers, not of the 'public service' and 'social obligation' that the founders of the publications he commands once embraced. 'There's a terrible amount of self-righteous claptrap about a sacred trust,' [says Black.] 'If the small guy's guardian is the media, then the small guy is in bigger trouble than I thought.'"[94] When Black lost out to publishing and real estate tycoon Mortimer Zuckerman in his attempt to buy the New York *Daily News*, in 1992, he was asked about whether he would have taken that paper further to the right if he had succeeded. "That's a paper whose readers are now seeking a rather more liberal view of things than the old Archie Bunker readers did . . . Let's all remember that newspapers are a service industry and you've got to give the people what they want or you're not going to be in business," he replied.[95]

Black comes to the defence of his fellow publishers, whom he says are maligned. Contrary to popular opinion, publishers are not connected to the establishment. "Publishers, like other employers, are usually identified by their organized employees with the establishment and the status quo, and generally this is not accurate. Reaction to the employer naturally encouraged what was until recently in this country an almost universal press sympathy for strikers, protestors, fugitives from justice, secessionists, disgruntled students and other visible elements in the broad spectrum of disaffected people." The influence of owners, publishers, and wealthy individuals is, in fact, quite limited, according to Black. "The most visible competitor the press has for influence over the elaboration of public policy and on politicians themselves is apparently the influence exercised by large corporations and wealthy individuals. In fact, this influence is largely a fiction, as politicians tend to be wary of seeming to be too much influenced by monied people and companies." Real power and influence, he says, lies with the working journalists. "Orson Welles, in his unforgettable portrayal of William Randolph Hearst in Citizen Kane, when his wife cautioned against a course of action 'because people will think' something or other, he said, 'people will think what I tell them to think.' It doesn't, I'm afraid, work that way, really. Stanley Baldwin's famous reference to Beaverbrooke . . . [was] 'Power without responsibility is the traditional role of the harlot' . . . Baldwin's comment has contributed importantly to the almost unshakeable mythology . . . [of the] baneful influence of the newspaper owner. This mythology is especially vigorous because it suits both the subject and the propagators. All those who in Stanley Baldwin's day would have had vast political influence because of the authority of the press owner are assuaged that they are still people of great influence, continuators of great prerogatives. And the working press which fosters such fictions maintains a straw scarecrow to attract public concern and divert attention from what I put to you is a more legitimately worrisome state of affairs: that the media have no rival and no countervailing force except the good sense of the public and the fairness of most individual journalists as an antidote to their potential for the capricious manipulation of public opinion."[96] How this squares with the other occasions on which Black has congratulated himself, for example, for buying up a great deal of political influence quite cheaply, is unclear.

Not surprisingly, Black also comes to the defence of the proprietor and publisher who exerts direct influence on his or her newspaper. "The absence of a controlling personality in a newspaper tends to encourage blandness and prolixity as most North American chain newspapers demonstrate every day."[97] Such influence is essential, according to Black, in order to counteract the influence of journalists. "As I have gradually risen through the ranks of the newspaper business . . . I have become an ever more vociferous advocate of the publisher, especially the proprietor publisher. Not as a ravening capricious despot or propagandist but as the needed countervailing influence to the proverbial working press."[98]

And of course that influence is a leftist one. Black says, "Except for the Toronto *Star* on the left and the Toronto *Sun* on the right, among major English-Canadian newspapers there is no countervailing executive influence on journalists. The proprietors at Southam and Thomson have, in effect, proclaimed their own virtue in allowing professional journalists, unanswerable and not necessarily representative, to administer to this country a dreary and unimaginative soft-left anaesthetic."[99]

In a column in *The Financial Post*, Black describes at length a demonstration of what he calls "the irresponsible power of journalists, unrestrained by publishers." He was attending the National Magazine Awards dinner in Toronto in May 1988, where he was nominated for an award. Black devoted most of his column on the affair to complaining about an award in another category, given to Elaine Dewar for her article in *Toronto Life* magazine about the Reichmann family. Black began with, "The Dewar article started from the improbable premise that there was something sinister and dishonourable in the origins of the Reichmann fortune, was unrelievedly nasty, and frequently prolix and boring as it meandered turgidly through more than 50,000 words to a tenuous conclusion. The best that could be said for it was that the author had gone to considerable inconvenience, traveling internationally for months, to prepare her material." From here, Black turned to the audience members, who had the temerity to applaud Dewar's award. "What nauseated me was the hallelujah chorus in favor of Elaine Dewar and her lengthy article about the Reichmann family, which is the subject of a defamation action . . . Like spiteful and rebellious children after placing a tack on the headmistress's vacant chair, our leading journalists leapt to their feet shouting and clapping when Dewar's triumph was announced." That the journalists did this despite the fact that the article may have been defamatory is beyond Black's ken. "Toronto's narcissistic media community was incapable of considering the possibility that the Dewar article might actually be defamatory," Black wrote. The fact that these journalists would give an award to Dewar, that in so doing they "would deal so flippantly with the reputation of the Reichmanns," was of tremendous concern to Black. Why? He explained. "Here, very graphically, was the malaise of our free press; the irresponsible power of journalists, unrestrained by publishers, who have made a virtue out of editorial noninterference. The working press proclaim Southam and Thomson (at least in the larger Thomson newspapers such as the *Globe & Mail*) to be ideal proprietors. And the proprietors record formidable profits while patting themselves on the head for their noninterference." Black went on to disparage a movement by working journalists to make Canadian libel laws similar to American ones, where the plaintiffs are required to prove malicious intent. "This is the latest stage in the attempt of elements of our working press, and some publishers they have dragooned to help them, to achieve a complete liberty to build and destroy reputations and manufacture public opinion. Having banished the owners and publishers from the editorial and news rooms, they will see off the litigants."[100] Black seems to feel that journalists have been granted too much freedom and that publishers such as himself should set matters straight. No more libel suits, and no more magazine awards, except possibly for the publishers themselves, such as Black.

This theme, the need for greater editorial interference by publishers, is one that Black has written about more than once. "There has been a general decline in the editorial role of the media proprietor and executive . . . the publisher has often become a local purser and paymaster . . ." he wrote in 1988. "Journalists, as a group, and like all other powerful groups, require some protection from themselves and their own excesses. I will not labor this point, but the first line of defence is the concerned, informed, responsible, publisher."[101]

Autonomy and Editors

Charles Bury, editor of the Sherbrooke *Record*, which is now owned by Pierre Péladeau's Quebecor Inc., once worked for Conrad Black. In 1996 he said that Péladeau "certainly doesn't tell me what to write in editorial columns or news columns. He said to me once, 'You put out a nice little paper in Sherbrooke. Keep on making me a little money, and you can do it for as long as you want.'" As for Black, Bury said the Sun chain, up for sale at the time by Ted Rogers, "would be better off in the hands of

Péladeau, by far. He wouldn't lay anyone off until he sees what each person does in the newsroom."[102]

With the 1995 acquisitions from Thomson, David Radler, president of Hollinger and partner to Black, was espousing his belief in the editorial autonomy of local publishers, all of whom, of course, are appointed by Hollinger. But we would do well to remember that this is the same David Radler who, in a less guarded interview with Peter C. Newman in 1992, said, "I am ultimately the publisher of all of these papers, and if editors disagree with us, they should disagree with us when they're no longer in our employ."[103]

Chairman Conrad Black used the 1996 Southam annual report, released in spring 1997, as a forum for his views on the company's recent history and future. In a five-page "Chairman's Statement," Black issued a condemnation of working journalists — specifically those at Southam. He described how Southam editors formerly had too much independence — a situation which met with the approval of working journalists, but not shareholders. "It was the view of Hollinger's managing share-holders, including me, for many years, that Southam had effectively adopted a policy of granting complete independence to editors, in budgetary and content matters, in tacit exchange for endless laudations as 'ideal owners' from the working press," he wrote. This is a system, according to Black, which could not work. "The objective quality of the product is too closely related to the financial results to be so completely separated from the activities of the chief executives."[104]

Also in the 1996 Southam annual report, Black said the new regime was firmly in control. One hundred heads had rolled at Southam's head office, saving $20 million annually. "The head office apparat has been dispersed," he commented. New profit margins had been set, and the people had been put in place to deliver them. "The publishers and other unit heads are work-ing out profitability and conceptual quality targets with us, committing to their achievement and receiving every assistance from us in achieving them," he wrote. The annual report indicated that in 1996 alone, new publishers were hired at ten Southam newspapers. An eleventh, in Windsor, Ontario, would have a new publisher in the spring of 1997.

"Responsible" Autonomy

At the Fairfax chain in Australia, in which Black held a minority share for a number of years, he encountered a charter of editorial independence, which, in part, precluded editors from sitting on the boards of parent companies. This contrasts with the situation in North America and Great Britain, where there are no such restrictions. Black complains about the charter in his memoirs, no doubt because he was not able to replicate in Australia the comfortable situation he had in the U.K. with "[the *Telegraph*'s editor] Max Hastings who, since becoming a member of the *Telegraph* board of directors, had shown an encouraging understanding of the commercial side of the business."[105]

In Black's view, installing editors who are in agreement with the proprietor would reduce, but not eliminate, the amount of interference that is necessary. "Much the best course, in my judgement, and the one that we try to follow, as do many others, is to hire editors with whom the principal shareholder, where there is one, is in general agreement, to minimize internal frictions. But the proprietor [still] should exercise an influence. Ideally, an influence to maintain standards of fair reporting and variety of opinion . . ."[106] As for the journalists, Black writes, "I believe in editorial autonomy provided it is exercised responsibly."[107]

In 1993 Tom Kent wrote about the rightward shift in *The Jerusalem Post* following Black's takeover of that newspaper.[108] Black denied that such a shift occurred. "The editorial stance of the Jerusalem *Post* is quite favorable to the present Labor government of Yitzhak Rabin," Black wrote. But reporting from Jerusalem for *The Toronto Star*, Bob Hepburn disagreed. "Black brought more than a change of ownership to the *Post*. He changed its liberal perspective, transforming the paper into a voice for the right. And, he oversaw the end of the careers of many of Israel's top journalists."[109] And Black's biographer (and employee at *The Financial Post*) Richard Siklos wrote, "no one disputes that there was a sudden and dramatic shift in [the *Post*'s] editorial direction. Radler argued it was merely a case of repositioning the paper to reflect its readership more accurately. 'Let's not play games,' Black huffed, when questioned on the matter by journalists. '[*The Jerusalem Post*] was universally perceived to be a very left-wing paper before. Well, the far-left isn't the only game in town.'"[110]

According to Black, too much editorial independence is especially bad when in the wrong hands. "I have written elsewhere, including in my submission to Keith Davey's committee, that Southam came long ago to an unspoken pact with its journalists and editors. In exchange for an absolute liberty of content the journalistic craft unanimously praised Southam as the ultimate ideal owners. When some of the more distinguished Southam publishers such as the late Ross Munroe had retired, this arrangement slowly degenerated, in most cases though not all, inexorably into soft, left journalistic pap for the readers and collapsing profits and stock prices for the shareholders. That arrangement no longer obtains at Southam."[111]

In the end, for Black, the publisher's influence is essential in order to maintain balance. "The fact is, journalists left absolutely without any challenge to produce whatever they want, in my experience, tend to produce unrepresentative and predictable and often rather biased comment, if not reporting. And where that occurs, whoever is the publisher, whether he is a proprietor or not, has a duty to try to raise the quality of the product, not to suppress or muzzle journalists, not to stifle, not to restrict opinion, but to do precisely the reverse."[112]

7

THE TYRANNY OF FEMINISM

"For the past 10 years at least, being a male has had aspects rather like being a Jew in Germany during the 1930s or a German in the postwar period."

— BARBARA AMIEL[1]

The women's movement has been called the single most important revolution of the twentieth century. Canadian women born in the early part of the century had minimal legal standing and few social rights. The pre-1917 Canada Elections Act said, "No woman, lunatic, idiot or child shall vote." Now, the great majority of women work outside the home at some point in their lives, and over half the law and medical schools are filled with women students. This profound change has arguably affected (and continues to affect) legislation and social policy more than any other single societal change of our time. The attitudes of influential press barons Black and Amiel toward feminism are therefore of crucial importance.

Conrad Black and Barbara Amiel share a view of the role of

women that could most kindly be termed old-fashioned. In reference to her marriage to British cable tycoon, David Graham, Amiel said, "In a woman, there is an urge to nurture and care for. It may not be biological destiny, but for me, I did want to look after someone."[2] Her single greatest fury is saved for those who question the traditional role of women and men. "There are some exceptions, no doubt, but most men and women enjoy being men and women. While gender roles have some drawbacks, they have great advantages, and only human beings would be so potty as to try to deny the existence of gender-specific behavior. I wish our anti-sexism police would turn their attention to nature and start a campaign for stags to behave like dogs."[3]

She notes that one of her strongest role models, Great Britain's former prime minister Margaret Thatcher, was unequivocal in her belief that the most important role for a woman is to raise a family and create a home. "Thatcher has an almost mystical belief, possibly correct, in the ability of a woman to instil and influence values in the home."[4] On why some career women choose not to have children, she states, "The idea that a man and a woman, each beginning the pursuit of serious careers, could somehow 'share' parenting is ludicrous."[5]

Women marry up, she explains, because it is what society expects, and marriage is a practical decision. "It seems to me that women don't get a fair shake, and it is about time we dismissed those ugly words of criticism (like 'meal ticket' and 'gold digger') that accompany a so-called 'good marriage' . . . All it means is that it would be practical to marry men who are making more money than we are — preferably at least twice as much . . . Racing pulses alone might have us all running off with beach boys and wildly unreliable bohemians. Such liaisons make for steamy novels but short unions."[6]

Nags and Hags

Amiel thinks men have had a bad rap with feminism. "What a sad figure is the male Canuck of the species: often nagged to death by ambitious wives, humiliated by potential dates, some-times left lonely in his testosterone haze by liberated females who criticize his sexual techniques as inadequate."[7] In fact, so thoroughly have men been dominated by feminists, they have been conscripted: "Not surprisingly, it is our feeble-minded, trendy, henpecked males who are leading this movement."[8]

Black men have it particularly rough. Amiel feels that the old world of hierarchies had a certain calming effect on the black underclass. "Equal opportunity followed by affirmative action took away this calm. Then, feminism and the sexual revolution hit black men in particular: as heads of households in a stable society they had some self respect. Now, their wives often took better-paying service jobs."[9]

Both Black and Amiel use stereotypical language about women and men, language that most now shun. "Among my many intel-lectual lapses is a weakness for watching beauty contests," says Amiel after a stint as a pageant judge. "There is for me a musical quality about the entire proceeding — the melody of whispering voices hesitantly giving audiences little thoughts about world peace from lip-glossed mouths perched on glowing bodies, all sun-streaked and swaying. It's so deliciously vulgar." She approv-ingly quotes fellow judge Diane Jones Konihowski, who, in "horror-stricken" response to the admonition by the organizers to refrain from making their decision based on the "generosity of figure" of the contestants, declared, "We can't send someone who is flat to represent Canada."[10]

Black describes the late Conservative leadership candidate, Claude Wagner, as "hag-ridden" by his "flaming red-haired harridan" wife, Giselle.[11] He has remarked that the "magnifi-cent" city of Beirut was "crowded with beautiful women with copper skin, doe eyes, and comely thighs"[12]; Argentina with women of "startling pulchritude."[13] In January 1992 Black had just bought into the Fairfax newspaper conglomerate in Australia. A journalist at a Sydney news conference asked Black what he thought was the best thing about journalism in

Australia. He replied, "If you will take this in the right spirit, there are a good many attractive women in the field."[14]

Black used his British paper, *The Daily Telegraph*, to launch an attack on longer skirts for women. "It is bunk to claim that long is in, short is out, and anything above the knee is dowdy . . . Apart from the welcome and long-deferred collapse of the anti-fur movement, the real fashion news is that, despite a massive campaign of contrived and oppressive conformity, the long skirt has had only very limited success . . . We applaud women's refusal to be cajoled or dragooned into a relatively unbecoming fashion . . .

"Women above 35 who have worked hard to maintain their shape and tone of their legs are attacked as stick-in-the-muds for not wanting to conceal them like Washington Square or Bloomsbury academic Bohemians . . . We have watched with confidence as women rejected the politically correct fatuity that to emphasize or reveal becoming shapes and curves was a demeaning pandering to leering men. We have noted with relief that the argument that short was a conspiracy of male voyeurism has been balanced by the even more asinine argument that long was a male conspiracy to deprive women of mobility. Most men do not rely on passing pedestrians for their physical appreciation of females."[15]

"Ardent desires"

In his autobiography, Black relates how he decided to court Amiel in the aftermath of his separation from his first wife. "As I observed from my conservatory the twilight of autumn and of conjugality, I scanned the range of women acquaintances in a way I had not over the eleven or twelve years in which I thought I had a reasonably happy marriage. Gradually, tentatively, and then with greater fixity and deepening conviction, and finally with intense determination, my thoughts and hopes settled on Barbara Amiel.

"Beautiful, brilliant, ideologically a robust kindred spirit, a talented writer and galvanizing speaker, chic, humorous, preter-naturally sexy, a proud though not religious Jew, tempest-tossed in marriage, disappointed in maternity, a fugitive from Canada assuredly making her way from and towards poles not unlike my own, a cordial acquaintance for many years, she shortly became the summit of my most ardent and uncompromising desires."[16]

When some Canadian media reports of their marriage were less than complimentary, Black pulls out the old shibboleth of female jealousy, and even impugns motives based on sexual orientation. "All those envious of Barbara's great talent and beauty, all those affronts by her ideological solidarity, all the forces of professional and 'lifestyle' and lesbian antagonism erupted splenetically. The British press was much more able to accept her editorial gifts and pulchritude and much less vulgar and contemptible than the Canadian newspapers."[17]

Amiel apparently shares his high opinion of her looks and their importance to her career. "I happen to be a woman — which is *In*, in itself. I also happen to be tall and considered shapely and attractive, and that makes me 'very merchandisable' — as one agent put it. I may have shuddered at the phrase but how can I deny that this 'packaging' has made my 'right-wing' views not only forgivable but intriguing — and given me access to forums that are closed to those of similar views but more standard appearance."[18] Yet elsewhere she complains that she and her ex-husband George Jonas were being shut out of the media. Writing about Jonas in 1987, Amiel said, "It disturbed me that we were never asked to contribute even guest columns to main-stream newspapers . . . As for the limitations on our access to the popular media, which continue to this day, well, this is in essence a social democratic country and we remain outside the main-stream. Fair enough."[19]

The Militant Fringe

Amiel has her own explanation for the former status of women as non-citizens and comes to the defence of patriarchy. While she applauds the "fine Liberal principles" of the vote and equality before the law, she asserts, "Society has never been overly ideological. It organized itself in the best way it could to survive. And clearly patriarchy used to be the best way."[20] According to Amiel, the unequal treatment of women can be attributed to differences in individual aspirations. "The problem with the Women's Movement in North America is that it is based on a totally false understanding of history. Its members see history as a male conspiracy to suppress women, and a conspiracy, moreover, that was carried out with force — both physical and economic."[21] The women's movement "became an ideology based on a perception that women's role in society was not the product of a mutual arrangement for the survival of both sexes but rather an oppressed role in which women had been victimized by a deliberate effort to keep them in the thrall of men . . . There is little patience with the idea that disparity may be caused by individual aspirations, needs or abilities." So women launched into an era of what Amiel calls, "'catch-up' time, which often seemed more like 'get-even' time."[22]

"There is a tiny hysterical band of militants in the fringe of the Women's Movement," she wrote in 1980, "who cannot cope with the notion that when God created people, men and women He made them: Having latched on to the great 20th century secret that the smallest pressure group can get its way if it co-opts the state machinery to implement its ideology, this little fringe of libbers has gone a long way toward institutionalizing the perverse minority views of radical feminism in our society."[23]

Radical feminists have taken over everywhere. They are in the schools, where Amiel warns they promote "ludicrous programs that call for the 'elimination of sexual stereotyping.'"[24] And what Amiel calls "Females of a Certain Type" are in great supply at the Canadian Broadcasting Corporation. "It might be useful to make it public that the CBC, which is maintained by Canadians of the most diverse opinions, has been captured by feminists bent on wiping out all distinctions between men and women."[25]

Radical feminists have even taken over the White House. "The

First Lady [Hillary Clinton] has emasculated America. I guess that is what radical feminists always wanted to do, but when the Bobbitt syndrome hits the only superpower left in the world, it's not only the Mr. Bobbitts who are in pain. We all are."[26]

Colour Them Red

Black and Amiel pin the usual Marxist label on feminists — as they do with other political enemies. In an article entitled "Coloring the Feminists Red," Amiel says that "some women in the movement were interested in women's issues only insofar as they could destabilize free enterprise, place an enormous burden on it with demands for special benefits and privileges, [and] advance sundry other left-wing causes . . . there was a significant segment in it for whom feminist goals were mere tools in the achievement of their real goal — a quasi-Marxist social revolution."[27]

In another, called "Today, courtesy of the WoMovement, ovaries can get you special status," Amiel declares, "The point is that the WoMovement is an elitist movement that recognizes achievement only among those women who subscribe to it, and achieve in acceptable fields — such as the WoMovement itself with all its educational monitoring and enforcement civil service jobs. It is a frankly Marxist-inspired movement."[28]

Amiel says, "Equality of opportunity becomes Russian roulette while society decides whether handicapped, female, homosexual, or short people are this year's in-group."[29] She trivializes the reality of society's minorities and implies that, when they are included in hiring, the quality of the workplace is diminished: "Group quotas will rule. In the name of human rights, all human rights (or common sense) will be set aside as percentages of sexually oriented purple people with at least one mental handicap will be required for admission to legal, medical and pilot-training schools. Availing oneself of legal and medical services (not to mention flying) will be a risky business, but it's one way to cut down on medicare and legal aid costs."[30]

Cloning Feminists

Women in non-traditional jobs are trivialized as well. A male companion nearly rear-ends the car ahead when he spots a young "female policewoman," described thus, one can only conclude, to ensure her gender is clear. "It was not her slim, blond being that made me pause," Amiel wrote, musing on the incident, "but rather the consequences this would have on her role as a police-woman. A policeman's function includes that of peacekeeping. The traditional reason for weight and height requirements has been the understanding that volatile situations — such as a pub brawl or a domestic fight — are better defused by the presence of a six-foot, four-inch beefy Irishman than a tiny Oriental woman. There is no dishonour in yielding to overwhelming force, but there is sure-as-blazes shame in a red-blooded male ending his macho brawling at the command of a slim policette." Amiel does not put her case against women in policing in terms of women's abilities, but rather in the shame to violent men of having to submit to female authority, authority being linked, in her view, to the presence of brute force. "Most cultures under-stand this . . . This is a familiar chord: if you want to incite shame and dishonour in the defeated enemy, turn them over to the women."[31]

Women lawyers come in for it too. Amiel wrote that a 1993 federal-provincial report that outlined the existence of wide-spread systemic discrimination against women in the Canadian legal system could only be produced in a country "ruled by lunatics and force-fed a menu concocted at the Mad Hatter's tea party . . . I am always amused when I read that a sign of the improved status of females is that more than 50 per cent of law school admissions are female. Law school has become — for both men and women — rather like the priesthood was in the past. If a child comes from a middle-class family or one with middle-class aspirations but has no special interest in anything, he or she is sent to law school . . ." Because women are in professions such as law, their daughters won't learn household skills. "The know-nothing male graduates become indifferent lawyers. The know-nothing women go into government agencies and become feminist issue lawyers. From there, these women go into a constant spin of self-perpetuation, drawing up programs for more women to become, yup, Status of Women lawyers. This marvellous report on sexism in the judicial system, for example, is a cornucopia for little feminists to reproduce and clone themselves. As for the daughters of the men and women who write these reports, the consequence is obvious: household skills are learned through apprentice in part, mother to daughter. But it is hard to apprentice with mom in the kitchen when she must be ever-vigilant at work for the human rights commission."[32]

On former prime minister Kim Campbell's public musings in her autobiography about having to sacrifice her private life for politics, Amiel says, "Campbell reminds me of the scores of females who these days choose law school and upon graduation moan that male lawyers work twelve-hour days while they as women have different requirements and must think about their biological needs or home duties and so, unfairly, lose promotions and are disadvantaged by gender."[33] (Neither Amiel nor Black had anything good to say about Campbell. Amiel describes listening to her giving a speech about the future of the nation, "her waterlogged face going on blah-de-blah-de-blah till I momentarily blacked out."[34] With rather violent imagery, Black called Campbell "a political torso without limbs."[35])

Attempts to implement pay equity programs come in for particular criticism. Amiel dismisses any notion of historical or systemic employment discrimination. The free market must be protected from such notions. For example, Amiel says janitors' wages must be protected from rapacious cleaning women who seek equality. "Of all the concepts that the totalitarian instinct of our times has bequeathed to society — including racial and gender job quotas and laws against free speech — the seemingly harmless slogan 'equal pay for work of equal value' is potentially the most destructive of a free society . . .

"What many advocates of the equal-pay thesis do not seem to realize is that they are proposing a fundamental change to the way our society operates. Market forces of supply and demand are neutral. When you replace them, you are not replacing an unjust system with a just one but, instead, introducing a conscious system to replace a spontaneous one. Ultimately, you are replacing the amorality of the free market with the immorality of the regulated society. What results is theft: you rob the janitors to pay the cleaning woman."[36]

Both Black and Amiel write copiously and derisively about what they call the cult of victimization. Says Black, "To read the press of Canada today it would be hard to avoid the conclusion that we are a society composed almost entirely of battered wives, molested children, humiliated ethnic groups, exploited workers and other groups despised for their sexual preferences or cultural attributes, all festering in a spoiling environment."[37] And, "This [tendency to put collective rights ahead of individual rights] is, and always has been, recognized as a matrix for dictatorship, whether we are purporting to protect society from Communists, Jehovah's Witnesses, assorted bigots, wife beaters, gay bashers, office voyeurs, or discriminatory hirers."[38]

Amiel laments that for women, psychological distress has become fashionable. "Turn on the television set these days and the noise of women's inner turmoil made manifest is positively deafening: match the celebrity to the disorder . . . Do you want to listen to a bulimic, an anorexic, an abused wife, an abused child or even a child abuser? Are you interested in a beaten wife or a battered Miss America? A martian would probably be forgiven for thinking that the primary problem of North Americans is a population of females totally absorbed with their personal misery — addictions, abusive experiences and pain . . . When was it that our values changed and being a psychological cripple became a mark of glamour?"[39]

Male Castration

All forms of violence against women are mocked. Amiel is opposed to the notion of women refugees who seek asylum based on violence and persecution they are suffering as women in their home countries. While admitting the existence of such violence, she trivializes it. "I haven't stoned anyone in an eternity."[40]

On the 1993 Canadian Panel on Violence Against Women, Conrad Black writes in his autobiography, "As this book is finished, a vastly expensive Royal Commission, the latest in a long sequence of institutionalized orgies of national self-reproach, has produced nearly 500 recommendations for the avoidance of violence to women. These include a universal pledge from the adult male population to avoid violent intent toward women and locally administered neighbourhood violence audits to incite and assess denunciations and tittle-tattle. Because of emergent definitions of rape, consent forms have become advisable between adult Canadians contemplating heterosexual intimacy, even if the parties are married. Freedom of expression no longer extends to many forms of disparagement or subjectively perceived harassment. As Chesterton wrote, the state has gone mad."[41] Of the same study, Amiel says it is Marxist and amounts to male castration. "Lenin, I recall, had a five-year plan to eliminate poverty. Mao's version claimed to eliminate flies and venereal disease. Now, Canada has an eight-year plan to eliminate violence against women. Our plan has the advantage that it seems to require the deaths of fewer people than the aforementioned schemes — unless you worry about the castration of the Canadian male."[42]

Amiel is strongly opposed to state and police intervention in what she calls "domestic strife between consenting adults." She is referring to societal intervention in the case of wife battering when the woman has not laid a charge. This is because, according to Amiel, some women willingly consent to an element of violence in their relationships. If we're going to accept the lifestyle choice of being gay, we should accept the lifestyle "choice" of a violent relationship. "The sado-masochistic relationship is another petri dish for violence. Some people have a psycho-sexual orientation that requires pain for full satisfaction."

She continues, "This is a sexual orientation that appeals to some people and I find it hypocrisy of the most unbelievable form to protect and promote one sort of sexual orientation, such as homosexuality, while simultaneously threatening everything from job loss to criminal penalties for consenting adults who happen to be of a different inclination, such as sado-masochists."[43]

Amiel writes with attempted humour about incest. "Let me confess straight up that I always wanted to sleep with my father. He was as magnificent as Zeus, genuinely courageous and a good tennis player and classical pianist . . . As I had barely reached puberty when he died, my attraction to his bed did not have a sexual component. In retrospect, I am certain it could have developed had we met when I was a 20-year-old with more snobbery about men than qualifications to attract them." She says that even though "there is nothing new about having an affair with your father at age 20," familial proximity discourages it. "If you are a functional family, the tedium of parenting a teenage daughter through those many years when her self-absorption is as pure as liquid air may abate your desire to penetrate her charms."[44]

Promoting Family Values

Amiel dismissed the 1984 Badgley report on Sexual Offences Against Children. While acknowledging the more gruesome problems of rape and torture, she trivializes the more common yet devastating crime of sexual abuse in families. "But what does it mean in the sorts of cases the Badgley report so often cites — an uncle occasionally fondling his niece when he tucks her into bed for instance. Such behavior is repellent, but does the committee honestly believe that a child will suffer less psychological trauma when mother's brother is reported for touching her in what may or may not have been a sexual manner and the family is disrupted and the child may be removed from the home?" To split up families over child abuse is to create a greater problem: the destruction of family values and the family itself. "The report has one significant ordering principle behind it. It is a further attack on the family by feminists and the state in the name of so-called 'experts' and social workers. As much as one may dislike authoritarian family structures, there is little doubt that it is the family — even in its most anarchic form — that provides the strictest moral standards for its children. To destroy further the autonomy of the family cannot help but ultimately breed even more promiscuity and immorality."[45]

Amiel's class politics become particularly evident over this issue. She laments that a social worker turned up on the doorstep of her "upper-middle-class" friends after receiving what she feels was an invalid complaint. No doubt false complaints do happen; Amiel's problem, however, is that she thinks they are happening to the wrong class. In her view, the problem is confined to the lower class and the upper class is subjected to false accusations. "Part of the hysteria of the child-abuse movement is its need to establish that child abuse exists among every group . . . because no one wants to acknowledge that there are lower-class people, we arrange laws and procedures to encompass them and then apply them to everyone." Amiel goes on to express her dim view of the basic competence of "lower-class" people, saying that "most social workers know that the real cases of abuse, with the occasional exception, are more likely to occur in a social stratum where the people are simply not competent to lead normal and adequate lives. There ought to be a way of helping those people without their care becoming our social standard. We should also be able to accept the fact, as a lesser evil, that because of the existence of such people, there will always be a number of casualties."[46]

The issue of workplace sexual harassment has, Amiel says with amusement, no "legs," and despite her years in the work-force, she complains she has never been sexually harassed. "No one has ever doubted that out of every one million men there are probably 1,000 genuine creeps, with pimply protuberances and sweaty extremities, and not even that minimum of courage required to pounce on a passing female from the bushes . . . Perhaps I'm just peeved. I've been in the labour force for over 20 years in every job from waitress to executive and no one has ever sexually harassed me. Maybe I just don't have any appeal."[47]

According to Amiel, if men have to put up with perfume and chattiness, women should put up with objectionable remarks and behaviour. "Men and women are different. An action that may seem reasonable to a man may not seem reasonable to a woman . . . Historically speaking, society has always recognized attitudinal differences between the sexes. That is why the Victorians had men go into the smoking room for their after-dinner cigars and ribald chat . . .

"Men have to live with the little peccadilloes of female behavior — our tendency to chattiness, the wearing of perfume. Women should put a good face on the fact that males will be themselves in our presence and at times will give objectionable glances or employ objectionable words. If equality in the workplace is to have meaning, it should not be an equality based on penalizing conduct that is objectionable to a reasonable woman but not to a reasonable man."[48]

Tolerance for abuse by males should be in direct relation to their productivity in other areas. "People in the workplace have different habits. Some smoke, some are annoyed by smoke. Some like dirty jokes, some people are prudish . . . If your star salesman tells dirty jokes, management ought to be able to say that since Jack sells more widgets than anyone else and we are in the widget business, that is more important than the sensibilities of a few secretaries."[49] Obviously under these rules, the boss would be given the most leeway.

"Barely fit for life"
Writing about the University of Toronto professor who was banned from using the university pool for five years because of

intense ogling of female swimmers, Amiel says the problem lies not with the male ogler, but with the subject of his ogling, the woman swimmer who should be able to deal with this situation herself. "I rather like stares from intelligent, humorous and tall men over 50, myself, although it is difficult to judge the sense of humour when swimming . . . Prolonged staring is probably rarer than moderate staring, but most of us have at one point or another encountered someone whose peculiar tastes seem to encompass our own fair forms, with the result that we have been the object of intensive staring. Unwanted staring can be uncomfortable, of course, but arguably any human being who is not equipped to deal with that kind of discomfort is barely fit for life." As for the complainant, although "one knows very little about Ms. Torfason," her complaint contains the language of "hardcore feminism . . . that rare sort of human being who seeks no sign of appreciation from men, women, or beached whales."[50]

Amiel also has no patience for Paula Jones's claim that President Bill Clinton sexually harassed her in a particularly crude way when he was governor of Arkansas. "In my view, any woman who can't cope with a non-violent man who unzips his trousers and politely invites you to do pleasurable things to their contents is scarcely fit to cope with life."[51]

Amiel praises American department store heir and founder of Diner's Club, Alfred Bloomingdale, as a role model. "Apparently Alfred had a penchant for hiring nubile young girls, tying them up, and having them gently beaten while his newest amoretto and he watched. There is nothing particularly remarkable about this. One simply has to read the literature of 17th- or 18th-century Europe to see the upper and lower classes enjoying all sorts of bizarre practices. One can only say that Alfred, being 66 at the time of his death and still, it seemed, very active, does more for the geriatric cause and the excitement of becoming a senior citizen than all the speeches of Senator David Croll laid end-to-end as it were."[52]

A *"Feminist Salem"*

In a column entitled "The tyranny of modern-day feminism," Amiel cites charges of sexual assault that she feels should never have been laid. Again, while there is no doubt that false charges are laid for this as for every crime, Amiel's analysis suggests a conspiracy comparable to Nazi Germany. "The feminist reign of terror in Canada is such that it is better to proceed with charges of sexual assault that are patently false than risk feminist wrath if support is withdrawn from a so-called victim . . . As evidentiary procedure changes to create kangaroo courts for accused males, our female judges, female Crown attorneys and female elites remain mostly silent . . . This reign of terror is their agenda . . . Meanwhile, good Canadians who found the silence of ordinary people shocking while the horrors of McCarthyism or Nazism were going on do nothing. 'What did you do, Mother,' Canadian children will ask in a decade or two, 'when men were imprisoned and reputations shredded in Canada's Feminist Salem?'"[53]

Amiel accuses women as a group of manipulation in this "time when the feminization of our culture is virtually complete."[54] "Most Canadian women don't believe they are sexual victims. But once they discover how to use these assumptions practically, they find they can get Joe dismissed or John shunted aside in hiring, or solve their child custody problems by quietly whispering 'child abuse.'"[55] In a column about the royal family, she says that Prince Charles "has accurately gauged that this is a grievance society and that if you want to get into its leading edge you pretty well have to be a victim . . . Playing the role of abused child is the ultimate in trendiness and that scam works for just about nine out of 10 people."[56]

Amiel and Black blame this trendiness for the decline of their homeland and save their ugliest comments to describe it. It seems feminists make Amiel's husband physically sick. "About a month ago, I was watching television one night when I came upon a group of talking heads including the feminist Judy Rebick.

Rebick was talking about the terrible plight of the dispossessed in Canada, specifically women, single mothers, 'minority persons' and other ill-treated groups in our land. I let out whoops of laughter. The only ill-treated groups in Canada I can see these days are hard-working Canadians of every socioeconomic class who fork over a lot of their money to the government so it can subsidize Rebick's various causes.

"'Please,' said my husband, Conrad Black, who was recuperating from flu, 'please change the channel or I'll be ill' . . . I went into the bathroom and found him lying on the floor turning green. He has a strong sense of Canadian patriotism and seeing the decline of rationality in Canada's political debate is a deeply unhappy experience for him. His response to Rebick was to evacuate a perfectly good supper."[57]

"The neuropathology of homosexuality"

Black and Amiel are particularly harsh in their references to gays and lesbians. Recalling her university experiences in her autobiography, Amiel describes the "havoc" that was sometimes caused among "normal" students when a female don invited them for long discussions about any special difficulties they might be facing — "or might not have thought of . . . The don's concern might have been genuine, but as a matter of fact, she was a lesbian and managed to impart her own confusion over sexual identity to several of the other girls, some of whom were not quite sure of their own. She also managed to equate confusion with 'sensitivity' and to hit on J.V., possibly the one genuinely disturbed girl in the group, who soon took an overdose of sleeping pills."[58]

Sixteen years later, little had changed in Amiel's views. Writing on "International Affairs" for Southam, Amiel, who has been married four times, turned her attention to the topic of same-sex marriages, and compared them to bestiality. "Marriage has a particular role in society. That role is by now so devalued that there seems to be no earthly reason why we should not include a commitment between same-sex couples or, frankly, between a human being and a house pet." She then went on to deliver her own clinical psychological assessment of gays. "The reason homosexual activists want same-sex *MARRIAGES* is to achieve the legal obliteration of any distinction between the normative sexual behaviour of society and the neuropathology of homosexuality that affects an estimated 5 per cent of the population."[59]

In a 1988 article on abortion ("all but impregnated rape victims could avoid the problem by behavioral restraint"), Conrad Black stated, "In the ultimate trenches of what calls itself in Canada the pro-choice movement, skulking behind more legitimate elements, is a prickly faction of maladjusted female opposition to heterosexuality itself. They are entitled to their opinions but not to govern us all."[60] In response to written criticism of this view, Black is defensive. "I do not think it is fair to accuse me of being ungenerous in referring to the presence of a stridently lesbian element within the pro-choice movement . . . There is room for every shading of opinion on this issue and I was only suggesting that a largely unsuspected consensus may exist between the more moderate views of both sides."[61]

As in her treatment of other groups, Amiel refuses to recognize the hurt caused to gays and lesbians by stereotyped language, claiming that only action can be legislated. She describes reaction to some highly controversial articles in a police journal. "The issue was sparked by the feeling of some Toronto homosexuals that they were being harassed by police, and by a few silly articles in a police association magazine that called homosexuals deviants and Jews terrible drivers and, for good measure, added that blacks worry about nothing but being black. The cry went up from the city hall task force for quotas of women, Jews, Italians and albinos in the police force as well as for a new oath swearing to love and honor homosexuals."[62]

When the United Church established a task force on homosexuality, Amiel took a sarcastic tone. "The church was not getting out of its traditional business of telling right from wrong, after all. It was merely redefining sin as a language comprehensible to

Freudian-Marxist-Systems-Analyst-Flow-Chart-Designers. Loving, non-exploitive fornication, socially responsible adultery, warm and genuine homosexuality were fine. Indecency was no longer gross if it was engrossing. Honesty conquered all, presumably even sadomasochism, pederasty and necrophilia — though the report did not specify them." Asserting that, until recently, the church measured behaviour not by contemporary mores, but by the revealed word of God, Amiel brings in her judgement on the place of gays and lesbians in the church. "The acid test had been how our fallible human ideas and appetites measured up to a higher moral law. It was when the church abandoned the test and began to render to Caesar not only what was Caesar's but also what was clearly God's that such things as the Concordat with Hitler became a possibility."[63]

Amiel says the archbishop of New York "is damn right" to refuse to sign an executive order outlawing discrimination against gays and lesbians in church hiring practices, as to do so would condone homosexuality. "As the marchers passed St. Patrick's Cathedral on Fifth Avenue, one sign was flashed that read, 'The Lord is my shepherd and He knows I am gay.' But that does not address the central point: does the Lord like it?"[64] She suggests that those who teach children about the human rights of gays and lesbians — a practice that is growing in schools — also give them totally age-inappropriate information on abortion. The latter charge is unfounded, but by combining these issues, Amiel cleverly mixes loaded issues for today's parents: "A parental rights amendment could allow parents to remove their children from school classes that teach nine-year-olds how to obtain abortions or suggest to six-year-olds that homosexuality is just another lifestyle."[65]

"Sexual perversities"

Amiel chides gay and lesbian couples who, wanting more than the freedom "to follow their sexual predilections," are seeking society's full recognition in law, a notion she calls "utter lunacy

. . . If the state can by a stroke of the pen, fundamentally redefine the old allocation of human roles — roles such as the heterosexual union, femaleness, maleness and the family, which have been reaffirmed in every historical period known to us — if it can redefine them willy-nilly without any indication that there has been the slightest change in real human behavior, then we are in Big Brother land . . . There has been no change in the amount of homosexual behavior in our society — it remains a minor sexual variation . . .

"Previous states, even the most tyrannical or authoritarian ones, drew certain lines based on human experience and the basic habit of our species . . . Here in the parliament of the limitless state there is nothing it cannot alter. When Caligula made a horse a consul, he did not do so because he thought his horse would be a good consul — he did it to show his power knew no limits. Ontario has declared two spouses can be of the same gender and by so doing they have imitated Caligula . . .

"The incidental result of this is that the legitimacy of the family will be diminished. Homosexual unions can be called 'families' but they cannot create children. The point is this: the family is the biological unit designed to propagate the species . . . You cannot retain the meaningfulness of the true biological family as an institution when you extend its advantages, such as spousal benefit packages, to outsiders."[66]

Amiel does not view homosexuality as even on the same continuum of behaviour as heterosexuality; rather, she lumps gays and lesbians in with sexual deviants. "Whatever we may think about them, adult sexual perversities or deviations are split into two categories. There are consensual perversities, which include everything from homosexuality to sado-masochism and arguably even necrophilia. [We wonder how necrophilia can be "consensual"?] Then there are assaults by perverted predators on non-consenting victims . . . Surely the dividing line is not the extent to which a perversity disgusts the observer, but consent. This society has decided to deal with most sexual deviations on the right side of this dividing line as sexual 'orientations' protected by law."[67] She later describes pedophilia and child abuse as fairly harmless, with no lasting trauma. "Pedophilia is a very ancient aberration that has existed since the dawn of time. While it affects a tiny minority of people, all children are warned about it and until the recent hysteria, there was a recognition that most sufferers were fairly harmless. A child is not lastingly traumatized by a pedophile making a lewd gesture or touching a child's buttocks if there is no force involved. People who do that should not be locked up for life and frankly, I don't think there is much that they can be treated for, any more than homosexuals can be treated for their sexuality. It is an aberration and having said that we need not go berserk."[68]

Amiel compares AIDS to the bubonic plague and leprosy, and says their victims should be quarantined. But as a society, we will not address AIDS, because we are afraid to offend the groups it has afflicted, claims Amiel. "If today, we were faced with a reappearance of the bubonic plague or leprosy, even though we now have medicines for their treatment, our first thought would be to make sure that no infected people were allowed in public places — we would scarcely force employers to hire them. But AIDS is different for a special reason. Unlike the bubonic plague or leprosy, AIDS is our first lethal *political* disease. What is muddying society's response to it are the two political strains in the virus — homosexuality and promiscuity . . .

"Today, homosexuals are surely unjustly and needlessly protected. If AIDS had been discovered as a disease predominantly among upper-income white Anglo-Saxon heterosexuals, it is a fair bet that the city of Los Angeles would not have rushed to make it unlawful to refuse them a job . . . Right now the most effective way to limit AIDS in an epidemiological sense would be to revert to the pre-sexual revolution mores of the 1950s so that people would stop copulating like bunnies . . . In the case of leprosy, society agreed to contain the disease by isolating the victims. Today, the operative phrase seems to be that we must not treat AIDS victims like lepers."[69]

For the victims of AIDS, Amiel shows little concern. "As for the victims of AIDS — who alas have only about three years at most to live — although it is incumbent upon this society to do everything that money can do to help alleviate their pain and suffering, our first responsibility must be to protect the healthy. That will include keeping children with AIDS out of regular schools for their last few months of life."[70]

And she makes it clear that she is singling out gays and lesbians and "various racial groups" when she lectures on the evils of promiscuity. AIDS victims are privileged, she seems to suggest, because of their race, nationality, and sexual preferences. "The major question in Canada seems not to be how we can prevent this awful disease from spreading and how we can protect the uninfected. Rather, it is how we can prevent Canadians from in any way discriminating against those people who are walking about with a fatal disease that can be communicated through bodily fluids and for which there is absolutely no cure . . . This lunacy reflects the political ramifications of AIDS. Had the disease first been associated with white heterosexuals instead of Africans, Haitians and homosexuals, it is certainly my view that our policies would have been swift and unequivocal . . .

"At some point, Canadian society will have to discuss the real issues here . . . It will also be necessary to talk to those various racial groups — as they have done in England — who have more flexible or looser groupings than the stable family unit. They must be urged to change their sexual habits. The alternative is to stand silently by and see them decimated by AIDS because we were afraid to be called racist."

According to Amiel, the state should bear down on those such as gays and lesbians who have immoral values. "It is, in part, because we allowed the anal practices of promiscuous homosexuals to become morally acceptable in this society that the disease has spread so rapidly. Now, the time has come to make promiscuity socially unacceptable or, when the AIDS epidemic finally makes its mark on the consciousness of this land, Canadians will cry out for the sort of hysterical measures that will condemn AIDS patients to Devil's Island."[71]

8

MALEVOLENT MINORITIES

"A certain amount of discrimination is the most basic of human rights."

— BARBARA AMIEL[1]

The face and colour of Canada are changing. Immigrants from Asia, Latin America, the Middle East, the Caribbean, and Africa are replacing the earlier waves, most, although not all, of whom hailed from Europe and the British Isles; for example, there are now more Sikhs in Canada than Presbyterians. Most inner city schools now deal with dozens of language groups; about half of Vancouver schoolchildren now use a language other than French or English at home. Racial tensions have become an issue of concern for governments at all levels, as has the issue of cultural identity.

At the same time, Canada's troubled past with its First Nations peoples is being called to account, as a majority slip deeper into poverty. In 1996, 50 percent of Indians living on-reserve were on social assistance. The Assembly of First Nations warns that the next generation will not tolerate such conditions without violence.

The issues of multiculturalism, racism, and native self-government are among the most pressing of our time, and Black and Amiel have no shortage of opinions on any of them. Their view is encapsulated by Amiel's conception of classical liberalism: "It is of some importance to understand that there is a human right, whether for individual human beings or for a person who defines himself as a faithful Roman Catholic, a fundamentalist Christian, a Sikh or a Protestant, to have discriminatory views on a number of subjects, from homosexuality to the sanctity of marriage, according to religious beliefs. That right — to discriminate and to hold those basic beliefs and act upon them — is a basic human right. It is the right of national or ethnic self-definition."[2]

Amiel feels that, rather than attempting to eliminate the natural tendency toward discrimination by implementing policy that would embrace different cultures, a modern liberal state should be based on the principle of "homogeneity of language and culture." The proof, she believes, is in the failure of Canada and Quebec to settle their differences of culture and language. "Myself, I think that the modern nation state cannot support biculturalism, let alone multiculturalism. This is a shame, but the truth. A sanitized, bloodless form of ethnic cleansing is the best we can hope for."[3]

The ingratitude of exiled writer Salman Rushdie — whose works are "incoherent, unreadable splurges illustrating the evils of life under white people" — proves that promoting the indigenous culture of minority groups is wrong. "The uncomfortable truth that the left-wing British intelligentsia is facing is that democracy and liberalism are incompatible with true multiculturalism — when your society is full of people who are in their values neither democratic nor liberals. (That, incidentally, is not a value judgment on the Moslems, only a description.)"[4] She ridicules Canada for trying to address its multicultural reality through government, comparing its attempt to do so to Hitler's Germany. "Nowhere in the world since the Third Reich has any country been quite as obsessed with color, ethnicity and religion as Canada."[5]

The Ethnic Joke

Conrad Black agrees, trivializing the cultural ramifications of racism: "Every regional, sexual, physical, ethnic, demographic and circumstantial shortcoming has enjoyed an endowed martyr-dom . . . The hectoring, Orwellian presence of the state and its volunteer auxiliaries, hounds not only the cigarette smoker and the impatient motorist but the devotee of the ethnic joke, the amateur of traditional folklore, such as those wishing to see the authentic musical Show Boat and almost anyone with a lin-gering nostalgia for the efficacy of the free market." He adds, "According to my reckoning, about 400% of Canadians now qualify as officially recognized victims."[6] (At a launch party to celebrate *The Financial Post*'s new status as a daily in Canada, minority-shareholder Black promised to give new meaning "to that nauseating expression, minority rights."[7])

Criticizing *The Globe and Mail* for issuing language guidelines on gender and race, Amiel says, "I find it ludicrous to say that it is wrong to describe somebody as 'part Indian' or 'part black' on grounds that this suggests that white is the standard . . . [T]he fact remains that just as in Africa the standard, numerically speaking, is black, or in the Orient the standard, numerically speaking, is Oriental, in Europe and North America the numerical standard is in fact white. What on earth is wrong with stating that?"[8]

Responding to those who say that Canada is no longer a pre-dominantly Anglo-Saxon society, Amiel says, "Canada was founded by such West Europeans as the Anglo-Saxons, the French, and the Celts. Its majority institutions and language remained — at last count — English. Its general culture, inas-much as it resembles anything, clearly resembles an Anglo-Saxon culture more than, say, a Hindu culture. People of other cultures come here to share in it, often because they found it preferable to their own."[9]

"It has always seemed strange to me that the principle of self-determination for the French in Quebec or the blacks in Africa — at the expense of immigrant groups or other tribes among them — is enthusiastically embraced by progressive social democrats, but is a principle that is viciously denounced when it emerges in the form of a Canada for the white liberal culture."[10]

"A homogeneous look"

Amiel comes to the defence of those in Italy who protested a black woman winning the coveted Miss Italy title in 1996, saying it is foolish. "Women and their physical attributes occupy a special place in the Italian soul. It may be difficult for Canadians to understand but Italy is not like Canada, the United States or Australia, all of which are multicultural countries. Italy is a fairly homogeneous society with a specific standard of beauty. Many countries in Europe or for that matter in Asia have a certain number of indigenous ethnic stocks. That is why there are recognizable types such as Mediterraneans or Scandinavians.

"When a contest has to do purely with celebrating the most beautiful example of a certain homogeneous look rather than any achievement, it would be hilarious to elect a Swedish blonde as Miss Japan or Miss Orient, even though she may be a resident of those countries. And it is rather foolish to elect a Miss Italy who is black."[11]

Amiel reiterates this theme of a "national type" in a column written soon after U.S. secretary of state Madeleine Albright discovered she was Jewish. "When I say that I had known that Albright was Jewish, I mean that one look at her features told me so . . . What is somewhat amazing to me is that such an intelligent and well-travelled woman would not have made that association herself many years ago. I would have made the association the first time I looked into the mirror." Amiel does go on to say that not all individuals conform to an ethnic type. "But national types do exist, and many individuals correspond to their ethnic types in appearance to the extent that it is evident the minute you look at them that they belong to that group. Albright happens to be the type of person whose attractive features correspond to her tribal affinity in an almost unmistakable manner."[12]

"Not in my house"

Amiel criticizes a poster promoting Canada's multicultural makeup: "Two of the five children are white. One assumes (though one is not allowed, of course, to make assumptions) that one of these two white children is also ethnic, or else the substantial Polish, Italian, German, and the-rest-of-us will have lost out completely. One assumes this because European ethnics clearly can't be represented by the three black and yellow members who by proportional representation in this illustration give a completely false picture of Canada's racial makeup.

"The point about all this, of course, is not that one disapproves of pictures with blacks or Orientals in them, but that one does disapprove of the attempt to depict Canada as a predominantly black or oriental country. It simply isn't true. Nor do I particularly disapprove of dad doing the dishes (though not in my house, thank you); I disapprove of presenting dad's doing the dishes to children as the norm when it clearly is not the norm."[13]

She also criticized the appointment in 1991 of the distinguished musician, Oscar Peterson, as chancellor of York University, ignoring the fact that university chancellors are almost always figureheads, appointed for their outstanding contribution to the community through politics, art, or business. "But what possible qualifications — other than his fashionable status as a minority member — does he have to be chancellor?" (Black received an honorary doctorate from the University of Windsor in 1979, from his friend, Richard Rohmer, who was then chancellor. Black didn't question Rohmer's qualifications.) Amiel continued, "When I spoke last week to Lionel Tiger, Charles Darwin Professor of Anthropology at Rutgers University and a distinguished writer on sex roles and social structure, I asked him why he thought accomplished blacks and Asians from mainstream American society were joining the politically correct movement and shouting 'discrimination.' He was matter-of-fact. 'Grievance,' he answered, 'has become the lingua franca of our times. Everybody craves victim status. And so the politically correct movement has to do with a kind of rolling adjustment of who is the greatest victim of our times.'"[14]

Amiel derides the promotion of multiculturalism by government or schools. "The Multicult bandwagon is very much a growth industry . . . it provides employment for a number of people whose main skill is a native ability to speak the dialect of Hercegovina or paint Easter eggs or process applications . . . It is also one of the more dangerous cults in Canada today."[15] Furthermore, she writes elsewhere, "if people stole or murdered, if they couldn't read, write, hold down a job, get their poems published or their loves requited, it was due to nothing but psycho-social conditions or, perhaps, the slanted, racist, sexist, capitalist way in which vested interests persisted in defining crime, literacy, or sexual attractiveness."[16]

"Commissars"

TVOntario's guidelines on race portrayal come in for special scorn: "I want to see a commercial with the marvellous Jamaican lilt saying 'Waha' appen jah' and subtitles to explain that it means, 'Hi. What's happening now?' . . . It is all madness. The language and image cops are using the pretence of reforming our sexist and racist language as a blatant attempt to enforce the twisted values of their extreme zealotry on the living body of our society."[17]

After sitting through a class on multiculturalism in a school with a "very mixed ethnic population," Amiel writes, "Educational egalitarianism teaches that the student who knows nothing is just as good and worthy of a hearing as the one who knows something . . . It is one of the most spiritually and mentally debilitating diseases of our time. It is not so much that it diminishes appreciation of people with special talents — talent is its own reward, like virtue — but that it debases taste and discourages the pursuit of excellence by society in general. It is, of course, the disease of choice in any society based on the politics of envy. Instead of teaching history, the helpless educator was opening floodgates and allowing — as he had to do — his students to sit through waves of their own illiteracy and ignorance."[18] Nor, of course, does the practice of employment equity find favour with Amiel: "There may be all sorts of reasons why certain groups — racial, sexual, and ethnic — dominate certain jobs, and these reasons may have only partially to do with inequality of opportunity, or sometimes, not at all."[19]

Amiel is particularly disdainful of "commissars" — her name for government-appointed human rights advocates. "Commissars are the bane of humanity. If they could be identified at birth and destroyed it would be a great help, but even this task could not be done without the aid of their own kind. Superficially, commissars are often indistinguishable from genuinely helpful and caring people.

"Indeed, they may be human beings in whom a genuine caring instinct has undergone a malignant change of growth. There is nothing you can do about the commissar type; just like cancer, the cure eludes us. They will exist in every society together with the aggressive, lecherous, creative, criminal and hundreds of other human types."[20]

"And if there is one thing worse than an ordinary bureaucrat it is a moralizing one with administrative powers. In black moments, I wonder if shooting all such meddlers and experimenting on their cadavers would be the most useful service they could perform for humanity."[21]

"Huns at the gates"
In 1977, Amiel created a national wave of protest over a *Maclean's* column in which she urged the British to find the same backbone to fight current economic adversity they had used to

rout invasion during the Second World War. "The Huns are gone," she said in the column,[22] refusing to acknowledge the concern that such language is derogatory to today's Germany and to German-Canadians. She stubbornly responded to her critics in her autobiography, using the very language they found objectionable. Their outrage, she said, "strengthened my belief that in our day the Huns at the gates are the ever increasing number of de-racinated, de-sexed Chairpersons of thought police designed to launder reality in order to enforce their own ideals of non-discrimination, non-violence, equal status or affirmative action . . . [T]he Huns were still very much at the gates when it came to establishing a large, arbitrary empire all over again, only now here in the green and pleasant vistas of Ontario."[23]

These "thought police" hide the real roots of the "explosion of urban violence in North America," which Amiel sees as including "changes in our immigration policies that have resulted in large influxes of people uprooted from their own culture base, encouraged to think of themselves as victims while we made no attempt to assimilate them into Canadian culture because that is regarded as cultural imperialism."[24]

Amiel makes it clear in much of her writing that there is a right and a wrong kind of immigrant. She raises concern over the declining birthrate in Canada, but it is evident she is not worried about an empty wilderness but about what ethnic groups will populate the country: "In Canada, while our geographical space would obviously be filled by some other people, most likely from the overpopulated areas of the world, Canadians — as we know ourselves — may be an endangered species in a few centuries . . . Will it matter if the people calling themselves Canadians a few hundred years down the road are largely of East Indian or African stock?" Perhaps not, if "replacement stocks" assume the values, attitudes, and habits of the "original people."[25]

An Endangered People

But, she asks, what if Caucasians disappear from the face of the earth, as they might if present trends continue? "How can we preserve these endangered groups? Well, we should recognize that those things we dismiss as 'traditional values' such as the family, the work ethic and motherhood, are a lot more than mere abstractions clung to for religious reasons. When we abandon these values in favour of abortion, hedonism, and the weakening of the family, we face far more than spiritual consequences: we face the practical implication that we may soon die out as a group."[26] Here Amiel associates family, the work ethic, and motherhood with whites — the group she views as the norm in Canadian, and indeed, Western society — and abortion, hedonism, and the weakening of the family with the "replacement stock."

Black is also concerned about the changing racial landscape, explaining that one of Quebec's most pressing problems is a collapsed French-Canadian birthrate coupled with "no assimilable immigrants (except a few Vietnamese, North Africans, and Haitians whom not all Quebecois, for obvious reasons, rushed to welcome.)"[27] He says opening up the "floodgates to Haitians and Moroccans . . . would create other problems."[28]

Amiel uses Canada's refusal to accept Jewish refugees during the Second World War to advance an argument for "gradual and assimilative" immigration. In one of her *Maclean's* columns, she acknowledges harm done by the dreadful policies and opinions of F. C. Blair, then head of Canadian immigration ("Pressure on the part of Jewish people to get into Canada has never been greater than it is now," he said, "and I am glad to be able to add, after 35 years' experience here, that it was never so well controlled.").[29] But she continues with an argument consistent with her oft-quoted belief that "racism is a common human vice."[30] "While no doubt there was that (racism) in (Blair's) attitude" she writes, to believe that is the whole problem "is to be wilfully blind about the entire human experience . . .

"Historically speaking, whenever two different cultural,

linguistic, religious or national groups were forced together for geographical or geopolitical reasons, the situation has been perilous so long as they maintained their own strong identities. Two weeks ago in Montreal, a taxi company wrote letters of dismissal to its 24 Haitian drivers on the grounds that the company was losing business because significant numbers of taxicab users would not tolerate black drivers. It takes only a quick historical look around the world to see the enmity between the Walloons and the Flemish in Belgium, the Tamils and the Sinhalese in Sri Lanka and . . . the fight in Africa between the Tutsi and the Hutu of Rwanda . . .

"In Canada the government has taken actions that to some of us seem designed or at least destined to create explosive cultural tensions in this country. Our government decided, first, to make Canada a country consisting of as many cultures as possible. Then it decided to include in our immigration quotas large numbers of races and cultures as remote as possible from our founding Anglo-Celtic-French groups. Thirdly, it has embarked on a program to make sure our immigrants maintain their cultural identity and separateness as much as possible forever and a day through the policy of multiculturalism. And fourthly, and most importantly, the government has obliged people under the penalty of law to disregard completely in their daily lives — business hiring, renting and selling of apartments, etc. — the very differences that it fosters and encourages . . .

"The solution to the problems still brewing in Canada among different cultural groups is to be sure not to misidentify the problem as simply one of bigotry. Canada ought never to close its doors to those of different cultures, but should bring them in with some regard for the concepts of gradualness and assimilation, which should not be dirty words. The more distant a culture is from our own Canadian culture, the more gradual the number of people from it you let in at one time."[31]

This is almost precisely the argument Blair used; he explained to his "Jewish gentlemen" acquaintances that if Jews would honestly try to "divest themselves of certain of their habits, I am sure they could be just as popular in Canada as our Scandinavians."[32]

Who is assimilable and who is not appears to depend on the perceived ideological compatibility between Amiel and the immigrant group in question. She called for Canada to open its doors to the Vietnamese Boat People being repatriated by the British from Hong Kong back to communist Vietnam. She implies that the West favours other, more pitiable refugees: "all those anxious, pushy Orientals with outstretched palms and camp-smarts, trying to worm their way into the West. They lack the stoic simplicity of African refugees who criss-cross that continent in eternal agony, seeking refuge from famine and civil war without bothering us for more than the odd blanket." Although Amiel states that their pain is not a contest and that "the West simply hasn't the means to rescue and take in that half of the world that lives in appalling conditions," she makes an exception for the Boat People. "As it happens, I cannot think of a better fix for the declining birthrate and labor shortage in parts of Canada."[33]

Similarly, she called on Canada to open its doors to the flood of white refugee applicants that she expected in the wake of the end of South African apartheid, a regime she has referred to as a "little villain."[34] She predicted that South Africa would replace the white regime with one "that will put the lives of the white majority in danger." These refugees would no doubt be opposed by some Canadians who would want to screen for racists, but Amiel counselled against this. "I am happy that after the Second World War Canada did not try to separate 'good' Germans from 'bad.' In the chaos after the war it was difficult enough to get into Canada without having people sit in transit camps for 10 years while evidence was gathered and analysed and every German was subjected to intense scrutiny. The lives of thousands of people who were essentially innocent of the events of Hitler's regime would have been ruined. Similarly, in the event of massive violence in South Africa, it would be a tragic error to create procedures to determine which immigrants were relatively 'innocent' of practising apartheid. Should 100,000 innocent victims waste away in detention centres in case 100 active racists get into Canada?"[35]

Amiel ignores the fact that massive and systemic violence was already taking place against the black majority under apartheid, saving her sympathy for potential white South African victims. "It is not even that the scope of South Africa's offenses against human dignity are greater than anywhere else: blacks in South Africa are restricted in their movements by passbook laws. Yet blacks in most African nations are just as restricted in their movements by current laws and roadblocks . . . We [Canadians] are perfectly happy to establish our moral superiority on the backs of white South Africans rather than having to go to the bother of defending the principles we spout. But we remain obdurately blind to what might happen if the most militant forces are permitted to take over in South Africa."[36]

(Black involved himself in post-apartheid South Africa when he flirted with purchasing some newspapers there. He was introduced to the Zulu leader, Mangosuthu G. Buthelezi, an anti-sanctions, pro-capitalist competitor of Nelson Mandela, by John Aspinall, a South African casino executive. [Buthelezi has since admitted that he was implicated, working alongside apartheid security forces, in the murder of African National Congress officials and supporters.] In 1990, Black hosted a black-tie dinner for Buthelezi to show his political support. Held at the Toronto Club, it was attended by lieutenant-governor Lincoln Alexander, Black's spiritual advisor and friend Cardinal Carter, the South African ambassador, and a who's who of the Toronto business establishment. The event was picketed by pro-ANC demonstrators. Black recalls, "On Buthelezi's first full night in Toronto, he came with us to Latham and Paddy Ann Burns's annual [Royal] Winter Fair dinner at their home and actually attended the equestrian show. Galen Weston had been relied on, as president of the fair and a friend of several members of the Royal Family, to fill the Royal Box with a suitable party, but wasn't able to do so. Paddy Ann, a lively soul, shrieked with delight when I sheepishly inquired if we could bring Buthelezi and his party to dinner. 'Isn't he a prince or something or other?' I assured her he was indeed a prince of the Zulus, by some reckoning a more formidable tribe than the Hanoverians.

"'That's it! You've found us a worthy occupant of the Royal Box!' Gatsha Buthelezi, with the jet-lagged John Aspinall dozing beside him like a clapped-out white batman, took the salute, brandished his tribal chief's baton, and played his assigned role to perfection. We repaired back to the Burnses' afterwards, and the day, on which angry Zulus were reported in the world's press to have 'scattered thousands of their ANC opponents in fright before them,' ended after two a.m. with Mangosuthu G. Buthelezi and his hostess, Paddy Ann Burns, singing 'When Irish Eyes Are Smiling' to the accompaniment of a well-known Toronto pianist."[37])

In February 1992 Black and Amiel were in Davos, Switzerland, when Henry Kissinger introduced them to South African President Nelson Mandela. In his memoirs Black mentions this and then adds the following footnote. "After this introduction, Henry, Barbara, and I sat down and started into a pot of tea when Kissinger started grumbling: 'Oh no, here comes that god-damned Indian again.' I accused him of quoting General Custer but the man he referred to, elegantly dressed and exquisitely courteous, proved to be a very senior official of the government of India, representing the prime minister of that country with whom Henry, as part of his constant practice of private sector state visits, then had a very satisfactory meeting."[38]

Helping the State

For a writer who would admonish members of the "pressure groups" she so maligns for their dependence on government to take individual responsibility for their positions in life, Amiel shows remarkable sympathy for the perpetrators of violence under oppressive states. For example, we have seen that in defence of her argument in favour of white South African refugees, she submits that it was next to impossible to sift out South African or wartime German racists from the "innocents" because most just accepted their governments' policies without question. Elsewhere she has argued that the government of Canada should not extradite suspected war criminal, Albert Helmut Rauca, for his complicity in the murder of almost 12,000 Lithuanian Jews as he was not an aberration, but part of his society of the time. She writes, "The whole chilling point about the Third Reich is that, although there may have been individual sadists and psychopaths within the Nazi edifice of murder and torture, the majority of people in it were ordinary men and women simply embodying the good citizenship qualities demanded of them by a murderous state. They acted in the belief that what they were doing — eliminating subhuman and subversive elements — was to help the state. Such people are, alas, not wicked sadists."[39]

And in a column on free speech ("Hitler was right, alas! You either have free speech for everyone or not. You cannot have a little free speech"), Amiel defends Ernst Zundel's right to promote his racist views. She acknowledges that Zundel is "obsessed with a lie." But rather than just give the traditional civil libertarian argument that all speech, no matter how awful, must be allowed in a free society, Amiel goes further and tries to understand the man. "Zundel himself may be a quite unpleasant person, but can we be entirely unsympathetic to the process that may have created him? What must it have been like for Zundel, a German child growing up at the end of the Second World War, with every radio station, newspaper and history book telling him he came from a race of hideous, bloody murderers?"[40]

Friendly Tyrants

When it comes to oppressive regimes, Amiel is unafraid to indicate her preferences. In an article entitled, "A difficult choice of tyrannies," she describes the dilemma of whether the West should have supported Corazon Aquino, then opposition leader in the Philippines, over dictator President Ferdinand Marcos. While she admits Marcos was a "tyrant," she (wrongly) predicted that an Aquino win would "assure delivering the Philippines into the hands of the Communists, which would mean a repressive regime worse than that of Marcos." The heart of her argument is that while both left- and right-wing dictatorships are distasteful, we do not live in Utopia, and cannot oppose both. Right-wing regimes, which she calls "our friendly tyrants" are preferable to left-wing regimes, which she calls "totalitarians." "Authoritarian regimes, such as Chile [then under dictator Pinochet's reign of terror] or the Philippines [under Marcos], have an intrusive state and police presence, but they concede a whole range of private activities. Citizens don't need permission to visit another city or to own a shop. Totalitarian regimes, such as the [then] Soviet Union or China, regulate every aspect of life. Further, we note that our tyrants are not only our geopolitical friends but they are better to the people they tyrannize than any of the alternatives . . . Given the choice between the two, we will continue supporting friendly tyrants." Amiel says there may be a third option, which would require "setting up the West as the moral police of the world." This would mean using our military to "come down like a ton of bricks" on any threat to a liberal democracy anywhere in the world. Although she says this would apply to tyrants of the left or right, she assures that "our" citizens would never have to put themselves on the line for a right-wing dictator, only to prevent a "Communist takeover."[41]

And she joins extreme right-wing American senator Jesse Helms in comparing Canada's opposition to the controversial U.S. Helms-Burton law against investment in Cuba to British prime minister Neville Chamberlain's 1930 appeasement of Hitler, and compares the plight of capitalists whose land was expropriated in Cuba to the fate of Jews in the Holocaust. "To my mind, such a law falls into exactly the same category that would have morally prevented Canadians or anyone else dealing in businesses that the Third Reich expropriated from Jews. I don't see the slightest difference between an offer Hitler might have made to businessmen to invest, trade and operate a business or help run a factory taken away from 'filthy Jews' than that of Castro offering businesses stolen from 'filthy capitalists.'"[42]

The notion that racist language and ethnic jokes are harmful is dismissed. "Only people whose ignorance of human psychology includes their total ignorance of history and languages can think that there is a direct connection between the words, grammatical forms and common expressions of a language and the value systems of the society in which it is used."[43]

A Malignant State

Like many children, Amiel used racist phrases and songs when she was small. "'Eeny meeny miney moe/Catch a nigger by the toe' sing Gillian and I with our skipping-ropes as we line up for Bromley in our nigger-brown uniforms. Such phrases are routine, like the simile 'mean as an old Jew' . . . It will be twenty-five years before those silly, harmless phrases are made significant, and mythical little black Sambo and Shylock become their real victims." But unlike most adults, she did not later reject this use of stereotypes. Amiel admits to going through a stage of questioning whether such childhood taunts are harmful, but found she learned nothing from the exercise. "Perhaps . . . we learned no lesson because there was no lesson to be learned. Perhaps we knew, instinctively, that (contrary to what the officious sterilizers of thought and language would now have us believe) there was no connection between our stereotypes or adjectives and the gas chambers of Auschwitz. The Nazis were not monsters grown big from our puppy-monsters of caricatures and silly nursery rhymes; they belonged to a different species altogether . . . The real connection was between the Gestapo and a State bringing in legislation and regulations about how other groups of people ought to be viewed . . . The malignancy would have been a State laying down the law about official opinions we were obliged to share.

"Much later I heard the difference expressed by an old man

who resisted the Nazis with much personal courage. 'I wanted Hitler to go,' he said, 'so that a gentleman could be an anti-Semite once again.'"[44]

As for the notion that racism or discrimination are part of the North American landscape, Amiel and Black have no shortage of scorn. Amiel does see black violence menacing whites. A friend shunted his "relentlessly blond and blue-eyed children" from school to school for his work. One was a thalidomide child who suffered from taunts, but, Amiel notes, "only in Spanish Harlem did his parents have to be sure that he had 'muggers' money' in his pocket."[45]

At the same time, however, Amiel cannot find anti-black racism or black poverty in inner-city America. All she sees is voluntary poverty. "How could poverty mean families with television sets, cars, and money for the numbers game? Surely people were free to choose whether to spend their income on luxury consumer appliances, liquor, drugs, or food? How could this be compared to the frightening hardships which faced the involuntary poor, like many of the elderly? How could unemployment mean an illiterate and belligerent youth refusing to take a delivery job on account of 'Man, I don't have to do that crap,' as one said so eloquently to the manager of the First Avenue D'Agostino's store where I grocery-shopped in Manhattan." Amiel downplays the relationship between poverty and crime, which she sees as incited by left-wingers. "What sort of insult was the left dishing out to the vast majority of working-class blacks who managed to survive their economic and social status without mugging and raping, when left-wingers called violence an inevitable by-product of a racist society, and practically exhorted black youths to prove them right at the cost of ruining their own lives."[46]

According to Amiel, a "small black underclass" was made miserable because it could no longer blame its failure on racism after the Civil Rights Act of 1964 rendered America "a land of equal opportunity." "In earlier times, the black underclass had a sense of belonging, with all black people, to the world of second-class citizens. This had a certain calming effect . . . left-liberalism justified the worst excesses of black men in their own eyes: after all, society told them they were dispossessed victims."[47]

The 1992 race riots in Toronto and Los Angeles were the work of "black activists who insult the great majority of the black community by emphasizing the so-called 'oppression' of those who take to criminal activities or vandalism," Amiel wrote in an inflammatory column entitled "Racism: an excuse for riots and theft." In the same piece she denied racism in Canadian society and compared those who say it exists to Nazis. "Both the march and the riot were informed by a fatally flawed liberal perspective on racism that for the past 30 years has sold blacks in North America the notion that nothing in life is their fault, and that they are entitled to vent their unhappiness by stealing or destroying what belongs to others . . .

"Why have black activists trotted out this tired rhetoric about systemic racism in Canada? Canadians know themselves, and they know Canadian society is not racist. One can only conclude that some black activists want to incite as much dissension and unrest as possible among us all, in order to build a power base for themselves. One sees a parallel in the Nazis who exploited the very real problems in Germany to build up their power . . .

"The real problem America and Canada must face is the growth of an increasingly violent underclass. Why is that under-class largely black? Clearly, it has nothing to do with race since so many blacks have achieved brilliantly in every possible field of endeavour, as well as creating stable working- and middle-class lives. Nor can the racism which long haunted the lives of U.S. blacks right up to the civil rights legislation of 1964 now be considered a cause: East Indians, Pakistanis and Koreans were not among the thousands arrested in Los Angeles. They work and prosper." Amiel implied that black culture itself may foster the problem, and the solution is to escape it. "'I believe,' one American sociologist told me, 'that blacks can achieve as well as any group with one difference: they must leave their communities and achieve as individuals, unlike Jewish, East Indian and Oriental people whose communities nurture excellence.'" Amiel said this may or may not be true, but society is not allowed to find out, as conducting the necessary race-based research she proposed would lead to an "unbelievable outcry."[48]

Writing in 1996 about Canada's disgrace in Somalia, Amiel's column in *Maclean's* carried the promising headline: "Whatever happened to military honor?" But in the column, although she refers to what happened in Somalia as "a disaster for Canada," she came to the defence of the soldiers who beat, tortured, and murdered unarmed civilians. "The Canadians were sent into a land of the primitive, desperate and dangerous who would regard any lenient or humane action as an invitation to rob, steal and ambush. One can't blame the Somalis: they are what they are and their situation is what it is. But if you try to turn active soldiers into heavy-handed jail guards, you must accept the possibility that they will occasionally act in a manner that is highly undesirable or even — as in Somalia — atrocious. All the Airborne's training and culture prepared them to be a professional aggressive force, not schoolteachers wielding the strap."[49]

In 1985, a committee struck by then Toronto mayor Arthur Eggleton studied alleged racism in *The Toronto Sun*. A subsequent study by the Urban Alliance on Race Relations in Toronto found the *Sun* to be racist after analyzing columns and editorials in the paper over an eight-year period, from 1978 to 1985. Amiel was editor of the paper for part of this time, and was named as one of the offending columnists, along with McKenzie Porter, Christie Blatchford, Ted Welch, and Claire Hoy. During the controversy, the City of Toronto threatened to pull $42,000 in annual advertising out of the *Sun*, in protest, through its mayor's committee on community and race relations.

In her autobiography, Amiel defended the work of Arthur Jensen of the University of California at Berkeley and others who published papers in the late 1960s and early 1970s citing research they claimed showed that heredity may be a strong factor in determining intelligence, and that blacks as a group scored lower than whites on IQ tests. Although Amiel claims that if such evidence were found to be true, it "should confer no special privileges or place no special burdens on us," she mocks the storm of criticism that Jensen's works elicited from what she called the "find-the-racists squad." She writes, "Liberals and socialists were outraged . . . Egalitarians were apoplectic . . . What the Black National Coalition of Canada failed to see, as they railed at and abused these men, was that only through the work of academics of intellectual curiosity, coupled with courage and integrity, was there any real chance of understanding or solving the problems about which they claimed to be concerned."[50]

Native Canadians: "A culture of victimization"

Amiel saves some of her most biting commentary for Canada's first people. Native problems are exaggerated, she says, by the leftist media, exemplified by Peter Gzowski. To keep up with Americans in their search for sources of guilt, "We rediscovered our native peoples, and drew all the wrong conclusions from their conditions, and tried accusing ourselves of at least small-scale genocide. Peter Gzowski took an appalling but isolated incident in North Battleford, Saskatchewan, in which an Indian was murdered by a gang of white thugs, and wrote a moving but quite-beside-the-point article which claimed with a hopeful note: 'This is Canada's Alabama. In the next few years we may have there, on a lesser scale, what the U.S. has had in the past few years in the South.'"[51]

Black agrees with Amiel. The problem is the culture of victimization. "Those who feel guilty over the displacement of native people will never expiate that guilt unless the entire country is given back to the descendants of those people. I am afraid that the principal motivation of many of those who encourage the culture of victimization and the industry of reparation that goes with it, is not so much a spirit of magnanimity as a lack of moral self-confidence."[52]

Again, stereotypes are harmless. Amiel reveals hers when she recalls events from her youth: "On week nights I was part of a group informally known as the Parkdale gang, consisting of a handful of ex-reform-school youths and native Indian girls. They were friendly and undemanding and adopted me as a sort of mascot. I clearly knew nothing about sex and used long words, while they knew everything about sex and were illiterate. We got along very well. After hanging out at the bowling alley on Parkdale Avenue in the east end of Hamilton we would pile into an old car and drive out to the roadhouses, where the Indian girls would move from booth to booth sitting with various men, drinking and getting lifts 'home' with them."[53]

She dismisses the world-renowned artwork of aboriginal and Inuit peoples. "And what about the primitive work of Eskimos, native peoples or Africans? It is of course of much anthropological or archaeological interest, if genuine. (If not, it is simply of no interest at all.) But it has the same relationship to art as an igloo to the Notre-Dame of Paris." Art collectors who think differently are "trying more to 'understand' their own little souls than to expand them."[54] In her memoirs Amiel comes to the defence of racial superiority theorist Paul Fromm. In 1977, Fromm favourably reviewed a book titled *Bended Elbow*, for *The Financial Post*. According to Amiel, Fromm's review "simply stated the problems which the book outlined"; that is, "the Indian problem in Kenora" and "the very real problems of Indian drunkenness and sexually explicit behaviour in public places."[55] As a result of the review, the Ontario Human Rights Commission had contacted *The Financial Post* to suggest that books and reviews such as this might be viewed by some as inappropriate. Amiel took this to be in keeping with the spirit of Human Rights Commissions, a spirit which she says encourages other bodies and individuals to "censor other people's views."[56]

Land claims, treaty rights, and the search for self-government are all held up to ridicule. Says Amiel, "By giving the appearance of legitimately considering such issues as self-government, sovereignty, land claim titles and special status for Canada's native people — solutions that would never be, and should not be, acceptable to the Canadian people — the government [takes] another step toward perpetuating the problems of our natives." When Europeans first arrived in what would become Canada, she writes, natives were "living a life with a tribal structure that had more in common with 10,000 BC than with the times in which the rest of the world was existing . . . Native culture was not geared to develop the continent into the geopolitical entity known as Canada."[57] She forgets, of course, the more advanced aspects of native culture which equipped the Iroquois to cure Jacques Cartier and his men of scurvy with herbal medicine 450 years ago.

Living in a Stone Age

The problem, according to Amiel, is that Canada's natives are still living in a Stone Age culture, furthered by giving natives special treatment. Full assimilation is the answer. "The . . . only genuine solution is a way that has been embraced by a number of individual Indians for some time. It is simply to join mainstream Canadian culture, claiming no special status and undertaking all the duties and privileges."[58] That this would wipe out ancient cultures seems not to bother Amiel at all: "I confess to a doubt that it is in the long-term interests of the native peoples to maintain a palaeolithic culture in the twentieth century and, personally, I'd prefer to see more of my tax money spent on helping Indian and Eskimo individuals to enter the mainstream of the dominant culture of this country. Historically no group has managed to retain a stone-age culture within a more advanced society, except as some sort of anthropological curiosity that delights sentimental writers who have read too much Rousseau when young. (And if some are offended by the value-judgement the word 'advanced' implies, so be it.) Still, if our native peoples wish to continue a life of extraordinary hardship and limited lifespan, there seems to be plenty of frozen tundra to go around without depriving the rest of us on this continent from access to the resources of the North."[59]

Natives who view themselves as trappers or hunters and take part-time jobs to support their way of life "make my psychiatrist friend in Toronto 'a fisherman' since he works in order to be able to afford to go back to his native island in the Maritimes to fish as his Acadian ancestors did hundreds of years ago."[60]

"Of all the sacred cows in Canada the most sacred is the caribou," Amiel writes, in reference to concern about the threat to wildlife posed by development. She mocks testimony before the 1970s Justice Thomas Berger inquiry into a proposed northern pipeline that development of the far north would devastate the environment because the arctic ecosystems are so fragile that of 23,000 species of fish, only 25 live in arctic waters, and of 3,200 species of mammals, only 9 are found in the high arctic. There are two inferences that can be drawn from this, says Amiel. "Berger chose to interpret it as indicating that so fragile an environment should have extra-special care and protection . . . The most logical would seem to be that, as a matter of policy, given the limited amount of wildlife able to survive these gruelling conditions, the benefits of technological development to the country and its population might outweigh the cost of harm to nature, since there is so little nature to harm."[61]

Amiel claims South American Indians were advanced; North American Indians were not. She forgets that the complex political structure of the Iroquois Five Nations was used as a model by the designers of the American Constitution. In an inflammatory column on the 1990 Oka dispute, Amiel was astounded that the Mohawks viewed themselves as a politically sovereign nation, "although I doubt that the Mohawks really understand all that decision would entail." Their view is based on a false reading of history. "The Indians . . . did not realize that in dealing with the French and English, they were dealing with a people on the verge of becoming an industrial civilization. Unlike the relatively advanced Indians in South America, North American Indians for the most part were simply a hunting and gathering culture. The Indians dealt with us as if we were simply another larger tribe. The peace pipe was smoked in the belief that each of us would hunt in their bit of land. We went along with this view." And Amiel ignores the fact that First Nations peoples in Canada were not conquered, but negotiated treaties with the government. "Canada will . . . have to face the fact that, like every other nation on earth, it is founded on conquest . . . if the Indians are claiming sovereignty, then there is simply nothing to negotiate or re-negotiate." Although she does not want to see men or women massacred, "it seems to me that a really strong show of force now is the only way to keep the casualties down to a minimum . . . Perhaps at long last, we will bite the bullet and understand that the gun barrel created this country and that once more it will have to be used if Canada is to remain our home and native land."[62]

9

THE CANADIAN
WASTELAND

*"Canada is still a better bet than a military junta, of
course, but only for the politically unfree. Canadians
themselves are becoming a sort of boat people, seeking
friendlier environments."*

— BARBARA AMIEL[1]

Canada is in the midst of a social revolution. The Liberal Party
that, under pressure from social groups, presided over the creation of the welfare state is in the process of dismantling it,
under pressure from corporations and the wealthy. The universal child benefits program and the universal retirement benefit
program have been eliminated and replaced by weak programs
targeted to the "needy." After thirty years, national standards
that guaranteed social assistance for anyone in need, regardless
of the cause, have been abandoned.

Provinces are free to cast thousands of welfare recipients to
their fates, and set up punitive "workfare" programs for the
unemployed. In 1989, the year the Canada-U.S. Free Trade
Agreement was signed, 87 percent of all employed Canadians

qualified for Unemployment Insurance; the number of Canadians who now qualify is less than 40 percent.

Health care budgets have been gutted. The federal government share of public health care spending has plummeted from 50 percent to well under 25 percent, leaving cash-strapped provinces to cut and restructure entire systems. Beds and hospitals are closing, services are being contracted out and privatized, and once universal services are being "delisted," opening the door to transnational health corporations. As a consequence of monopoly protection for corporate drug patents, drug prices have soared through the roof, royalty payments to foreign patent holders have skyrocketed, and universal drug insurance programs for seniors and those in need are being destroyed.

This is the Canada Barbara Amiel and Conrad Black have been fighting for and in which they find themselves more comfortable to operate after their self-imposed exile in Margaret Thatcher's England.

Black's decision to leave Canada was caused by "the cultural bigotry in Quebec, the inexorable erosion towards the left in Ontario, the constitutional quagmire, the pandemic envy, mediocrity and sanctimony, punctuated in my own experience by countless defamations and a public police witch-hunt."[2] "The 'caring and compassionate' model for Canada's national vocation effectively excludes all of us who are not socialists, which is one of several reasons why I ceased to be a Canadian resident some time ago."[3]

Amiel lamented, at the time of his departure, "Canadians may not miss Conrad Black who now lives in England because they never realized what he stood for and what they were losing when a man of his calibre gives up the battle. They will."[4]

A Society of Addicts

Of her own decision, she explained that "the nanny state" had gone too far in Canada. "My allegiance is not to any piece of earth or particular set of rock outcroppings. My allegiance is to ideas, and most especially to the extraordinary idea of individual liberty. That idea is still there in the North American landscape, a landscape I have come to love. I do not wish to leave. But my suitcase is packed. I do not feel bound to any country or any popular will more than to my own conscience. I would leave here as easily as I would have left Germany when its people elected Hitler to power."[5]

The reason for such an extraordinary comparison? Canada has been in the grip of what Amiel calls "bleeding heart liberals" who have created the "warm bath of Canadian life with its equity this and unemployment that"[6] and what Black calls "the great Canadian sloth, the spirit of smug entitlement . . . envious whingeing people,"[7] "a society of over-compensated self pitiers."[8]

Black minces no words in his contempt for Canadians. "In Canada, government-designated victims outnumber the entire population because of the possibility of accumulating conditions of victimization like food stamps."[9] Canada is "uncompetitive, slothful, self-righteous, spiteful, an envious nanny-state, hovering on the verge of dissolution and bankruptcy,"[10] "a population composed almost entirely of self-proclaimed geographic, ethnic, behavioural, and physiological victims,"[11] "an international laughing stock"[12] because of its dour, politically correct reputation.

Black writes, "Canada effectively created a political ethos of official pandering and a society of addicts to government largesse . . . Each new category arose, became vocal, and was pandered to: for women government adjudication of job worth and forced elimination of salary differentials with men regardless of merit. Homosexuals were officially encouraged in the armed forces. Japanese Canadians were compensated for their detention after the attack on Pearl Harbour. Native people have a federal government department whose budget is now over $12,000 for every designated man, woman and child in the country."[13]

Amiel explains, "The Trojan horse of . . . [s]tatism, very much the trend of our century, is the modern version of feudalism, in which the citizen is subservient to a state that controls or regulates virtually every aspect of his private and public life."[14] In her critique of the state, Amiel makes little distinction between moderate social democracy and communism. "There is, of course, a difference between orthodox communists and democratic socialists, but it boils down chiefly to this: the communists are ready to liquidate everyone who stands between them and total power, while the democratic socialists would not go that far."[15] But the effect is the same, she argues, for it is the state, any state, that stifles the search for true liberty — by which she means economic freedom. "[The state] may acquire its mandate through guns (China) or even the popular vote (England). It may perform with hysterical tyranny or some civil sophistication . . . but it cannot do without coercion. It cannot co-exist with liberty."[16] Amiel compares the welfare state in Canada to the former Soviet Union under communism: "A planned society can range from the brutal coercion of the Gulag to the so-called moral suasion of the [Canadian] human rights commissions."[17]

The Flat-Earth Society

Since Black and Amiel see all of these regimes as cut from the same cloth, politicians of all but libertarian stripes are maligned. On Pierre Trudeau, Black says, "His incitement of ethnic, occupational, regional, and sexual groups debased public policy and ultimately almost bankrupted the country. He, more than anyone, turned Canada into a people of whining politically conformist welfare addicts."[18] "Audrey McLaughlin is Bob Rae in drag, mouthing crypto-Marxist platitudes that have about as much contemporary relevance as the utterances of the Flat-Earth Society."[19]

The Tory party on Brian Mulroney's departure fares no better. "The collapse of the Progressive Conservatives indicates the country is disgusted with a party which calls itself conservative but is, in fact, socialist,"[20] Black says. Amiel agrees: "The Progressive Conservative party is lost, filled with candidates it thinks are meaningful who flirt with feminism, eco-ism, and every other half-baked idea under the sun."[21]

Few other Canadians escape their disdain. In his attacks, Black includes "bureaucrats, journalists, academics, left-wing clergy, labor leadership and trendies in business and the learned professions . . . who swaddled their inability to compete with their American analogues in patriotic sanctimony."[22]

Says Amiel, "But to blame legislators alone is scapegoatism. Canadians sui generis seem to suffer from a reflex forelock-tugging that makes us the most passive lot in the Western world, with the possible exception of the great automaton society of Swedes who manifest their rebellion every now and then by jumping off roofs at a considerably higher rate than we do . . . We are almost German or Japanese in our obedience to regulations, as if the great movements of individualism that swept Britain, France and America froze when they hit the St. Lawrence River."[23]

Although Amiel "nod[s] off whenever I hear intimations of 'The Future of Canada,'" she does attend a lecture on that "rivetting" subject by her new husband, Conrad Black, because she is "in love." "Black's diagnosis of the Canadian Disease was accurate, all right — a virus made up of special interest–group politics, bad political leadership, danegeld to Quebec and so on — but his identification of the carrier of the virus was a little short. He was laying the whole mess in the country on the failure of the elites — rotten political leaders, less-than-rigorous journalists, hope-less academics, churches with their attention on moral relativism, and that sort of thing . . .

"But surely, a small voice inside me whispered, the fault is with the Canadian people, not only the elites: the fault is with our complacent citizens who don't read, don't think, don't want to face reality and don't want to know . . . I'll bet most Canadians still haven't a clue why their country is in a mess and, if you told them what has to be done, namely, end universality of benefit programs, minimum wage laws and transfer payments to harder-up regions of Canada, dismantle labor legislation that makes Canadians' costs uncompetitive and strangles the produc-ers of wealth — in a word, end Canada living beyond its means —

they'd mumble some dishonest mantra about the compassionate caring Canada and disinter the CCF."[24]

"In some curious way," Amiel wrote on another occasion, "part of our intellectual development was arrested in the 1960s. In spite of all the changes in the world, including the utter discrediting of socialism, Canada remains a backwater where wealth and success are regarded with suspicion . . . Canadian voters seem not to understand that public policy, which represses the human right to enterprise, is an offence against human dignity and leads to economic, political and moral decline . . . [It] stifle[s] the economic well-being and wealth of a society and drain[s] its moral and physical capital."[25]

"Canada is a cultural backwater. It views the events in the world the way it sees a faraway star — not as it actually is now, but rather as it was when its image began to travel light years ago."[26]

"I couldn't live here for a minute"

Black returns to this theme time and again in his speeches and columns: "I have a ghastly, sinking feeling that the Canadian academic-bureaucratic-journalistic complex has foisted on us the notion that Canada's national identity must be preserved because we are more 'caring and compassionate' than Americans (for which read, of course, more socialistic) . . . Mrs. Thatcher has told me that one of her most fervent desires is to do to the word 'compassion' what she says she has done in Britain to the word 'planning' . . . In English Canada, there is almost no literate dissent from the righteous, envious, soft-left conventional wisdom foisted and consumed throughout the country."[27]

"There is something about the Canadian mentality that cannot stand an unbroken string of successes, unless it comes after a long life or after evident ordeal . . . [P]resent Canadians with too much success too soon and it's just unbearable."[28]

To Black, as we've seen, Canada is synonymous with "caring and compassion," a phrase which he detests. Now it has become a "flimflam." "The greatest of Canada's problems is the mean

spirit of the country. At the best of times, envy is our most baneful characteristic and it need not be emphasized that these are
not the best of times . . . Our countrymen have been failed by their
academic, journalistic, and bureaucratic elites, who sold them
the myth of the 'caring and compassionate' society. This is a
euphemism for what has become a ruinously exaggerated process
of taking money from those who have earned it and giving it to
those who haven't. The nationality that has acquiesced, indeed
wallowed, in this flimflam for 30 years should reflect on how we
brought this magnificent country to the brink of disaster."[29]

When in London, Amiel often tried to "tart up Canada's significance," but had a hard time. "There is no practical reason why
any country in the world should bother learning about Canada
when there are so many significant and pivotal international
issues that require attention . . . Canada is an immigrant's country
and most often we have attracted people whose priorities are not
very adventurous. Those intrigued by challenge chose the United
States. This country's western frontiers were opened up by
government and the railway, not by rugged individuals . . .
[R]omantics either die young or live in Canada, which is much
the same."[30]

"I am a tourist in this Canada," Amiel says, without regret.
"Once Canadian politicians simply irritated me with their
personal greed for power at the expense of responsible policies.
Now, I couldn't live here for a minute. I'd be a maniac or a criminal — as most Canadians have become out of sheer necessity to
survive."[31]

Drunken Sailors

Canadian social programs and the concept of universality —
what Black calls "plundering and bribery" — come in for special
attack. Amiel: "We have spent like drunken sailors in order to fill
the sense of 'entitlement' that our weak-tea socialism has created.
We have become a country of feuding special-interest groups in
which envy and resentment play more than their natural roles . . .

"We extended the safety net to encompass not simply the genuinely unfortunate, but rather anyone who is second-rate. We would rather take care of the second-rate people than reward first-rate ones for their initiative . . . If you reward mediocrity and discourage excellence, the consequences can be no surprise. One can hardly blame mediocre politicians, our frightful church leaders and a hopeless intellectual establishment for endorsing this system — it works very well for them."[32] Besides, Amiel would remind us, harkening back to the accepted doctrine of the nineteenth century, "We do have orphans and the handicapped to consider."[33]

Says Black, "Instead of controlling the welfare state, the Canadian government has consented to be controlled by it . . . Instead of grovelling to every aggrieved group — disparate Indian bands, World War II Japanese Canadians, homosexuals in the armed forces — and promising economic equality to all Canadians, wherever they are, we should provide an affordable safety net with incentives to work. Universality is a sacred cow that should be put humanely to sleep and replaced with a means-based system."[34]

Transfer payments to less advantaged regions are relentlessly criticized. Black: "In regional economic equality, we have signed on to an impossible dream."[35] "The end will come eventually because otherwise the entire gross domestic product of Canada will be a mighty transfer payment of money from people and regions who have earned it to those who have not."[36]

For Black and Amiel the unofficial relocation program moving Newfoundlanders to the mainland is inadequate. Says Black, "The fact is that if Newfoundland wants to have the same standard of living as Calgary, then half the Newfies have to pack up and move to Calgary."[37] But that's not likely to happen, says Amiel. Newfoundlanders "could make better lives for themselves, and especially for their children, if only they would move to where the better jobs and housing are. But they won't."[38]

Both speak out against universal health care. Amiel reminisces about her childhood in England, before the "mindless egalitarianism" of public health when "patients were treated like clients rather than liabilities." She objects to the "tendency to abolish better services that people can elect to buy, whether private hospital rooms or first-class airplane seats, because the mere existence of such facilities is thought somehow offensive to the poor — or the parsimonious . . .

"When health care becomes a free commodity like air and water it is treated less seriously by people. It is abused in major or minor ways." Amiel says that when health care is universal, society pays with a loss of liberty, and individual freedoms are removed. "However, coercion not only is possible, but becomes natural and the only way out of the government's dilemma . . . The citizen's liberty to engage in certain practices is curtailed on the basis that it is a health hazard and therefore a legitimate subject for regulation by the community." This is the thin edge of the wedge of statism for Amiel. "[Public funding for health care] may yet be invoked to restrict the consumption of fatty foods or to introduce compulsory jogging. *Categories of treatment may be classified to tailor the expense to the citizen's usefulness to the community or the government.* Hospital beds or rare medicines may be allocated on this basis, as in the Soviet Union."[39]

Amiel is direct in expressing her views on the merits of public health and public education. "I prefer a society in which there is private medicine and private schools because their policies are decided by the people in charge of them."[40] And on the subject of burdens on the health care system, she writes, "It is marvellous that we can transplant organs and, instead of cutting off limbs, we can sew them back on. But an amputated limb is infinitely cheaper than the cost of all the hospital facilities required to sew it back."[41]

Legislation to rein in extra billing by doctors was an attempt to make political hay by taking on a powerful group in society. "It pays to play to the worst instincts of greed and envy in voters — in the short run at least — and the government's promise that not one Ontario citizen would have to put filthy lucre into the sweaty palms of overpaid and grasping doctors must have sounded like votes in the ballot box to the backroom boys."[42]

Parents have rights to their children that should be unimpeded by government. Amidst much controversy in Canada over the recent deaths of many young children at the hands of their parents, Amiel praised a U.S. state amendment affirming the "natural, essential and inalienable right of parents to direct and control the upbringing, education, values and discipline of their children" that has "whipped the various U.S. 'caring' and educational establishment members into a frenzy of opposition. If passed, it could stop social workers going into homes at will to remove children or to give parents lectures on how to raise their offspring."[43]

Where most people are calling for more intervention by Children's Aid Societies in these cases, Amiel calls for less. When she worked for the CBC in the late 1960s, Amiel did a story on a "horrific" incident of child abuse, in which Children's Aid sent children back to the abusing foster home. But the problem was not with "a particularly inadequate Children's Aid Society staff *but the very existence of such organizations as the Children's Aid Society.*

"Any organization that requires victims if it is to survive has a vested interest in maintaining the dependency of its clientele. In the United States journalists would soon uncover the shocking story of children kept from adoptive homes by social workers whose jobs (and grants) depended on having a good supply of non-replaceable kids to administer . . . today, the militancy of many social workers inside government organizations for such hideous pieces of legislation as a Children's Bill of Rights is clearly directed at expanding their own power base."[44]

Rae-Style "Communism"
Social democrats, particularly "the drivelling left" typified by Bob Rae's former NDP government in Ontario, come in for heavy fire

from Black and Amiel, even though, according to Black, "Bob Rae is only marginally to the left of David Peterson and he was only marginally to the left of Bill Davis."[45] Rae's platform is "lobotomous drivel," his party filled with "petty functionaries and derelicts," Rae himself a "swinish, socialist demagogue," a "perennial millionaire-baiting anti-corporate agitator," an "insolent, impudent, reckless, dangerous little upstart" who is preaching "soft, left pablum."[46]

In his memoirs, Black describes Canada as falling behind international developments. "At a time when most of the rest of the world was celebrating the victorious end of the Cold War, or replacing repressive with liberal regimes, Canada's two largest provinces, two-thirds of the country, were led by mindless stooges of a corrupt antediluvian labour movement in Ontario, and by craven ethno-narcissists in Quebec. Even from the safety and distance of London, it was painful to see so great a country laid so low by the lassitude, faddishness, and philistinism of its own voters."[47]

Just days after the NDP government of Bob Rae was elected in Ontario, Black waxed apoplectic. "The Ontario election provides the apotheosis of the Canadian left, the triumph of the forces of envy, slothfulness, fiscal confiscation and misplaced sanctimony that have been enfilading the province for decades, creeping forward on hairy little feet. The Marxist tinkerers in the NDP deserve the responsibility of governing. Red Tory and Liberal palliations were stations on our political Calvary."[48] Black spoke and wrote copiously on this topic once he got started. "Bob Rae's government is a howling mob of single-issue fanatics: militant homosexuals, feminists, abortionists, eco-geeks, worker radicals and social agitators, standing and shrieking on each other's shoulders."[49]

"Bob Rae is the Salvador Allende of Canada, trying to translate a 36% vote into a mandate to strangle, disembowel, and immolate the vestiges of the incentive-based economy and then pursue 'co-operation' with survivors."[50]

"Only in Ontario in the entire democratic world, is the cant and hypocrisy of union-dominated soak-the-rich, anti-productivity, politics of envy officially approved and po-facedly presented as 'caring and compassion' . . . Only in Canada, especially in Ontario, are the Prig stormtroopers of the old, soft, anti-capitalist left still taken seriously when they insolently strive to communize industry, confiscate wealth, and discourage economic growth . . . what has died in Russia has lived on in Ontario."[51]

Getting to the Airport

Not to be outdone, Amiel flayed away at the Ontario "socialists" from her own perch in *Maclean's*. She didn't know whether it was "scientific socialism" or "economic communism," but she didn't like it. "Canada's Liberals and Progressive Conservatives may have had half-wits in power, but it is the NDP that wants to legislate what foods I may eat, how females should be depicted on television or what the composition of my employees or board of directors ought to be."[52]

"The only place where scientific socialism has still got a gun at the throats of the economy are [sic] in South Africa — where the executive of Mandela's African National Congress is dominated by the South African Communist Party — and Ontario, where NDP Leader Bob Rae is introducing economic communism through such policies as his proposed amendments to the Ontario Labour Relations Act."[53]

Rae's modest proposals for labour reform — reforms already in place in a number of other provinces — came under strong fire. Black said that Rae "plans a union usurpation of the means of production, expropriation without compensation . . . a 'scorched earth, take no prisoners' annihilation of capital by labor . . . this is legislated conquest . . . it is communism . . . war on the private sector . . . The damage to Ontario . . . would be irreparable, a terrific price to pay for Bob Rae's submissive bondage to Bob White . . .

"If anything resembling the proposed changes is enacted,

private-sector capital spending in Ontario will cease sine die . . . [Members of Ontario's business community] are mere economic victims, as the government of Hong Kong says of most of the wretched Vietnamese boat people who fetch upon its shores."[54] "The provincial government seems to think that those who are interested in commerce are like scavenging animals riffling through the garbage."[55]

Amiel says that it is "rot" to think people will adhere to these "crazy and witless" policies. "Stupidity should not be taken lying down, and the Canadian that votes with his feet by, for example, cross-border shopping or paying in cash and letting the government try and collect the GST is merely performing an act of good citizenship."[56]

Black goes further. "I rejoice in our democratic society as much as Bob Rae does. We do indeed make our 'choices' and I made my financial 'choices' well before Ontario chose him. I followed David Peterson's exhortation to me to 'export capital' and exported it to places where the return on it and the tax treatment of that return are much more generous than they will be in Ontario where that capital originated, especially while Ontario is under the hobnailed fiscal jackboot of Bob Rae."[57] In fact, at a dinner he and Hal Jackman gave for Preston Manning on the eve of Rae's election, Black "jocularly" explained that he wasn't all that worried about a Rae win. "I can get to the airport before Bob Rae can get to the lieutenant-governor's office."[58] And he did.

Appeasing Quebec

Black believes that "Ontario has the distinction of being practically the only jurisdiction in the world except for Cuba and North Korea that officially discourages the incentive system."[59] He pulled his investments out of the province with a public announcement, threatening that "Ontario will pay dearly and long for its mindless submission to the NDP," adding, "When it becomes advisable again to invest in Ontario, we will happily do so."[60]

Says Amiel, "Those who can leave, have, and those who stay,

suffer. That is one hell of a social contract."[61] But Black knew that he and his allies would defeat Rae and "today's stimulant will be tomorrow's anaesthetic and ultimately, a most effective physic, an enema in fact."[62] "The burning question is whether there will be anyone left in Ontario to turn out the lights after Bob Rae and Bob White have finished making the province into a no-fault, equal-opportunity, Sabbatarian bicycle-repairing commune."[63]

Socialism is also the root of Canada's constitutional problems, according to Black. Quebec, with its "avaricious, bourgeois instincts,"[64] has not only influenced the country to be less individualistic in its ideology and its policies, but has also been the cause of expensive transfer payments from consecutive federal governments trying to buy constitutional peace. "As the British connection faded and the French fact became more nationalistic and abrasive, an unorganized consensus developed in the media, academia and public sector bureaucracy of Canada that our new raison d'etre was to be more 'caring and compassionate' than the United States . . .

"The federal government's effort under succeeding prime ministers culminating in Trudeau to prove its relevance to the average voter, especially in Quebec where its relevance was most in question, led to a huge proliferation in social spending . . .

"Once we were embarked on the objective of demonstrating our compassion by the profligacy of our social programs and once we had accepted that large sections of the country would only be persuaded of the virtues of federalism by buying their votes with money from other regions, progress towards our present impasse became predictable and in a sense, even logical. It was inevitable that Quebec would demand more and more in jurisdiction and in money and it was probably inevitable that Ontario, the source of half of Canada's gross national product and of 80% of the equalization payments, would move steadily to the left."[65]

Black was born in Montreal, studied law in Quebec City, and

owned his first newspapers in rural Quebec. He wrote an M.A. thesis and a book on former Quebec Premier Maurice Duplessis. While he was studying Duplessis, the Quebec-Canada question was becoming quite clear to him. "I was coming to the tentative conclusion that French Quebec's interest in social democracy was a preparedness to accept Danegeld from a federal government whose enduring relevance to Quebec was increasingly unclear. It was also a subscription to a fashionable method of redistributing money between socio-economic groups whose lines of demarcation had a providential resemblance to the province's ethnic divisions, i.e., to the French from the non-French, from each anglo or Jewish Quebecker according to his means, to each 'authentic' Québécois according to his relative lack of means, with the vocal approval of English-Canada's premier and most fashionable Quebec-watchers."[66]

For Black, the Canadian disease of "caring and compassion" reaches plague-like proportions in Quebec. There, polls consistently demonstrate that social democratic and egalitarian values are at the highest levels in our country, and are most distant from the elitist and individualist values of his beloved United States. Hence, for Black, the Canadian problem is a Quebec problem writ large. The transfer of funds from governments to individuals in the form of social programs such as unemployment benefits, welfare, subsidized health, and education has a parallel in federal-provincial relations and equalization payments. For these reasons, French-speaking Quebeckers represent everything that is "wrong" with Canada. "Canada has deluged Quebec with money and good will. Under relentless pressure to buy popularity for federalism in Quebec and to promote sociological modifications elsewhere in the country, Canada has become an overtaxed, deficit-ridden, semi-soft-currency, desperately politically correct socialist state."[67] "The back-breaking federal transfer payment system really developed momentum in the 1950s and 1960s . . . In the late 1960s, Pierre Trudeau set out to buy the adherence of Quebec to Confederation."[68]

The "Futile Expense" of Quebec

Now that "the federal Santa Claus's bag of toys is empty," Black wrote in 1995, Quebec federalists should "consider seceding from Quebec, as West Virginia seceded from secessionist Virginia in 1863," and Quebec should be divided in two. "I doubt that these five million Quebeckers would find independence quite as uplifting as they expect, but we would. Canada would be truly liberated from its age-old ambivalence and a back-breaking obligation to futile expense."[69]

Francophones who move from other parts of Canada to settle in the new Quebec state would not be missed. "An ambitious immigration policy would replace the departed Quebec nationalists in a few years with more appreciative citizens."[70] And just what would these more appreciative citizens be like? "The departed Quebeckers would be swiftly replaced by suitable immigrants happy to be assimilated to an English-speaking free-enterprise democracy. Canada would not be out of the G-7 for long, if at all."[71]

Black has hardened his position toward Quebec nationalism in recent years. For a long time, he urged Canadians to drop the "non-starter" of ten equal provinces ("It is as obvious that Quebec is a 'distinct society' as it is that Louis St. Laurent was mistaken thirty-five years ago when he said, 'Quebec is a province like the others'"[72]), and to seek a special relationship with Quebec worked out on asymmetrical lines. Now, however, he charmingly says, "Sovereignty-Association was a political fairyland and Quebec's separatist leaders shouldn't be allowed to suck and blow simultaneously for ever."[73]

Without Quebec, "the absolutely mad concept of trying to define a nationality and a country by its social programs" would be over. "Without Quebec, a majority of Canadians would be electors of Ralph Klein and Michael Harris."[74] (Black's preoccupation with the values of liberty and freedom — values he sees as Anglo-Saxon and therefore lacking in Quebec society — is echoed in the publications of the right-wing lobby group, the

National Citizens' Coalition, which in 1987 gave Barbara Amiel its highest award. The NCC has vehemently opposed bilingualism and says Canada should abandon the attempt to keep Quebec in Confederation. Quebec leaving Canada, the NCC says, would have the added bonus of eliminating the Liberal Party, kept in power "by the habitual voting prejudices of Quebeckers." A recent NCC publication claims that democracy is an Anglo-Saxon institution.)

"One country rather than two"

Without Quebec, Black maintains, the rest of Canada would finally be able to follow its destiny. "English Canada could also, if it chose, make a much better deal with the United States than it has had with Quebec, a population with which most English-speaking Canadians have less natural affinity than they have with Americans."[75] "I used to say to my separatist friends at Laval University that every vote for the secession of Quebec was a vote to make me a citizen of an expanded United States, a not altogether disagreeable fate."[76]

But elsewhere Black touts the benefits of an Americanized Canada with more conviction. "We could also draw officially closer to the United States, with whom, if we choose, we could make a much more rewarding arrangement than we have had with an unappreciative Quebec. Canada could negotiate arrangements with the United States that would preserve our regional distinctiveness as Texas and New England have preserved theirs, would raise our standard of living, lower taxes, reduce our debt burden and doubtless involve a translation into U.S. dollars from Canadian that would be very advantageous to us. Just 220 years after its founding, the most conceptually and materially powerful country in history would be virtually born again geopolitically by gaining access to Canadian resources and population."[77]

"If the lure of the U.S. proved irresistible, this would not be a tragic fate either. Next to a bicultural country, the most interesting political option we possess is to do what we can to ensure that

English-speaking, North American, democratic, capitalism continues, without jingoism or arrogance, to be the world's greatest political influence. Arguably, this could be best achieved in one country rather than two . . . I suspect that most Canadians would prefer an American Canada to a socialist one and would rather deal with George Bush than Robert Bourassa (or Brian Mulroney)."[78] Noting that Black refused to allow his *Daily Telegraph* to criticize a U.S. bombing attack on Libya in 1986, the *Wall Street Journal* has said that Black is "more pro-American than many Americans."[79]

For Black, the attraction of the United States lies in its position as a global superpower and global cop. Although he admires its tax structure, free enterprise mentality, and so on, he appears to be transfixed by its power. Just as he admires powerful individuals — Napoleon, Duplessis, Hearst — Black reveres powerful nation states, with huge bankrolls for 'defence' budgets that produce giant, technologically advanced military forces (and wealthy corporations).

Writes Black, "I have always loved the United States; as a youth I was impressed by its power and showmanship. From an early age I had felt that it possessed all of Canada's strengths on a geometrically greater scale without being unoriginal, mean-spirited, or self-conscious."[80] "Whether the bedraggled Canadian left likes it or no, the United States is by far the most successful and powerful country in the world."[81]

"The U.S. is the only pre-eminent power in world history that in its prime has had almost no discernible imperialist ambitions, and it is the only democratic political society in history that has simultaneously maintained a reasonably comprehensive social security and welfare system, a heavy national defence commitment, and a dominant private sector."[82]

To Amiel, the whole notion of "Canada" is artificial. "Perhaps there is an additional explanation for our anti-Americanism. This land of ours is an artificial entity. We are nothing but a political idea. Apart from the French, we have no ethno-cultural or geographic distinctiveness to separate us from the United States. Only an arbitrary line on the map, which is not even defined by a range of mountains or continuous river. We share the same culture and language. It takes a professor of linguistics to discern the two dozen words we may pronounce differently. In fact, there is no good reason for Canadian nationalism or our separate identity from the United States." While Amiel goes on to say that she still has the desire to remain Canadian, "it does require a certain kind of fairly witless nationalism."[83]

The United States, for Amiel, is all about individual liberty: freedom to roam the western frontiers, but mostly freedom from meddling governments which insist on hobbling hard-working entrepreneurs and decent citizens who just want to be left alone. "Americans aren't quite like Canadians. They have more than some dim ancestral memory of individual liberty. Meddling governments that can't tackle basic issues like the safety of citizens but can enforce irksome regulations that ought to be none of its business are not really part of the American dream. Just read some of the bumper stickers: 'Make building permits as easy to get as welfare.'"[84]

"My own allegiance," she writes on another occasion, "goes to whatever country most highly cherishes individual liberty. In my lifetime, that has always been the United States . . . America does not redistribute its income through transfer payments based on some collective national welfare scheme. If you want the living standard of Phoenix, Ariz., you move there. You do not stay in Halifax and wait for the taxpayers of Calgary to look after you. All in all, for Canada to join the United States, unlikely and impossible as that may be, seems to me a very good idea."[85]

But while Amiel appreciates the U.S. government's hands-off approach to domestic affairs, she is not opposed to its imposing its will on foreign shores. "The United States is unique — it is the world's only nation based on the idea of individual liberty . . . Whatever its shortcomings, it has managed to create a society which docilely assumes guilt about its past and manages to work towards individual liberty without different groups, tribes or religious members putting bombs in letter boxes, occupying cathedrals on Fifth Avenue and routinely massacring each other. If any nation is to impose peace on the world order to further its own self-interests, can one name a more worthy occupier of the role than America?"[86]

America as aggressor gets full marks. Says Amiel, "There is no point in running for the presidency of the United States unless you have the taste of blood in your mouth."[87] Black, who as we've seen knows a good navy when he sees one, says, "There is nothing wrong with tying oneself to the mast of an American aircraft carrier in a good cause."[88] And Amiel insults the Canadian men and women of two world wars when she claims Canada always lets the U.S. fight its causes. "Canada has always enjoyed the special luxury of never having to take responsibility for major geopolitical decisions . . . Canada has never had to take the first step in fighting fascism or communism in the battle to save the values it enjoys."[89]

Black did temporarily despair over the U.S. when the Democratic Party "handed [power] over to Gay Liberation, Jane Fonda, Shirley MacLaine, the eco-geeks, militant abortionists, and assorted rabble-rousers,"[90] and when liberalism swept the country in the 1960s and 1970s: "From the assassination of President Kennedy through the purgatorial years of Vietnam and Watergate and the righteous inanities of the Carter era, I almost wept for America, an optimistic and generous country gnawed by the liberal death-wish within and the spiteful envy of foreigners . . . She was the greatest of all nations, humbled every night in 60 million American living rooms by the liberal media with the magnified facts of racial violence and inequity at home, ineffectuality abroad."[91]

But Ronald Reagan restored sanity. "After Vietnam, Watergate, and the inanities of the Carter era, the presidency had to be restored to a position of natural leadership, and the United States, which had suffered the most precipitate decline of influence of any great power since the fall of France, was to be restored to its rightful place of world leadership."[92]

(In a speech he gave in 1988 Black clearly saw the same "improvements" ahead for Canada. He praises the National Citizens' Coalition, the Reform Party, and the Fraser Institute, and chillingly foretells their ideological victory. "I believe that slowly, quietly, almost imperceptibly, most of the values the Fraser Institute seeks to promote will achieve greater acceptance in Canada. There will be neither outright victory nor the equally deserved rout of conservatism's opponents. There will be no triumphalism other than of the most discreet and sportsmanlike variety."[93])

"Folkloric distinctions"

Around 1990, Black began, in his writings, to quietly moot the idea of unification with the United States. (Provided, of course, we could be spared their "inner-city welfare cases," who would be attracted to our "extravagant social programs." One solution to this problem has been to snip the Canadian social safety net, adapting it to the American way of life.) Usually, such musings were wrapped in the appropriate disclaimers to the effect that this should only be pursued if things don't work out with Quebec.

By 1996, when Black made a presentation in Vancouver to politicians and international businessmen at a gathering of the influential Trilateral Commission, many of the disclaimers and caveats had fallen away.

While he admits "economic and cultural dependence would increase steadily and we would be resistless against the benign magnetic power of the American civilization, which repels and frightens some, but fascinates, impresses, and affects the whole world," he suggests that "English Canada should prepare to submit, to its great profit and comfort, and, ultimately, possibly even relief, to what Mackenzie King described, also to General de Gaulle, in 1944, as the gentle but 'overwhelming contiguity' of the United States."[94]

Although few Canadians favour such a union today, Black

feels we could be convinced. "Current polls show fewer than twenty per cent of Canadians wish to join the United States, about the same percentage as those East Germans who . . . favoured reunification. This figure would rise quite quickly if it became a less far-fetched hypothesis."[95]

For Black, a Canada-U.S. union would — well, it would be efficient. And after all, the only obstacles to its happening are a few "folkloric distinctions" such as universal medicare and strict gun control measures. He writes, "North American, English-speaking, capitalist liberal democracy remains . . . the world's leading political influence . . . best achieved in one country and not two . . . Canada's natural and human wealth, together with its geographical position, make it an area so strategic that the world will be more than passingly curious to see if concern for universal public-sector medicare, strict gun-control, and a few other public-policy and folkloric distinctions (which could be accommodated in a fuller embrace with the United States anyway) will suffice to prevent a continentalist political process from succeeding as a sequel to the economic foundation of free trade."[96]

Of course, if a union were to occur, Black suggests, "Canada would have to retain some control of immigration to prevent an unbearable influx of America's inner-city welfare cases, seeking to take advantage of Canada's extravagant social programs."[97] And while the U.S. would benefit from our natural resources, Canadians would gain in an area dear to Black — power and influence.

"Such a union would have a good deal more strategic importance than the reunification of Germany, as English Canadians are more numerous and sophisticated and occupy a larger, richer and more strategic land mass than the benighted East Germans. Ironically, Canada would exercise more political influence in the world in taking such a step and operating within the American political system than it has enjoyed as a founding member of the British Commonwealth, the United Nations, NATO and as a G-7 country."[98]

As for the future of the country, Black takes a tough stance. "Quebec must stop being coy and accept or reject Canada. Canada will embrace either Quebec or, failing Quebec, the United States. North America will be divided geographically or linguistically."[99]

10

DEMOCRACY'S OXYGEN

*"Legislation may not change the heart, but it can
restrain the heartless."*

— MARTIN LUTHER KING

Citizens in a democracy depend upon the media to understand and
evaluate public policies and social issues — in theory, the media
are democracy's oxygen. However, the increasing concentration
of media ownership in fewer and fewer hands, the underfunding
of public service broadcasting, the rising commercialization of
news and information, and the commercial exploitation of the
new communications technology all threaten to limit the
accountability of the media, the diversity of views given public
expression, and the ability of citizens to access the news and
information we need to participate in and make informed decisions about our social, economic, and political affairs.

We have written this book to catalogue the views of the most
powerful couple in print journalism in Canada today. Conrad
Black and Barbara Amiel are not typical commentators, presenting their views in a marketplace of competing ideas. Through

their control of Canada's newspapers, they have bought themselves the right to influence the political landscape in a way that distorts freedom of the press. We believe that the stunning domination of Conrad Black over the Canadian print media presents a clear and present danger to the future of democracy, such as it now exists.

How We Got Here

Several factors have contributed to the development of both Black's personal control base and corporate media concentration in general. The first of these is the prevailing neoliberal thinking that sees the so-called unfettered free market system — more aptly known as the law of the jungle — as paramount. Government regulation is treated as unnecessary interference, instead of the only means by which the vast majority of the public can influence the conditions of their existence. These attitudes permeate the media in the form of code words for corporate freedom, such as "free trade," "free market," "globalization," and the "information highway."

The second, related factor is the unprecedented privileged status now enjoyed by huge corporations. A prevailing approval of corporatism has produced an environment that fosters and encourages not only mergers, takeovers, and concentration, but also record profits and the wholesale discarding of workers. And layoffs are only part of a war on workers that has effected the erosion of their wages and standard of living for decades, culminating in a dramatic reduction in the social safety net.

The Canadian situation is part of a system of corporate rule in which governments all over the world use their still-considerable power to deliver an economic system that is beneficial to the private sector. Just 200 giants now control over a quarter of the world's economic activity. Their combined sales are bigger than the combined economies of all countries minus the biggest nine; that is, they surpass the combined economies of 182 countries.

Of the world's 100 largest economies, 51 are corporations —

only 49 are countries. Wal-Mart is bigger than 161 countries, including Poland, Israel, and Greece. Mitsubishi is larger than the fourth most populous nation on earth — Indonesia. General Motors is bigger than Denmark. Ford is bigger than South Africa. Philip Morris is larger than New Zealand. Toyota is bigger than Norway. The Top 200, with a combined revenue of $7.1 trillion, have almost twice the economic clout of the poorest four-fifths of humanity, whose combined income is only $3.9 trillion.

However, in spite of their enormous wealth and clout, the Top 200 are net job destroyers — altogether, they employ less than a third of one percent of the world's people. For layoffs, CEOs are paid big bonuses, and they make millions of dollars in the increased value of their stock options after the layoffs are announced.[1]

In a striking illustration of the world's skewed distribution of wealth, Ed Finn of the Canadian Centre for Policy Alternatives, writing in *Canadian Forum* in summer 1997, cited a study conducted in 1996 at Simon Fraser University. The researchers decided to "shrink" the Earth's population to a village of one hundred people, with the relative size of human groups and incomes remaining the same. Said Finn, "They found that, in such a global village, six people would have half the world's wealth, 50 would suffer from malnutrition and 80 would have to live in substandard housing."[2]

In 1995 Canada saw $77.4 billion in corporate mergers and acquisitions, up 60 percent from 1994, which in turn was up by more than 100 percent from 1993 — three record-breaking years in a row. Canadian corporate profits are at a twenty-year high; first quarter profits in 1997 for selected companies hit a record $6.9 billion, up 44 percent from the same period a year earlier.[3] Yet corporations continue to lay off huge numbers of workers and wage increases for remaining workers run far behind the record earnings of corporate CEOs. Since 1975, executive pay has jumped over 100 percent; some CEOs now earn one thousand times more than their workers.

And while ordinary Canadians pay 22 percent more in income tax than they did a decade ago, corporations pay less; they now account for less than 12 percent of all tax revenues collected in Canada.

A third element contributing to concentration in news media ownership is stealth. The amassing of power by only a few has been going on for decades, but not surprisingly has received little coverage in the corporate news media. Warnings on this subject were sounded early — by journalist Carleton McNaught in *Canada Gets the News*, in 1940, and the Royal Commission chaired by newspaper publisher Gratton O'Leary in the early 1960s. Immersed in this gradual but relentless concentration, Canadians are oblivious, not unlike the frog in the pot of water on the stove.

A fourth factor is the myth that journalistic independence from government alone is a necessary and sufficient condition for freedom of the press, which itself is essential to democracy. Indeed, the very meaning of "true press freedom" is limited to the absence of government interference. Hence, by definition, it is not possible for corporations, advertisers, publishers, managers, and so forth to impinge on press freedom.

But this view assumes that the private sector is neutral, benign, and without its own ideologically driven interests to promote — a totally false premise. While maintaining an arm's-length relationship to government is crucial to a free press, it is not enough — we ignore at our peril the corporate relationship to government and the dominant position of big business in our society. And there is an important distinction between preventing undue government influence over news content and having government take reasonable actions to protect the rights of citizens to diverse opinions, particularly in the light of the anti-democratic reality of corporate rule. By ignoring this difference, which is not a subtle one, the media preserve their monopolies from public influence.

A fifth factor is another myth, that of journalists' independence from ownership. Journalists are taught that they are professionals, protected by strong unions, free to practise their profession without undue influence from management. While most working journalists strive to maintain this ideal, it is increasingly difficult to do. Academic and case studies and interviews with working journalists have documented that owners and managers exert tremendous influence over news content, beginning with the hiring and firing process and extending through to sources, editing, and story placement. Sometimes this is subtle, sometimes direct. Journalists are human beings with mortgages and children and a need to keep their jobs. Faced with instructions from the boss, they have little recourse.

And it's not just Conrad Black. John Bassett, when he was publisher of the now defunct Toronto *Telegram*, was asked by a television interviewer, "Is it not true you use your newspaper to push your own political views?" Bassett replied, "Of course. Why else would you want to own a newspaper?"[4]

A sixth element is the claim by owners that they are merely interested in profits, and not in content. The reality is that the two are inseparable. If you eliminate all of the wire services, you won't have a good newspaper, as Ken Thomson has proven. If you have wire copy, and nothing else, the result is similar. Increasingly, profits come at the expense of journalists. It's a simple equation, although they try to make it appear complex: the fewer journalists, the lousier the content.

It's Time for Legislation
Canada is virtually alone in the industrialized world in having no legislation to prevent the concentration of newspaper ownership or cross-media concentration. This should come as no surprise, for the Competition Act, which regulates mergers and acquisitions, was drafted for the Mulroney government by the Competition Policy Task Force of the Business Council on National Issues.

Representing the interests of the 160 most powerful corporations in Canada (many of them branch plants of American transnationals), the BCNI is the most important corporate lobby group in the country. The mother of all special interest groups, the BCNI has been the primary influence behind government policies on trade liberalization, privatization of public assets, deregulation of environmental protection, transportation, tele-communications, investment, and corporate-friendly taxation competition practices.

The BCNI's recommendations were, according to its committee mandate, to "establish a cooperative and mutually supportive approach between the business community and the government on the contentious issues of competition policy in order to ensure that the public interest in having Canadian business compete vigorously in domestic and international markets can be served."[5] Consequently, the mandate of the Competition Bureau, which administers the Competition Act, is very narrow, pitifully inadequate to protect the public interest, and skewed in favour of big business; it can only rule against a merger if the local "commercial" competitiveness of advertisers has been compromised. The Bureau refuses to examine whether editorial and news content diversity will be compromised, whether local news and the use of local reporters and columnists will be diminished, or even if a national chain will be able to control national advertising markets, thereby creating a monopoly and effectively diminishing competition at that level.

We can do no better than to quote once again from Conrad Black, when he was the owner of only one daily newspaper, on the need for legislative action. "The anti-monopoly provisions of the Combines Investigations Act should be applied to the media as zealously as they have been to other industries. It is high time the media divisions of the Power Corporations group, and perhaps the Irving media interests also, had their day in court."[6]

Exacerbating the problem of a weak legislative framework is the fact that public advocacy intervention in Competition Bureau proceedings is discouraged. In fact, when the bureau granted Hollinger control over Southam, it did not even hold public hearings or grant the public access to its written decision. And the Competition Bureau joined the legal counsel of Hollinger to defeat an attempt by the public interest group, the Council of Canadians, to challenge the lack of public participation in the Hollinger decision. Clearly, the federal government, through the Competition Bureau, views newspapers as being no different than widgets; newspapers are simply commercial products to be bought and sold in the open market by corporate interests.

There is no law to prevent Conrad Black from buying every newspaper in Canada and every private radio and television station as well. Even his current level of ownership is unacceptable to the democratic interests of Canadians. Legislation to curb the concentration of media ownership is long overdue.

Countering the Apologists

Media owners and their apologists in academia argue that legislative measures: 1) are unnecessary because we are living in a multimedia universe, with hundreds of diverse voices available over the airwaves and the Internet; 2) are an inevitable development given the economics of a dying newspaper industry which has been outpaced by technology and plagued by inadequate profits; 3) infringe upon their individual rights as proprietors, whose properties were obtained under the legitimate rules of the free market; 4) transgress the Charter guarantee of freedom of the press by allowing public interference with their private property rights.

We have already addressed the first point in the introduction, where we noted the extent of Conrad Black's reach into the broadcasting media of this country, through the Canadian Press, Press News, and Broadcast News services. His daily newspaper content finds its way into all of the broadcasting media of this country and virtually all of our daily newspapers.

As for the World Wide Web and the Internet, these do hold tremendous potential as alternative resources. But as it now stands, there are serious limitations, such as: only about 7.5 percent of

Canadian homes currently have access; many of the news and information sites are (even briefer) rehashes of the news from the mainstream, corporate-run providers; while alternative information is available,[7] searching out this information requires more time than most people have, with the exception of students working on projects, or computer addicts. For the time being, then, the available alternatives are inadequate and inaccessible.

In reference to newspaper economics, we quoted Hollinger's chief financial officer, Jack Boultbee, who says that many Southam properties can be made to realize 35 percent profit margins. This obviously outpaces just about any other industry in the country. Conrad Black is not the "only game in town," as he says, but he is tremendously successful when it comes to acquisitions. The reason? He can usually afford to offer more for newspapers because he implements cost-saving measures that others can't — or wouldn't — even imagine. And the current laws of corporate finance favour people like Conrad Black, who can leverage their next buyout with the last one, a method Black has used for thirty years.

Black describes this low-risk acquisition technique: "[His Eastern Townships Publishing Company] bought the *Sherbrooke Daily Record* for $18,000 in 1969, and the *Record* founded Sterling Newspapers in 1971 and expanded it on the basis of borrowing half the purchase price of acquired newspapers and retiring the rest of the purchase prices as declining balances of sale in the hands of the vendors. I was like the man who went to the horse races and kept winning, parlaying up his initial $2 bet by re-enlisting the winnings in each subsequent race. Apart from years of effort and personal credibility, I was not gambling more than my original $500 in 1966 on the Argus project."[8]

Clearly, then, profits in the newspaper industry, especially in Black's case, are far from inadequate. And rather than being outpaced by technology, newspapers are in on the ground floor of the development of, for example, the Internet and web sites. Newspapers' demise was predicted almost thirty years ago in the

Davey Report, but the end is still nowhere in sight.

As to whether legislation limiting concentration of ownership constitutes an infringement on the rights of newspaper proprietors, it is the case that private, individual property is expropriated in the public interest on a daily basis in this country. There is no reason why fair market value cannot be ensured, as stipulated in the report of Tom Kent's Royal Commission on Newspapers in 1981, in cases where owners have to divest because they do not fall within legislated guidelines.

Regarding a potential violation of freedom of the press, we disagree. The media have a public role and social responsibility that makes them unlike other commercial activities. Freedom of the press is not just the proprietary right of those with the money to buy newspapers as they see fit. It is the right of the Canadian people. To quote from the opening words of the Kent Commission report, "Freedom of the press is not a property right of owners. It is a right of the people. It is part of their right to free expression, inseparable from their right to inform themselves."[9]

What Others Have Done

Other countries and jurisdictions have recognized this basic principle and have developed measures to confront the threat of media ownership concentration.

- The European Commission is proposing legislation to restrict the reach of big media corporations and control the spread of cross-media ownership.

- In Britain, television broadcasters are limited to 15 percent of the national audience. In the case of newspaper mergers, the British Monopolies and Mergers Commission, unlike Canada's Competition Bureau, is required to assess the impact on "the accurate presentation of news and free expression of opinion" when deciding whether or not to approve a merger.

• Sweden has a long-standing press subsidy scheme whereby a diversity of newspapers, not always supported by private corporate advertisers, are provided public financing.

• The Italian Broadcasting Act of 1990 sets concrete limits on media concentration. Under the law, no one person or company may own or control more than 20 percent of all the media.

• In Germany, whenever a merger enables a company to control a specific press market or strengthen its already controlling position, the federal cartel office is required to intervene to prevent the merger. The regulations have been used several times and with some notable success. Most recently, the cartel office prevented Springer from acquiring monopoly control of the Munich newspaper market.

• The French government restricts any group or individual from owning more than 30 percent of the daily press. However, if a company or individual has substantial interests in the broadcast media, it may only control up to 10 percent of the daily press.

• U.S. anti-combines and anti-trust laws have more teeth than our Competition Act. Historically, the U.S. Supreme Court has not allowed the First Amendment guarantee of freedom of the press to be used as a refuge for those who promote concentration and monopolization. A landmark decision in 1945 addressed, in part, the exclusive contract for providing news between the Canadian Press and the Associated Press, an agreement which the U.S. government viewed as monopolistic and in violation of the Sherman Anti-Trust Act. The court agreed. Justice Black (first name Hugo) wrote, in the decision for the majority, "It would be strange indeed however if the grave concern for freedom of the press which prompted adoption of the First Amendment should be read as a command that the government was without power to protect that freedom. The First Amendment, far from providing an argument against application of the [anti-combines] *Sherman Act*, here provides powerful reasons to the contrary. That amendment rests on the assumption that the widest possible dissemination of information from *diverse and antagonistic sources* is essential to the welfare of the public, that a free press is a condition of a free society. Surely a command that the government itself shall not impede the free flow of ideas does not afford non-governmental combinations a refuge if they impose restraints upon that constitutionally guaranteed freedom.

"*Freedom to publish means freedom for all and not for some.* Freedom to publish is guaranteed by the Constitution, but freedom to combine to keep others from publishing is not. Freedom of the press from governmental interference under the First Amendment does not sanction repression of that freedom by private interests. The First Amendment affords not the slightest support for the contention that a combination to restrain trade in news and views has any constitutional immunity."[10] (Emphasis added)

Early in 1997 the U.S. Justice Department forced Toronto-based Thomson Corp. to sell forty-five legal publications before it could acquire West Publishing Co. Thomson agreed to divest its holdings — worth about $200 million — as a response to an anti-trust lawsuit charging that the merged company would have reduced competition in the field of legal journalism. The regulator said the decision was taken "in the public interest."[11]

As well, the U.S. has a Newspaper Preservation Act that authorizes two competitive newspapers to combine all but their news and editorial functions, provided one of them is in financial trouble. As the troubled newspaper revives its fortunes, it is supposed to publish as an independent again. (However, there is some debate over whether these so-called Joint Operating Agreements preserve or inhibit competition. Some see a number of disadvantages to the agreements: they need not be re-examined if the market changes; they protect existing publications from competition from a third paper; they tend to lead to similar, uncompetitive editorial products; and they encourage monopoly, or duopoly, profits.)

Canada is lagging behind the rest of the developed world when it comes to regulating media ownership. This has contributed to concentration levels that make those of other countries pale in comparison. Concentration of media ownership in the U.S., for example, falls far short of the levels reached in Canada. The two largest U.S. newspaper chains, Knight-Ridder and Gannett, each control about 10 percent of national circulation. You have to add up the circulation of eleven American corporations to reach 50 percent of daily newspaper circulation in the U.S., where there is a total of about 1,750 dailies. In Canada, one man controls about 50 percent of English-language daily newspaper circulation, and we have only 105 dailies.

Canada's federal government must take action that has three broad goals: to limit and eventually reverse the current level of media ownership concentration; to provide measures that will promote a diversity of media ownership; and to encourage the media to more effectively live up to their social responsibility and provide a wider range of coverage and content.

Proposals for limiting and reversing media ownership concentration

Specific restrictions on ownership limits are required. However, the Competition Bureau must also take a more active role in protecting the public from the adverse effects of mergers in the media sector. We recommend that:

- the total number of daily newspapers, radio stations, or television stations owned by one company or individual in any province not exceed 50 percent within each medium;

• no one company or individual control more than 25 percent of the circulation of daily newspapers in Canada;

• to limit cross-media ownership concentration, no one person or company own or control more than 20 percent of all the media in the country, or in any one province, region, or city;

• the Competition Act be amended to contain this clause: "The Director of Research and Investigation shall report whether or not a merger involving media interests may potentially operate against the public interest, taking into account all matters which appear in the particular circumstances to be relevant and having regard to the need for accurate presentation of news and free expression of diverse opinion."

Proposals for encouraging diversity of ownership

Limiting the amount of holdings one company can control is an important step toward protecting freedom of expression. However, it will only be effective if accompanied by measures to encourage new owners to enter the market and to promote alternative forms of ownership. There is now considerable evidence available to suggest that a high degree of concentration of ownership makes it virtually impossible for new parties to enter the market. We recommend that:

• legislation be enacted to provide special tax inducements and interest-free loans for the establishment of new newspapers by small local investors, community groups, and non-profit organizations (modelled, for example, on the Canadian Film Development Corporation, which successfully promoted the Canadian film industry facing fierce American competition);

• tax inducements and interest-free loans be provided to encourage employee purchases of media properties;

• full, stable, multi-year funding be restored to the CBC with a renewed mandate clarifying its public service goals.

Proposals for encouraging corporate responsibility and diversity of content

Media concentration breeds a number of dangers: one-dimensional perspectives on major events and debates; information manipulation; and the disappearance of alternative views and opinions. The impact on journalistic independence is particularly troublesome. Fear of layoffs and reprimands from management can put pressure on journalists to self-censor. Moreover, the increasing degree of media concentration is matched by an equally alarming movement toward conglomeration. This occurs as non-media corporations directly or indirectly gain holdings in the media sector, a development that raises the spectre of potential editorial interference. The increasing reach and power of these corporations gives new urgency to concerns about who controls them and whose interests they serve. We recommend that:

• a code of professional practice be established to protect journalists and other media workers from interference by owners;

• in concert with a reform of the current libel law, legislation be enacted to establish a right of reply to inaccurate or misleading reporting (Currently, this is left to the whim of the editor. Black says magnanimously, "We have consistently offered our ideological opponents a full right of reply in our own pages, and this is our principal outlet for pressure groups that feel aggrieved by our treatment of them,"[12] as if this rare and totally arbitrary gesture is a substitute for fair representation in his papers.);

• because the self-regulatory press councils and the Canadian Broadcast Standards Council have often proven to be ineffective in dealing with public complaints about media coverage, an independent and publicly accountable body, a Media Commission, be established to investigate such complaints, report publicly on its findings, and order any redress where it has decided an infraction has occurred;

• media corporations, particularly those involved in other sectors of the economy, be required to provide full details on their ownership holdings as well as a statement of the relationship to be maintained between the editorial department, including the editor and publisher in the case of newspapers, and the corporation;

• as with broadcasters, who are currently required to set aside a small amount of time for public service organizations and community groups, a similar policy be developed whereby daily newspapers would be required to set aside a modest amount of space for community groups and local non-profit organizations. Such a requirement would help ensure more diversity of voices and issues in the press.

These modest legislative proposals would go a long way toward encouraging wider diversity, openness, and choice in our media; they would also start the essential process of rolling back the holdings and power of Conrad Black and other powerful media moguls in Canada. Canadians must press the government to take action.

Conrad Black per se is not the problem. Whatever one might think of Black's actions, he is merely taking advantage of opportunities presented to him under Canadian laws. With his odious methods and views, and his love of the limelight, Black is bringing a great deal of attention to the problem, and may well crystallize opposition and action in a way which less visible and less intrusive personalities such as Ken Thomson or Paul Desmarais would not, were they to exercise a similar degree of control.

While Black alone is not the problem, he has certainly exacerbated the situation. Our laws need to be changed to rectify the general problem of media concentration and the problems related to the particular example of Conrad Black and Barbara Amiel.

A Citizens' Agenda

Meanwhile, those of us concerned about the relentless rightward tilt of the mainstream press in Canada must find ways to influence the process. We must recognize the difficulty of demanding legislative changes from the federal Liberals, who are closely allied to the corporate power brokers inside the media and elsewhere and are not likely any time soon to bite the financial hand that feeds them. We remember the outcome of the Kent Commission, which made a number of similar suggestions and was stillborn due to political machinations arising out of the very power infrastructure it had no mandate to address.

But the citizens of Canada ultimately hold the key to the type of society we want. When we as a society realize the nature and extent of the problems created by corporate domination of our news media, we will come together and foster meaningful change in our democratic interest. We have justice and legitimacy on our side. They have only greed and self-interest.

As citizens, we can support or start newspapers and radio stations and put forward alternatives to the monoculture of values and ideologies that currently dominate the media. We should explore the public, community ownership of local newspapers, in place of, or in addition to, absentee chain ownership; they would be self-financing and established at arm's length from local councils, and overseen by a broadly representative board of citizens, who would hire an editorial board and give it independent autonomy. If communities can own local hockey arenas, why not newspapers?

The pension funds of unionized Canadian workers now stand at almost $400 billion — the kind of investment capital that could start a new national daily in this country, or buy radio stations, if the holders would see fit to use the funds in this way. Rather than investing these funds in gold "finds" in brutal dictatorships like Indonesia, these funds could go into socially responsible projects like local newspapers.

Further, the groups that have come together to form the Campaign for Press and Broadcasting Freedom could set up an independent Citizens' Commission on Media Concentration, composed of working journalists, academics, and other concerned citizens, to hold hearings, conduct studies, and report their findings, to the Canadian people. Such a commission might also consider the advantages of a professional association of journalists that would provide editors, managing editors, and those who guide the newspaper's editorial content, with national guidelines, long-term contracts, and guaranteed non-interference from publishers and owners.

It is time for Canadians to choose their nation's future. Conrad Black, Barbara Amiel, and their collaborators are clear in their own vision, and now have sufficient control of our news media to impose it. The challenge, for those of us who hold a profoundly different, more equitable and diverse vision of our nation's future, is to take action.

NOTES

Prologue

  1 C. M. Black, F. David Radler, and Peter G. White, "A Brief to the Special Senate Committee on the Mass Media from the Sherbrooke *Record*, the voice of the Eastern Townships," November 7, 1969, p. 10.

  2 Ibid., p. 4.

  3 Ibid., p. 28.

  4 Conrad Black, *A Life in Progress* (Toronto: Key Porter Books, 1993), p. 51.

  5 Quoted in *The Toronto Star*, May 28, 1997.

  6 *The Ottawa Citizen*, May 28, 1997.

1/ Citizen Black

  1 Figures provided by Gerry Fairbridge of the Canadian Press office in Toronto, April 3, 1997.

  2 This information was provided by Norm Graham of the Canadian Press office in Toronto, April 3, 1997.

  3 This information is taken from the CBC World Wide Web Site Map, in April 1997. (http://www.cbc.ca/commnhtm.webmap.html)

  4 *The Globe and Mail*, September 9, 1995.

  5 Peter C. Newman, *The Establishment Man* (Toronto: Seal Books, 1983).

  6 Conrad Black, *A Life in Progress* (Toronto: Key Porter Books, 1993), p. 36.

  7 Ibid., p. 504.

  8 Ibid., p. 393.

  9 Ibid., p. 371.

10 Richard Siklos, *Shades of Black: Conrad Black and the World's Fastest Growing Press Empire* (Toronto: William Heinemann Canada, 1995), p. 43.

11 Quoted in *The Globe and Mail*, February 27, 1997.

12 Quoted in *The Financial Post*, April 25, 1995.

13 Reported in *The Jerusalem Post*, January 17, 1997.

14 Ibid.

15 Quoted in *The (Montreal) Gazette*, March 9, 1993.

16 Quoted in *The Globe and Mail*, October 8, 1996.

17 *The Globe and Mail*, March 1, 1997.

18 Quoted in *Frank* magazine, April 1, 1997.

19 Quoted in *The Toronto Star*, August 31, 1996.
20 See Mordecai Richler, "Of Scots, Quebecers and a gaffe-prone Parizeau," *The Windsor Star*, May 5, 1997, p. A6.
21 Black, p. 424.
22 *The Financial Post*, October 26, 1990.
23 Black, pp. 424–426.
24 Ibid., p. 467.
25 Ibid., pp. 467–468.
26 Ibid., p. 468.
27 Ibid., p. 469.
28 *The Globe and Mail*, March 5, 1997.
29 *The Globe and Mail*, April 24, 1997.
30 Quoted in *The Toronto Star*, August 31, 1996.
31 Black, p. 51.
32 Ibid., p. 125.
33 Ibid., p. 374.
34 *The Financial Post*, October 11, 1991.
35 *The Financial Post*, October 26, 1996.
36 Quoted from "The Paper King," *The National News Magazine* (CBC-TV), October 21 and 22, 1996.
37 *Maclean's*, November 25, 1991.
38 *The Ottawa Citizen*, August 21, 1996.
39 *The Globe and Mail*, May 1, 1997.
40 Quoted from CBC Ontario's *Radio Noon* program, May 31, 1996.
41 *Maclean's*, June 17, 1996.
42 *The Globe and Mail*, April 22, 1997.
43 *Maclean's*, June 10, 1996.
44 *The Globe and Mail*, April 23, 1997.
45 Black, p. 314.
46 The Southam Inc. Annual Report, 1996, p. 6.
47 Quoted in James Winter, *Democracy's Oxygen: How Corporations Control the News* (Montreal: Black Rose Books, 1996), p. 94.
48 These conclusions obtained from Jim McKenzie, "Content Analysis of the Regina Leader-Post under Hollinger Ownership," School of Journalism and Communications, University of Regina, December 1996, p. 21.
49 Ibid., p. 21.
50 *The Globe and Mail*, May 8, 1996.
51 This national campaign was sponsored in the spring of 1977 by the Communications, Energy and Paperworkers Union, the Newspaper Guild, the Canadian Media Guild, Friends of Canadian Broadcasting, the Canadian Teachers' Federation, the Ontario Secondary School Teachers' Federation, the B.C. Teachers' Federation, the Canadian Labour Congress, Rural Dignity, the Canadian Union of Postal Workers, the Saskatchewan Federation of Labour, the B.C. Federation of Labour, the Council of Canadians, the National Farmers' Union, the Jesuit Centre for Social Faith and Justice, GCIU, the Canadian Union of Public Employees, the National

Anti-Poverty Organization, the Periodical Writers Association of Canada, the Writers Union, ACTRA, the Assembly of First Nations, the Canadian Autoworkers (CAW), MediaWatch, and the Action Canada Network.

52 Linda McQuaig, *Shooting the Hippo: Death by Deficit and Other Canadian Myths* (Toronto: Viking, 1995), p. 12.

53 Canadian Daily Newspaper Association, *Statement of Principles.* Adopted in 1977, revised in 1995. Revised version adopted by the Canadian Newspaper Association. Of interest is the fact that the 1977 version read, "Conflicts of interest, and the appearance of conflicts of interest, must be avoided. Outside interests that could affect, or appear to affect, the newspaper's freedom to report the news impartially should be avoided." This was in effect for eighteen years, but was excised from the revised version in 1995.

54 White wrote on February 26, 1997, to say, "Our country desperately needs a strong and effective alternative voice to the Liberals."

55 Black, p. 165.

56 Black describes this as "a costly operation to which I made a significant contribution." Ibid., p. 309.

57 Ibid., p. 312.

58 Ibid., p. 163.

59 Ibid., p. 322. Black notes that he has known Turner since 1963, and that Turner's wife Geills Kilgour is his father's goddaughter, whom he has known all his life.

60 Quoted in Newman, pp. 272–273.

61 Black, p. 504.

62 Ibid, p. 51.

63 See, for example, Linda McQuaig, *Shooting the Hippo: Death by Deficit and Other Canadian Myths* (Toronto: Viking, 1995), or Noam Chomsky, *Deterring Democracy* (New York: Verso, 1991), or for that matter Maude Barlow and Bruce Campbell, *Straight Through the Heart: How the Liberals Abandoned the Just Society* (Toronto: HarperCollins, 1995); Maude Barlow and Heather-jane Robertson, *Class Warfare: The Assault on Canada's Schools* (Toronto: Key Porter Books, 1994); James Winter, *Democracy's Oxygen: How Corporations Control the News* (Montreal: Black Rose Books, 1996); or James Winter, *Common Cents: Media Portrayal of the Gulf War and Other Events* (Montreal: Black Rose Books, 1992).

64 Quoted in *The (Montreal) Gazette*, November 4, 1993.

2/ *Wanting to Be Liked*

1 Quoted in Richard Siklos, *Shades of Black: Conrad Black and the World's Fastest Growing Press Empire* (Toronto: William Heinemann Canada, 1995), p. 36.

2 Quoted in Siklos, p. 40.

3 Siklos, p. 400.

4 Quoted in Siklos, p. 35.

5 Quoted in Scott Disher, "Conrad Black, Press Lord Redux," *Books in Canada*, Summer 1996, p. 30.
6 Conrad Black, *A Life in Progress* (Toronto: Key Porter Books, 1993), p. 22.
7 Quoted in Siklos, p. 227.
8 Siklos, p. 396.
9 Quoted in Siklos, p. 227.
10 Black, p. 38.
11 Ibid., p. 184.
12 Ibid., p. 92.
13 Ibid.
14 Siklos, p. 399.
15 Quoted in Siklos, p. 45.
16 Black, p. 140.
17 Quoted in Peter C. Newman, *The Establishment Man* (Toronto: Seal Books, 1983), p. 191.
18 Black, p. 417.
19 Ibid., p. 402.
20 Ibid., p. 401.
21 Ibid., p. 506.
22 *The Financial Post*, November 25, 1988.
23 Quoted in Siklos, p. 40.
24 Ibid., p. 398.
25 Quoted in *The (Montreal) Gazette*, November 4, 1993.
26 Black, p. 79.
27 Ibid., p. 81.
28 Ibid., p. 185.
29 Quoted in Siklos, p. 275.
30 Ibid., pp. 275–276.
31 Black, p. 461.
32 Quoted in Siklos, p. 277.
33 Ibid. pp. 277–278.
34 Ibid., p. 281.
35 Barbara Amiel, *Confessions* (Toronto: Totem Books, 1981), p. 41.
36 Quoted in Siklos, p. 281.
37 Barbara Amiel, interviewed on the CBC Television program, *Authors*, Toronto, 1980.
38 Siklos, p. 282.
39 *Maclean's*, May 25, 1987.
40 Ibid.
41 Ibid.
42 Amiel, p. 99.
43 *Maclean's*, May 25, 1987.
44 *The Windsor Star*, March 3, 1997.
45 Amiel, pp. 56–57.
46 *Maclean's*, May 25, 1987.
47 Quoted in James Winter, *Democracy's Oxygen: How Corporations*

Control the News (Montreal: Black Rose Books, 1996), p. 41.
48 Quoted in Siklos, p. 283.
49 Ibid.
50 Ibid.
51 Barbara Amiel, interviewed on the CBC Television program, *Authors*, Toronto, 1980.
52 Siklos, p. 283.

3/ To the Manner Born

1 Peter C. Newman, *The Establishment Man* (Toronto: Seal Books, 1983), p. 263.
2 From *Report Card 1996*, produced by Campaign 2000, a national coalition of child advocacy organizations in Canada.
3 Newman, p. 263.
4 Conrad Black, *A Life in Progress* (Toronto: Key Porter Books, 1993), p. 175.
5 Ibid., p. 20.
6 Ibid., p. 144.
7 *The Financial Post*, May 29, 1989.
8 Black, p. 142.
9 Ibid., p. 189.
10 Ibid., p. 48.
11 Ibid., p. 173.
12 Ibid., pp. 170, 171.
13 Ibid., p. 185.
14 Ibid., p. 196.
15 Ibid., p. 341.
16 Ibid., p. 465.
17 Ibid., p. 251.
18 Ibid., p. 310.
19 Ibid., p. 307.
20 Ibid., p. 80.
21 Ibid., p. 226.
22 Barbara Amiel, *Confessions* (Toronto: Totem Books, 1981), p. 3.
23 Ibid., pp. 100, 101.
24 Ibid., p. 110.
25 *Chatelaine*, November 1985.
26 *Maclean's*, July 31, 1995.
27 Black, pp. 300, 301.
28 *Maclean's*, January 4, 1993.
29 Amiel, p. 34.
30 Black, p. 8.
31 *Canadian Business*, November 1991.
32 Black, p. 371.
33 *The Financial Post*, October 26, 1990.
34 *Maclean's*, August 1, 1994.

35 *The Financial Post*, November 13, 1993.
36 Quoted in *The Toronto Star*, June 28, 1989.
37 Quoted in *The Financial Post*, October 1, 1994.
38 Richard Siklos, *Shades of Black: Conrad Black and the World's Fastest Growing Press Empire* (Toronto: William Heinemann Canada, 1995), p. 232.
39 Black, p. 460.
40 Siklos, p. 389.
41 *Maclean's*, January 13, 1997.
42 From Black's address to the Fraser Institute, August 1988, printed in *Canadian Speeches*, November 1988.
43 Quoted in *Maclean's*, November 15, 1993.
44 *Maclean's*, October 23, 1989.
45 *Maclean's*, January 22, 1996.
46 *Maclean's*, March 7, 1988.
47 *The Financial Post*, May 9, 1988.
48 Black, p. 395.
49 *The Financial Post*, March 24, 1988.
50 Ibid.
51 Black, p. 279.
52 Ibid., pp. 279, 280.
53 *Maclean's*, February 24, 1992.
54 *Maclean's*, April 3, 1995.
55 Black, p. 420.
56 Ibid., p. 133.
57 Ibid., p. 299.
58 *Maclean's*, January 4, 1993.
59 Amiel, p. 71.
60 Black, p. 475.
61 Amiel, p. 66.
62 *Maclean's*, March 14, 1983.
63 Amiel, p. 35.
64 *Maclean's*, March 14, 1983.
65 *Compass*, Summer 1987.
66 Black, p. 105.
67 *The (Montreal) Gazette*, November 4, 1993.
68 Black, p. 465.
69 *The (Montreal) Gazette*, November 4, 1993.
70 *The Financial Post*, November 30, 1988.
71 Ibid.
72 Amiel, p. 234.
73 *Maclean's*, February 4, 1991.
74 *Maclean's*, September 27, 1982.
75 Black, p. 153.
76 *Maclean's*, August 26, 1991.

4/ Business Is War

1 Quoted in *The (Montreal) Gazette*, November 4, 1993.
2 Conrad Black, *A Life in Progress* (Toronto: Key Porter Books, 1993), p. 25, 26.
3 Richard Siklos, *Shades of Black: Conrad Black and the World's Fastest Growing Press Empire* (Toronto: William Heinemann Canada, 1995), p. 391.
4 *Canadian Business*, November 24, 1991.
5 Siklos, p. 390.
6 Peter C. Newman, *The Establishment Man* (Toronto: Seal Books, 1983), p. 145.
7 Quoted in *Maclean's*, May 11, 1992.
8 Black, pp. 214, 215.
9 Quoted in *The (Montreal) Gazette*, November 4, 1993.
10 Black, pp. 218, 219.
11 Ibid., p. 220.
12 Ibid., p. 239.
13 Ibid., p. 238.
14 Ibid., p. 240.
15 Ibid., p. 253.
16 Ibid., p. 262.
17 Ibid., p. 266.
18 Quoted in *Maclean's*, August 1, 1994.
19 Black, p. 467.
20 Ibid., pp. 286, 287.
21 Ibid., p. 295.
22 Ibid., pp. 218, 325.
23 Ibid., p. 357.
24 Ibid., pp. 354, 355.
25 Ibid., p. 326.
26 Ibid., p. 358.
27 Ibid., pp. 123, 124.
28 *The Financial Post*, September 2, 1991.
29 Black, p. 316.
30 Ibid., p. 360.
31 Ibid., p. 361.
32 *Maclean's*, July 29, 1991.
33 *Maclean's*, September 9, 1996.
34 *Maclean's*, May 1, 1995.
35 Ibid.
36 *Maclean's*, March 4, 1991.
37 Ibid.
38 *The Nation*, March 11, 1991.
39 *Maclean's*, November 5, 1990.
40 *Maclean's*, March 4, 1991.
41 *Maclean's*, June 28, 1982.

42 *The Vancouver Sun*, January 17, 1997.

43 *Maclean's*, March 29, 1982.

44 Black, p. 65.

45 Ibid., pp. 156, 157.

46 Ibid., p. 158.

47 Ibid., p. 268.

48 Ibid., p. 48.

49 *Maclean's*, June 10, 1985.

50 *Maclean's*, November 23, 1981.

51 Ibid.

52 *Maclean's*, March 1, 1993.

53 *Maclean's*, November 10, 1980.

54 Hollinger Inc. Annual Report, 1996, p. 8.

55 *The Ottawa Sun*, June 27, 1997.

5/ News Without Journalists

1 Quoted in Richard Siklos, *Shades of Black: Conrad Black and the World's Fastest Growing Press Empire* (Toronto: William Heinemann Canada, 1995), p. 24.

2 Conrad Black, *A Life in Progress* (Toronto: Key Porter Books, 1993), p. 17.

3 Nicholas Coleridge, *Paper Tigers*, cited in Scott Disher, "Conrad Black, Press Lord Redux," *Books in Canada*, Summer 1996, pp. 30–38.

4 Quoted in Siklos, p. 21.

5 Black, pp. 123–124.

6 Ibid., p. 124.

7 Quoted in Siklos, p. 34.

8 Black, p. 326.

9 Ibid., p. 418.

10 Ibid., p. 420.

11 Ibid., p. 415.

12 Ibid., p. 416.

13 Ibid.

14 *The Financial Post*, June 25, 1991.

15 Quoted in *The Globe and Mail*, August 15, 1991.

16 Quoted in *The Financial Post*, April 22, 1994.

17 *The Financial Post*, May 22, 1992.

18 *The Financial Post*, September 10, 1990.

19 *The Globe and Mail*, February 21, 1995.

20 *The Financial Post*, February 26, 1988.

21 Black, p. 406.

22 C. M. Black, F. David Radler, and Peter G. White, "A Brief to the Special Senate Committee on the Mass Media from the Sherbrooke *Record*, the voice of the Eastern Townships," November 7, 1969, p. 16.

23 From a transcript of Black's speech to the Canadian Association of Journalists (CAJ), Chateau Laurier Hotel, Ottawa, April 9, 1994.

24 Quoted in *The Globe and Mail*, March 1, 1997.

25 Black, p. 464.
26 Ibid., p. 472.
27 Ibid., p. 513.
28 Quoted in *The Vancouver Sun*, March 7, 1997.
29 Quoted in *The Globe and Mail*, October 2, 1996.
30 Southam Inc. Annual Report, 1996, p. 5.
31 *Maclean's*, January 27, 1992.
32 Barbara Amiel, *Confessions* (Toronto: Totem Books, 1981), p. 78.
33 From Black's address to the Fraser Institute, August 1988, printed in *Canadian Speeches*, November 1988.
34 Black, p. 396.
35 *Maclean's*, February 20, 1984.
36 *The Globe and Mail*, May 6, 1997.
37 Black, p. 405.
38 Ibid., p. 51.
39 Ibid., p. 71.
40 Ibid.
41 Ibid., p. 73.
42 Ibid.
43 Ibid., p. 77.
44 Black et al., p. 12.
45 Quoted in *Maclean's*, February 3, 1992.
46 *Report on Business* magazine, August 1994.
47 *The Globe and Mail*, July 28, 1995.
48 Quoted in Siklos, p. 198.
49 Quoted in *Report on Business* magazine, August 1994.
50 Siklos, p. 209.
51 Black, pp. 393–394.
52 Ibid., p. 70.
53 *Report on Business* magazine, October 1993.
54 *The Financial Post*, September 18, 1991.
55 Black, p. 120.
56 Ibid., pp. 120–121.
57 Ibid., p. 490.
58 *The (Montreal) Gazette*, November 13, 1992.
59 Black, p. 491.
60 Ibid., pp. 490–491.
61 Quoted in *The Globe and Mail*, October 8, 1992.
62 Quoted in *The Globe and Mail*, May 6, 1997.
63 Black et al., p. 73.
64 Siklos, p. 347.
65 *Maclean's*, October 3, 1994.
66 Black, p. 399.
67 Quoted in Siklos, p. 212.
68 Siklos, p. 367.
69 This account is drawn from a review of Richard Siklos's biography of

Black. The review is by Scott Disher, "Conrad Black, Press Lord Redux," *Books in Canada*, Summer 1996, pp. 30–38.
70 *The Globe and Mail*, May 1, 1996.
71 *The Globe and Mail*, May 8, 1996.
72 Black, p. 71.
73 Ibid., p. 51.
74 *Maclean's*, October 23, 1989.
75 Siklos, p. 336.

6/ Vampire Journalism

1 Conrad Black, *A Life in Progress* (Toronto: Key Porter Books, 1993), p. 504.
2 C. M. Black, F. David Radler, and Peter G. White, "A Brief to the Special Senate Committee on the Mass Media from the Sherbrooke *Record*, the voice of the Eastern Townships," November 7, 1969, p. 1.
3 Ibid., p. 2.
4 Ibid.
5 Ibid.
6 Ibid., p. 3.
7 Ibid., p. 4.
8 Quoted in *The Vancouver Sun*, March 7, 1997.
9 Black et al., p. 26.
10 Black, *A Life in Progress*, p. 332.
11 Ibid., pp. 385–386.
12 *The Financial Post*, May 9, 1988.
13 Quoted in *Maclean's*, April 15, 1993.
14 Quoted in *The Toronto Star*, May 30, 1996, p. B1.
15 Quoted in *The Toronto Star*, May 30, 1996, p. B18.
16 Quoted in *Maclean's*, June 10, 1996.
17 Black, *A Life in Progress*, p. 501.
18 Black et al., p. 5.
19 Quoted in *The Globe and Mail*, May 6, 1997.
20 Black, *A Life in Progress*, pp. 376–377.
21 Black et al., p. 12.
22 *Maclean's*, April 15, 1985.
23 Black et al., p. 7.
24 Barbara Amiel, *Confessions* (Toronto: Totem Books, 1981), p. 142.
25 *Maclean's*, November 26, 1984.
26 *Maclean's*, December 31, 1990.
27 Ibid.
28 *Maclean's*, February 1, 1993.
29 Black et al., p. 8.
30 Ibid., p. 14.
31 *Maclean's*, February 18, 1985.
32 Black et al., p. 20.
33 *The Financial Post*, October 26, 1996.

34 Ibid.
35 *The Financial Post*, October 14, 1995.
36 Black et al., pp. 16, 17, 19.
37 *The Financial Post*, July 18, 1991.
38 *The Financial Post*, February 6, 1991.
39 *Maclean's*, April 29, 1991.
40 *Maclean's*, February 8, 1988.
41 *Maclean's*, April 29, 1991.
42 Ibid.
43 Amiel, p. 80.
44 Ibid., p. 78.
45 *The Financial Post*, February 26, 1994.
46 Amiel, pp. 77–78.
47 Ibid., pp. 69–70.
48 Ibid., p. 71.
49 Ibid., p. 79.
50 Ibid., pp. 76–77.
51 *Maclean's*, April 28, 1986.
52 *Maclean's*, June 23, 1986.
53 Ibid.
54 *Maclean's*, April 28, 1986.
55 *Maclean's*, February 19, 1996.
56 Black et al., p. 23.
57 Ibid., p. 25.
58 Siklos, p. 58.
59 Ibid., p. 67.
60 Quoted in Black, *A Life in Progress*, p. 182.
61 Ibid.
62 Ibid., pp. 345–346.
63 Ibid., p. 365.
64 Tom Kent, *The (Montreal) Gazette*, March 9, 1993.
65 Conrad Black, *The (Montreal) Gazette*, March 9, 1993.
66 Black et al., p. 10.
67 Conrad Black, "A view of the press," *Carleton Journalism Review*, Winter 1979–80.
68 Black, *A Life in Progress*, pp. 74–75.
69 From a transcript of Black's speech to the Canadian Association of Journalists (CAJ), Chateau Laurier Hotel, Ottawa, April 9, 1994.
70 *The Financial Post*, (letters), July 18, 1989.
71 Quoted in Richard Siklos, *Shades of Black: Conrad Black and the World's Fastest Growing Press Empire* (Toronto: William Heinemann Canada, 1995), p. 293.
72 Ibid.
73 Ibid., p. 294.
74 Amiel, p. 41.
75 Amiel, p. 68.

76 Southam Inc. Annual Report, 1996, p. 8.
77 Quoted in *The Globe and Mail*, October 2, 1996.
78 Ibid.
79 Quoted in *Canadian Business*, July 1996.
80 Ibid.
81 Quoted in *The Toronto Star*, May 30, 1996.
82 Quoted in Siklos, pp. 292–293.
83 Black, *A Life in Progress*, p. 388.
84 Ibid., p. 387.
85 From Black's speech to the CAJ, April 9, 1994.
86 Quoted in Siklos, p. 337.
87 Siklos, p. 337.
88 Black, *A Life in Progress*, p. 450.
89 Quoted in Siklos, p. 337.
90 Black, *A Life in Progress*, p. 388.
91 Ibid., pp. 389, 396.
92 Ibid., p. 396.
93 Ibid., p. 389.
94 Siklos, p. 399.
95 Quoted in *The Globe and Mail*, October 8, 1992.
96 From Black's speech to the CAJ, April 9, 1994.
97 Ibid.
98 Ibid.
99 From Black's address to the Fraser Institute, August 1988, printed in *Canadian Speeches*, November 1988.
100 *The Financial Post*, May 19, 1988.
101 *The Financial Post*, May 9, 1988.
102 Quoted in *The Globe and Mail*, June 6, 1996.
103 *Maclean's*, February 3, 1992.
104 "Chairman's Report," Southam Inc. Annual Report, 1996.
105 Black, *A Life in Progress*, p. 435.
106 From Black's speech to the CAJ, April 9, 1994.
107 Conrad Black, *The (Montreal) Gazette*, March 9, 1993.
108 Tom Kent, *The (Montreal) Gazette*, March 9, 1993.
109 *The Toronto Star*, November 15, 1992.
110 Quoted in Siklos, p. 199.
111 From Black's speech to the CAJ, April 9, 1994.
112 Ibid.

7/ The Tyranny of Feminism

1 *The Ottawa Citizen*, November 24, 1996.
2 Quoted in *Chatelaine*, November 1989.
3 *Maclean's*, August 28, 1995.
4 *Maclean's*, January 16, 1989.
5 *Maclean's*, December 23, 1985.
6 *Chatelaine*, November, 1985.

7 *Maclean's*, August 23, 1993.
8 *The Ottawa Citizen*, November 24, 1996.
9 *Maclean's*, October 23, 1995.
10 *Maclean's*, October 13, 1990.
11 Conrad Black, *A Life in Progress* (Toronto: Key Porter Books, 1993), p. 84.
12 Ibid., p. 152.
13 Ibid., p. 46.
14 *Maclean's*, January 13, 1992.
15 *The Daily Telegraph*, December 31, 1992.
16 Black, p. 463.
17 Ibid., p. 464.
18 Barbara Amiel, *Confessions* (Toronto: Totem Books, 1981), p. 129.
19 *Maclean's*, May 25, 1987.
20 Amiel, p. 136.
21 Ibid., p. 135.
22 *Maclean's*, February 23, 1987.
23 *Maclean's*, September 7, 1980.
24 Amiel, p. 14.
25 *Maclean's*, September 7, 1980.
26 *Maclean's*, April 11, 1994.
27 *Maclean's*, May 9, 1983.
28 *Maclean's*, October 8, 1979.
29 Amiel, p. 140.
30 *Maclean's*, January 7, 1980.
31 *Maclean's*, August 28, 1995.
32 *Maclean's*, July 26, 1993.
33 *Maclean's*, April 15, 1996.
34 *Maclean's*, October 18, 1993.
35 *The Toronto Star*, November 3, 1993.
36 *Maclean's*, August 5, 1985.
37 From Black's address to the Canadian Club of Toronto, October 1992, printed in *Canadian Speeches*, January 1993.
38 Black, pp. 513–514.
39 *Maclean's*, October 28, 1991.
40 *Maclean's*, March 29, 1993.
41 Black, p. 514.
42 *Maclean's*, August 23, 1993.
43 *Maclean's*, November 10, 1996.
44 *The Ottawa Citizen*, April 20, 1997.
45 *Maclean's*, October 29, 1984.
46 *Maclean's*, August 22, 1988.
47 *Maclean's*, July 4, 1979.
48 *Maclean's*, September 3, 1984.
49 *Maclean's*, September 14, 1983.
50 *Maclean's*, April 19, 1989.
51 *The Ottawa Citizen*, June 14, 1997.

52 *Maclean's*, October 26, 1982.

53 *Maclean's*, July 11, 1994.

54 *Maclean's*, July 31, 1989.

55 *Maclean's*, August 23, 1993.

56 *Maclean's*, October 31, 1994.

57 *Maclean's*, March 6, 1995.

58 Amiel, p. 42.

59 *The Hamilton Spectator*, September 21, 1996.

60 *The Financial Post*, February 22, 1988.

61 *The Financial Post*, March 14, 1988.

62 *Maclean's*, July 30, 1979.

63 *Maclean's*, April 14, 1980.

64 *Maclean's*, July 9, 1984.

65 *The Ottawa Citizen*, November 3, 1996.

66 *Maclean's*, June 6, 1994.

67 *The Ottawa Citizen*, November 17, 1996.

68 *The Ottawa Citizen*, February 16, 1997.

69 *Maclean's*, September 30, 1985.

70 *Maclean's*, December 8, 1996.

71 Ibid.

8/ *Malevolent Minorities*

1 *Maclean's*, July 9, 1984.

2 Ibid.

3 *Maclean's*, November 20, 1995.

4 *Maclean's*, March 13, 1989.

5 *Maclean's*, May 27, 1991.

6 *The Financial Post*, November 6, 1993.

7 Conrad Black, *A Life in Progress* (Toronto: Key Porter Books, 1993), p. 390.

8 *Maclean's*, December 31, 1990.

9 Barbara Amiel, *Confessions* (Toronto: Totem Books, 1981), p. 221.

10 Ibid., p. 115.

11 *The Ottawa Citizen*, September 15, 1996.

12 *Maclean's*, February 17, 1997.

13 Amiel, p. 170.

14 *Maclean's*, June 24, 1991.

15 Amiel, p. 165.

16 Ibid., p. 67.

17 *Maclean's*, November 26, 1984.

18 Amiel, p. 167.

19 Ibid., p. 139.

20 *Maclean's*, September 5, 1994.

21 *The Ottawa Citizen*, December 15, 1996.

22 *Maclean's*, April 4, 1977.

23 Amiel, pp. 205, 213.

24 *Maclean's*, April 3, 1995.
25 *Maclean's*, October 28, 1985.
26 Ibid.
27 Black, p. 127.
28 *The Financial Post*, February 23, 1989.
29 *Maclean's*, May 14, 1984.
30 *Maclean's*, August 8, 1986.
31 *Maclean's*, May 14, 1984.
32 Quoted in *Maclean's*, May 14, 1984.
33 *Maclean's*, November 20, 1989.
34 Amiel, p. 128.
35 *Maclean's*, February 3, 1986.
36 *Maclean's*, September 2, 1985.
37 Black, pp. 493, 494.
38 Ibid., p. 497.
39 *Maclean's*, November 22, 1982.
40 *Maclean's*, April 15, 1985.
41 *Maclean's*, March 3, 1986.
42 *The Toronto Sun*, February 2, 1997.
43 *Maclean's*, November 26, 1984.
44 Amiel, pp. 11, 12.
45 Ibid., p. 94.
46 Ibid., p. 95.
47 *Maclean's*, October 23, 1995.
48 *Maclean's*, May 18, 1992.
49 *Maclean's*, September 9, 1996.
50 Amiel, pp. 185–187.
51 Ibid., p. 94.
52 From Black's speech to the Canadian Club of Toronto, October 1992, printed in *Canadian Speeches*, January 1993.
53 Amiel, p. 37.
54 *Maclean's*, February 5, 1979.
55 Amiel, pp. 228, 229.
56 Ibid., p. 229.
57 *Maclean's*, April 11, 1983.
58 Ibid.
59 Amiel, p. 160.
60 Ibid., p. 162.
61 Ibid.
62 *Maclean's*, September 10, 1990.

9/ The Canadian Wasteland

1 *Maclean's*, January 17, 1994.
2 Conrad Black, *A Life in Progress* (Toronto: Key Porter Books, 1993), p. 398.
3 *The Financial Post*, September 10, 1990.

4 *Maclean's*, October 2, 1990.
5 Barbara Amiel, *Confessions* (Toronto: Totem Books, 1981), p. 131.
6 *Maclean's*, March 19, 1984.
7 Black, p. 507.
8 Quoted in *The Toronto Star*, November 12, 1994.
9 *The Globe and Mail*, February 21, 1995.
10 *The Financial Post*, February 6, 1991.
11 Black, p. 507.
12 *The Globe and Mail*, November 3, 1993.
13 *The Financial Post*, May 22, 1992.
14 *Maclean's*, March 19, 1984.
15 Amiel, p. 120.
16 Ibid., p. 118.
17 *Maclean's*, December 20, 1982.
18 Black, p. 113.
19 *The Financial Post*, August 13, 1991.
20 From Black's speech to a combined meeting of the Canada and Empire Clubs, reported in National Citizens' Coalition newsletter, *Consensus*, December 1993.
21 *Maclean's*, October 18, 1993.
22 *The Financial Post*, May 22, 1992.
23 *Maclean's*, November 5, 1979.
24 *Maclean's*, November 15, 1993.
25 *Maclean's*, October 8, 1990.
26 *Maclean's*, September 25, 1989.
27 From Black's address to the Fraser Institute, August 1988, printed in *Canadian Speeches*, November 1988.
28 Quoted in Peter C. Newman, *The Establishment Man* (Toronto: Seal Books, 1983), pp. 166, 167.
29 *The Financial Post*, August 13, 1991.
30 *Maclean's*, January 23, 1984.
31 *Maclean's*, January 17, 1994.
32 *Maclean's*, December 23, 1991.
33 Amiel, p. 146.
34 *The Financial Post*, May 17, 1989.
35 From Black's address to the Canadian Club of Toronto, October 1992, printed in *Canadian Speeches*, January 1993.
36 *The Financial Post*, November 18, 1988.
37 *The (Halifax) Chronicle-Herald*, October 1, 1993.
38 Amiel, p. 87.
39 Ibid., pp. 29, 30, 31.
40 *Maclean's*, December 18, 1995.
41 *The Ottawa Citizen*, December 2, 1996.
42 *Maclean's*, July 21, 1986.
43 *The Ottawa Citizen*, November 3, 1996.
44 Amiel, pp. 73, 74.

45 *The Financial Post*, September 10, 1990.
46 *The Financial Post*, September 10, 1990; *The Financial Post,* June 25, 1991; *The Globe and Mail*, August 15, 1991.
47 Black, p. 416.
48 *The Financial Post*, September 10, 1990.
49 *The Financial Post*, August 3, 1991.
50 *The Financial Post*, July 18, 1991.
51 *The Financial Post*, September 18, 1991.
52 *Maclean's*, April 20, 1992.
53 *Maclean's*, February 24, 1992.
54 *The Financial Post*, September 2, 1991.
55 From Black's address to the Canadian Club of Toronto, October 1992.
56 *Maclean's*, January 17, 1994.
57 *The Financial Post*, June 25, 1991.
58 Black, p. 415.
59 *The (Halifax) Chronicle-Herald*, June 20, 1992.
60 *Calgary Herald*, June 22, 1991.
61 *Maclean's*, May 24, 1993.
62 *Calgary Herald*, June 22, 1991.
63 *The Financial Post*, August 13, 1991.
64 *The Financial Post*, October 11, 1991.
65 From Black's address to the Canadian Club of Toronto, October 1992.
66 Black, pp. 91–92.
67 *The Globe and Mail*, November 7, 1995.
68 *The Financial Post*, February 23, 1989.
69 *The Globe and Mail*, November 7, 1995.
70 *The Ottawa Citizen*, January 28, 1997.
71 *The Globe and Mail*, November 7, 1995.
72 *Saturday Night*, September 1990.
73 Black, p. 130.
74 *The Globe and Mail*, October 27, 1995.
75 *The Financial Post*, September 23, 1995.
76 Black, p. 114.
77 *The Globe and Mail*, October 27, 1995.
78 *The Financial Post*, February 6, 1991.
79 *Wall Street Journal*, November 8, 1994, cited in Edward Herman and Robert McChesney, *The Global Media: The New Missionaries of Global Capitalism* (London: Cassell, 1997), p. 157.
80 Black, p. 29.
81 From Black's speech to the Metropolitan Toronto Board of Trade, January 26, 1997.
82 *The Financial Post*, January 9, 1989.
83 *Maclean's*, January 4, 1992.
84 *Maclean's*, December 5, 1994.
85 *Maclean's*, March 6, 1995.
86 *Maclean's*, April 1, 1991.

87 *The Ottawa Citizen*, October 13, 1996.
88 *The Financial Post*, March 12, 1991.
89 *Maclean's*, July 8, 1985.
90 Black, p. 248.
91 Ibid., p. 400.
92 Ibid., pp. 250–251.
93 From Black's address to the Fraser Institute, April 1988.
94 *Saturday Night*, September 1990.
95 Ibid.
96 *The National Interest*, Summer 1992.
97 Ibid.
98 Ibid.
99 Black, p. 515.

10/ Democracy's Oxygen

1 Sarah Anderson and John Cavanaugh, *The Top 200: The Rise of Global Corporate Power* (Washington: Institute for Policy Studies, September 1996).
2 *The Canadian Forum*, July/August 1997.
3 *The Globe and Mail*, May 13, 1997.
4 *Maclean's*, August 22, 1988.
5 Quoted in David Langille, "The BCNI and the Canadian State," *Studies in Political Economy*, Autumn 1987.
6 C. M. Black, F. David Radler, and Peter G. White, "A Brief to the Special Senate Committee on the Mass Media from the Sherbrooke *Record*, the voice of the Eastern Townships," November 7, 1969, p. 26.
7 See, for example, Flipside, the Canadian Alternative Media Homepage, at http://www.uwindsor.ca/newsstnd/flipside/index.htm, or the linked home-pages of the Council of Canadians and the Canadian Centre for Policy Alternatives.
8 Conrad Black, *A Life in Progress* (Toronto: Key Porter Books, 1993), pp. 229–230.
9 Tom Kent, *The Royal Commission on Newspapers*, 1981, p. 1.
10 *Associated Press v. United States*, U.S. 326 (1945).
11 *The Toronto Star*, January 30, 1997.
12 Black et al., p. 12.

INDEX